Who Wins?

Who Wins?

Predicting Strategic Success and Failure in Armed Conflict

Patricia L. Sullivan

Oxford University Press, Inc., publishes works that further
Oxford University's objective of excellence
in research, scholarship, and education.

Oxford New York
Auckland Cape Town Dar es Salaam Hong Kong Karachi
Kuala Lumpur Madrid Melbourne Mexico City Nairobi
New Delhi Shanghai Taipei Toronto

With offices in
Argentina Austria Brazil Chile Czech Republic France Greece
Guatemala Hungary Italy Japan Poland Portugal Singapore
South Korea Switzerland Thailand Turkey Ukraine Vietnam

Published by Oxford University Press, Inc.
198 Madison Avenue, New York, NY 10016

www.oup.com

Library of Congress Cataloging-in-Publication Data
Sullivan, Patricia L., Ph. D.
Who wins? : predicting strategic success and failure in armed conflict / Patricia L. Sullivan.
p. cm.
Includes bibliographical references and index.
ISBN 978-0-19-987833-8 (hbk. : alk. paper)—ISBN 978-0-19-987835-2 (pbk. : alk. paper) 1. Strategy.
2. Military policy—Case studies. 3. Conflict management—Case studies. 4. Military history—20th century.
5. War. I. Title. II. Title: Predicting strategic success and failure in armed conflict.
U162.S874 2012
355.4—dc23 2011047117

1 3 5 7 9 8 6 4 2

Printed in the United States of America
on acid-free paper

This book is dedicated to those who bear the costs of war.

TABLE OF CONTENTS

LIST OF TABLES AND FIGURES

TABLES

FIGURES

ACKNOWLEDGMENTS

At every stage of this project, I benefited greatly from the generous assistance of numerous individuals. I have many people to thank at the University of California, Davis, where I completed my Ph.D. in political science. First, I must express my deepest gratitude to my exceptional advisor, Scott Gartner. Without his unfailing support, advice, and encouragement over the last decade, I would not be where I am today. I am also grateful to the other members of my dissertation committee, Robert Jackman and Josephine Andrews. Their guidance and support were especially critical as this research first took shape.

I could not have wished for a more supportive and collegial atmosphere than I found in my first academic position at the University of Georgia's School of Public and International Affairs. Chris Allen, Jeff Berejikian, Gary Bertsch, Markus Crepaz, Loch Johnson, Han Park, Jaroslav Tir, and Howard Wiarda welcomed me into the department and provided every possible form of support. I must especially thank my junior colleagues, Mia Bloom, Sherry Lowrance, Doug Stinnett, Brock Tessman, and Maurits Van der Veen. I owe much of my happiness and success at UGA to their friendship, assistance, and advice.

This book would not exist without the particularly persistent encouragement of several exceptional scholars and mentors. Zeev Maoz, Kelly Kadera, Mark Crescenzi, and Irfan Nooruddin, in particular, urged me to develop this project into a book and provided much needed feedback, guidance, and advice over the years it took to accomplish that. The final product is much better than it would otherwise have been because of the helpful discussions I had with countless other colleagues as well. I am especially grateful to Scott Bennett, Keith Dougherty, Hein Goemans, Stephen Gent, and several anonymous reviewers for their exceptionally thoughtful critiques and suggestions. Very special thanks are also due to my editor at Oxford University Press, David McBride, for his unflagging support of this project, and to Production Editor Marc Schneider for skillfully shepherding the manuscript through the publication process.

For the material support that made this book possible, I am indebted to the National Science Foundation (NSF), the Smith Richardson Foundation, the Office of Naval Research, the University of Georgia Research Foundation, the Institute for Global Conflict and Cooperation (IGCC), and a University of California Dissertation Year Fellowship. An NSF Dissertation Research Improvement Grant was essential in providing funding for the research assistance I needed to collect detailed data on international military interventions. Data collection for the analysis in chapter 6 was an enormous undertaking, and I could not have done it without the able assistance of many talented undergraduate and graduate student research assistants at the University of California, Davis, and the University of Georgia. Special thanks go to Matthew Anderson, Murat Bayar, Michelle Dowst, Frank Grau, Johannes Karreth, Xiaojun Li, Aimee Lodigiani, Connor McCarthy, Joshua McLaurin, Emily Myers, Julie Patel, Lauren Pinson, Kristen Pope, Giray Sadik, Sonal Sahu, Allison Shelton, Nitya Singh, Szymon Stojek, Kyle Tingley, and Joshua Watkins. The Smith Richardson Foundation's Junior Faculty Research Grant in International Security and Foreign Policy provided an especially critical year of funding at a time when long-term efforts were finally evolving into this book. I would also like to thank the American Political Science Association's Centennial Center for Political Science and Public Affairs in Washington, D.C., for hosting me during the summer of 2006 while I did research at the National Archives and at George Washington University's National Security Archives. Additional research into the military strategies states employed was supported in part by the Office of Naval Research (ONR) United States Navy Grant No. N00014-09-1-0557. Any opinions, findings, conclusions, or recommendations expressed in this book are those of the author and do not reflect the views of the Office of Naval Research or any other funding agency.

I am grateful as well to many audiences for insightful comments and challenging questions whenever I presented this research. Parts of the work in progress were presented at annual meetings of the American Political Science Association, the International Studies Association, and the Peace Science Society International, where I received excellent feedback from both discussants and audience members. I shared my research at the University of South Carolina and benefited a great deal from comments by Zaryab Iqbal, Harvey Starr, and Chris Zorn. I was also fortunate to have the opportunity to present my research at the 2007 Journeys in World Politics Workshop at the University of Iowa. The organizers, Kelly Kadera and Sara Mitchell, my discussant, Karen Rasler, and the other workshop presenters deserve special acknowledgment for their insightful questions and enthusiastic critiques of the ideas presented here. I am especially indebted to Columbia University's Summer Workshop on the Analysis of Military Operations and Strategy

(SWAMOS), where the idea for this project was born, and the Triangle Institute for Security Studies (TISS) New Faces Conference, one of the first broad audiences for the argument I present in this book. I must also offer my sincere thanks to Richard Betts, Steve Biddle, Steve Rosen, and Peter Feaver for creating and nurturing these stimulating intellectual environments.

Parts of the argument presented in this book and an early version of the statistical analysis presented in chapter 6 were first published as articles: "War Aims and War Outcomes: Why Powerful States Lose Limited Wars," *Journal of Conflict Resolution* Vol. 51, No. 3 (June 2007): 496–524 and "At What Price Victory? The Effects of Uncertainty on Military Intervention Duration and Outcome," *Conflict Management and Peace Science* Vol. 25, No. 1 (March 2008): 49–66. Thanks are due to Sage Publications for permission to publish revised versions in this book.

Finally, I must thank the people whose constant support has been central to my ability to write this book, my family: Paul and Lynne Sullivan, Cindy Wunder, Hailey Wunder, and Rory Sullivan.

Who Wins?

CHAPTER 1

Introduction

On Christmas Eve of 1979, in response to growing domestic opposition to the Afghan government, the Soviet Union invaded Afghanistan, flying airborne units into Kabul, Bagram, Shindand, and Herat with the intention of securing the Marxist regime against the rebel threat posed by the Mujahideen. A month later, the Russians had over 80,000 troops in Afghanistan and had occupied its major cities. At the height of the occupation, more than 600,000 Soviet troops fought for control of the country. But after ten years and the loss of more than 14,000 soldiers, the Soviet government decided that the cost of sustaining the war was too high and withdrew its troops from Afghanistan without eliminating the rebel threat.[1]

On October 7, 2001, just over a decade after the Soviet withdrawal, American troops were deployed to Afghanistan to overthrow the fundamentalist Taliban regime and destroy a global terrorist network's base of operations. This time, the foreign intervention accomplished many of its immediate-term goals quickly and at a relatively low cost, in spite of the dire predictions of many observers. In less than three months, the U.S. military, in cooperation with indigenous opposition forces on the ground, succeeded in routing Taliban forces and removing the regime from power—a feat that a six-year insurgency waged by a coalition of tribes opposed to the regime had been unable to accomplish. Fewer than 60,000 U.S. troops were committed to the war effort, and only twelve were killed in action. The "Afghan Model" was hailed as a "revolutionary, new tool in the United States' foreign policy arsenal."[2] By 2005, there were only 20,000 U.S. troops in Afghanistan, and a report by the Secretary-General of the United Nations concluded that security in the country was sufficient to allow UN personnel to begin reconstruction efforts.[3]

The rapid, decisive removal of the Taliban regime by the U.S. military and its Northern Alliance allies was an impressive achievement. However, al Qaeda and Taliban forces resurfaced, and violent opposition to the new Afghan regime grew as the United States shifted its attention to Iraq. By the time a new American president was sworn into office in 2009, U.S. military leaders were concerned that the situation in Afghanistan had deteriorated to a critical level. U.S. President Barack Obama decided to respond to the insurgency by escalating the country's commitment, sending an additional 17,000 troops to Afghanistan in February and another 33,000 in early 2010. By the summer of 2011, as the tenth anniversary of the U.S. war in Afghanistan approached, approximately 100,000 American troops were engaged in the counterinsurgency and polls showed a majority of Americans did not support the war.[4] Although President Obama promised to begin withdrawing U.S. troops, both military and political leaders were expressing grave concerns about the survival of the Afghan government and its ability to deny terrorist groups safe haven in the country.[5]

Where did the United States go wrong in its efforts in Afghanistan? Is Afghanistan unique as the "graveyard of empires"? Or can the difficulties encountered by both the Americans and the Soviets be attributed to flawed strategies or insufficient effort?

War-fighting is a high-stakes enterprise. At times, states that use military force are able to achieve their objectives at human and material costs they consider acceptable. Frequently, however, they fail to obtain their war aims and bear higher-than-expected social, economic, and political costs in the war effort. Even the most powerful states in the international system do not always attain their war aims. Between 1945 and 2003, Britain, China, France, Russia, and the United States (the five permanent members of the UN Security Council) failed to achieve their primary political objectives in almost 40 percent of their military operations—despite their immense war-fighting capacities and the relative weakness of their state and nonstate adversaries.

Why are states with tremendous advantages in capabilities and resources often unable to attain even limited objectives when they use force against much weaker adversaries? More broadly, under what conditions can states use military force to attain political objectives, and what conditions limit the utility of military force as a policy instrument? How accurately can we predict the outcome of a war before the fighting begins?

This book presents a widely generalizable theory of armed conflict outcomes based on a unique integration of insights from deductive models of war initiation and modern military doctrine. Scholars and military leaders have argued that poor strategy choices, domestic political constraints on democratic governments, or failure to commit sufficient resources to a war effort can explain why the materially strong do not always prevail in war. This book argues that the key to understanding strategic success in war lies in a better understanding of the nature of the political objectives that states pursue through the use of military force. Although I do not deny the importance of military strength, strategy, or resolve, I attempt to provide both a coherent argument and substantial empirical evidence that the effects of these factors on war outcomes are dependent on the nature of the belligerents' political objectives.

Throughout this book, strategic victory in war is defined as attaining the primary political objectives for which an actor chose the costly and risky tool of military force. A central thesis is that strategic success in war requires that an actor's goals, available means, and strategic approach be aligned. This idea will not be surprising to anyone familiar with military doctrine. But I build on this simple conceptual framework by identifying precisely how ends, ways, and means must align—developing a theory about the nature of state (and nonstate) political objectives (ends), the qualities of a state's political and military capacity (means) that matter most, and how actors' political objectives and resources determine both the military strategies (ways) most likely to be adopted and war outcomes. I argue that a critical characteristic of war aims—the degree to which attaining them is dependent on target compliance—determines whether *war-fighting capacity* or *resolve* has a greater impact on a war's outcome. Combining a typology of war aims and military strategies with measures of relative military capacity and cost tolerance produces a model capable of predicting when states are likely to achieve their political objectives through the use of military force, and when they are likely to fail.

WHY STUDY WHAT DETERMINES WAR OUTCOMES?

Should political scientists even be attempting to predict who will win wars? Aren't armed conflicts best understood by those who have experience fighting them? Or is it perhaps the case that war is such a complicated and idiosyncratic phenomenon that it is impossible to predict how a war will end before it has begun? I agree that it is difficult to predict war outcomes—in fact, we would not be likely to observe many wars if it was easy to forecast the outcome ex ante, because rational actors who anticipated losing a war would make the concessions necessary to avoid its occurrence. Nevertheless, even the most complicated phenomena have some systematic patterns that can be identified. If we can improve upon our ability to predict the outcome of a war before it has been initiated, we could prevent the unnecessary loss of life and all the pain and suffering caused when decision-makers choose to escalate a conflict to violence because they have overestimated the probability of success or underestimated the cost.[6]

Both state and nonstate actors resort to the use of military force in an attempt to obtain political objectives. But we know from observing the outcomes of wars that the political leaders who opt for war are frequently wrong about their ability to attain their war aims at an acceptable cost. High social, economic, and political costs are borne by both the war initiator and the target, without the intended results. The United States' intervention to prevent a communist takeover of South Vietnam and the Soviet Union's tremendously costly and ultimately futile use of military force to maintain a communist government in Afghanistan are two of the most well-known examples, but there are many others. Neither Iraq nor Iran attained its war aims despite the incredible human and material costs of the eight-year war between them. France was unable to hold onto its most treasured North African colony despite committing almost 1.5 million soldiers and suffering over 15,000 combat casualties to defeat independence movements in Algeria between 1954 and 1962.

Whether the objectives of a state that initiates a war are positive or negative in a normative sense, it is always best if military operations that will inflict pain and suffering without achieving their aims are avoided in the first place. Although peace activists in many countries implore their governments to avoid the use of military force abroad, knowledge about the conditions under which the use of military force is unlikely to achieve its objectives is more likely than moral exhortation to encourage governments to seek alternative means of conflict resolution.

Unfortunately, national leaders lack a systematic theory or sufficient empirical evidence upon which to base their decisions about the use of force as an instrument of statecraft. Frequently, decision-makers "reason by analogy," applying the lessons of the last war, or a prominent case considered to be "similar" to the current situation, in order to determine the likely effectiveness of their various military options.[7] But policymakers need far more than analogous cases and recent experiences to make informed decisions about whether or not to employ force in a particular situation. Better theory and empirical evidence on the factors that affect the ability of states to achieve their political objectives through the use of force might at times allow decision-makers to design more effective military operations. At other times, such knowledge and information might caution them against the use of force altogether. Before accepting the immediate and long-term risks of war-fighting, national leaders should have access to systematic empirical evidence on the utility and limitations of military force.

WHAT DO WE KNOW ABOUT THE DETERMINANTS OF WAR OUTCOMES?

The present state of our knowledge about the determinants of war outcomes presents a puzzle. The vast majority of military doctrine is predicated on the assumption that troop strength, firepower, and military effectiveness determine war outcomes. Recent scholarly research is inconclusive—alternatively pointing to war-fighting capacity and military effectiveness, military strategy, or the strategic selection of "winnable" wars as the most important determinants of victory and defeat.[8] But none of these factors can fully explain why powerful states frequently fail to prevail in the armed conflicts they initiate against materially weak targets.

Military doctrine, realist theories of international relations, and conventional wisdom all suggest that states that possess superior technology, more numerous and better-trained troops, better tactical capabilities, higher quality leadership, a wider range of options for delivering firepower, and vastly greater resources and production capabilities than their weak adversaries should prevail over those adversaries in war. When powerful states lose wars that they *initiated* against much weaker foes, the outcome is even more difficult to explain. Strong states face far fewer material constraints on the military capabilities and resources they can bring to bear in a conflict than their weak targets. What prevents these states from using their overwhelming military might to attain their war aims? And—whatever those constraints are—why can't they be anticipated before the troops are committed to battle?

Some scholars have pointed to the imbalance of resolve that frequently exists between actors with disparate levels of military capacity to explain cases in which the materially weak prevail over the materially strong. Observing a number of cases of failed counterinsurgency operations, Andrew Mack notes, "In every case, success for the insurgents arose not from a military victory on the ground . . . but rather from the progressive attrition of their opponents' political capability to wage war."[9] And case studies of individual conflicts often attribute otherwise puzzling conflict outcomes to an imbalance of resolve or "asymmetry of motivation" between the combatants.[10]

The "balance of resolve" perspective is intuitively appealing, and it certainly fills in a piece of the puzzle. When states have only limited interests at stake in a particular conflict, they are likely to commit only limited resources. But this class of explanations cannot predict when a militarily strong actor is likely to prevail and when it is likely to abandon its war aims in the face of a militarily weak, but highly resolute, actor. In sharp contrast to conventional theories of war outcomes—which assume that "God is always on the side of the larger battalion" and have trouble explaining how the weak win wars—theories that emphasize political will have difficulty explaining how strong states with relatively little at stake ever prevail over weak adversaries fighting for their survival. How are policymakers to know if a military campaign is destined to fail because of an "asymmetry of motivation" before the troops are sent?

A final school of thought that has the potential to explain why the most militarily capable states do not always prevail in war draws attention to the military strategies the belligerents employ. Many scholars and military leaders have advanced arguments suggesting that strong states can lose wars to much weaker actors when they employ the "wrong" military strategy.[11] This too bears some truth. But most of these theories cannot explain why powerful states make poor strategy choices. Powerful states generally possess the technology, tactical capabilities, leadership, and troop quality necessary to successfully execute even the most difficult and complicated military strategies. Although the weak may not have the physical ability to choose an optimal strategic response to their adversary's military strategy, strong states undoubtedly do. What prevents a strong state from exchanging its losing strategy for a winning one when it becomes clear that its initial strategy is ineffective?

In the following sections, I critique three prominent arguments about the determinants of war outcomes—explanations based on relative war-fighting capabilities, military strategies, and resolve—and introduce my own theoretical approach to the puzzle of who wins wars.

Capabilities

The material capabilities of states have figured prominently in much of international relations theory, but military power has held a particularly privileged place in theories of war and peace. The assumption that military strength largely determines conflict outcomes underpins many theories about war initiation, war termination, arms races, alliances, and even international trade. For example, while disagreeing about whether power parity or preponderance makes war more likely, both balance-of-power and power-preponderance theorists implicitly agree that the balance of military capabilities between two states is the primary determinant of war outcomes.[12] Relative capabilities also play a prominent role in theoretical work on the success and failure of deterrence and coercive diplomacy.[13] In fact, the relative lack of attention to war conduct and termination among political scientists may be due in part to a tacit acceptance of the realist paradigm, in which it is assumed that the distribution of power—by which most scholars mean material resources and military capabilities—explains war outcomes. If the stronger state wins all but a handful of wars, then perhaps there is nothing very interesting to say about what determines victory and defeat in war.

But the empirical evidence of a direct relationship between relative material capabilities and war outcomes has been mixed. Bruce Bueno de Mesquita notes that the *less* powerful state prevailed in 41 percent of the wars in the last two hundred years.[14] Zeev Maoz tests two competing models of militarized interstate dispute outcomes: one that explains conflict outcomes based on the balance of capabilities between the two sides, and another that predicts that the balance of motivation or resolve among the disputants will determine outcomes.[15] In his statistical analysis, Maoz finds that the capabilities variables he employs (military expenditures and personnel) are unrelated to dispute outcomes, but that there is a statistically significant relationship between his measures of resolve and favorable outcomes. In a later study, he argues that the relationship between "control over resources and control over conflict outcomes is either weak or nonexistent."[16]

Other scholars, however, have found a robust relationship between military capabilities and the ability to prevail in violent conflicts. The results of empirical tests reported by Bueno de Mesquita in a 1981 publication indicate that military power is an important predictor of success in war.[17] Likewise, Cynthia Cannizzo finds that the state with the largest military won all but nine of the thirty wars between two states from 1816 to 1965.[18] More recent research by Al Stam provides a particularly convincing case for the importance of material capabilities.[19] In *Win, Lose, or Draw*, the author argues that the industrial and military resources available to a state play a critical role in determining victory and defeat in war. In his empirical analysis, he demonstrates that a state's proportion of the combined military-industrial capabilities of two warring parties has a significant positive effect on the probability that the state will prevail in the war, even after controlling for military strategy, distance, terrain, regime type, and issue area.

The fact that the historical record is mixed suggests that we should begin asking questions about the *conditions* under which the balance of military capabilities between adversaries is most likely to affect conflict outcomes, and when other factors are likely to mitigate the impact of an actor's advantage in material capabilities. There are also good theoretical reasons for questioning traditional assumptions about the relationship between military capabilities and war outcomes. First, many theories about the effect of relative capabilities on war outcomes are built on the implicit assumption that both sides commit either the full force—or at least equal proportions—of their capabilities to the fight. The primary predictors in most theories of war outcomes are factors like industrial production, population, military expenditures, and troop strength in the year a war begins.[20] But these variables measure *potential* military power rather than *applied* military power. Assuming a one-to-one relationship between latent capabilities and applied military power is reasonable enough in wars in which both sides value the issues at stake to a similar degree, but many wars are characterized by an imbalance of both military capabilities and interests at stake. When strong states use force against weaker states, their military operations are frequently initiated to achieve limited aims, in the absence of a credible claim to self-defense, and in a context of numerous competing international concerns and commitments. Clearly, the resources and capabilities that are actually committed in any particular conflict are not always equal to the resources a state is capable of bringing to bear in a conflict.

Conventional theories of war outcomes are also based on a second assumption that is problematic for many conflicts. These theories assume that military victory is equivalent to political victory and that winning battles inevitably leads to winning the war. Alastair Smith, for example, assumes that states attain victory in war by defeating their enemies in a series of battles that gradually reduce the opponent's capacity to resist.[21] Although the relationship between winning battles and winning wars may appear self-evident, many violent conflicts defy this logic. Dan Reiter and Al Stam quote Frederick the Great's claim that "[w]ar is decided only by battles and it is not decided except by them" and cite the importance of Inchon in Korea and Tet in Vietnam—but the victor-and-vanquished relationship established in these battles did not translate into victory and defeat in the larger wars of which they were a component.[22] In fact, Steve Rosen finds that the "winner" lost more lives in battle than the "loser" in eighteen of the forty interstate wars between 1815 and 1945.[23] U.S. Department of Defense figures indicate that the North Vietnamese suffered twenty battle deaths for every one American battle death, losing an almost unprecedented 3 percent of the population in their war with the United States and South Vietnam. Likewise, the Algerians lost approximately ten soldiers for every one soldier lost by the French.[24] Despite their overwhelming destructive capacity and battlefield military effectiveness, in each of these conflicts, a strong state failed to achieve its war aims.

I will argue that battlefield military effectiveness is likely to be a poor predictor of war outcomes when states use military force in pursuit of political objectives that can only be attained with target compliance. Whenever possible, the target of a stronger challenger is unlikely to attempt a direct defense strategy, relying instead on an indirect strategy of imposing costs while evading enemy firepower. The greatest advantage of guerilla armies is that they can use the natural terrain and the civilian population to conceal themselves and avoid pitched battles with stronger foes. The leaders of weak states can also avoid the head-to-head battles they are almost certain to lose if the object at stake in a conflict cannot be physically seized. No matter how strong a state is militarily, a target with exceptionally high tolerance for pain and suffering can deny the more powerful state victory if the state needs the target to change its behavior. An actor's overwhelming destructive capacity can raise the cost of resistance for a weak adversary, but greater firepower will not necessarily convince that adversary to change its behavior. In some cases, greater destruction is even counterproductive to the attainment of a state's political objectives.

Military Strategy

Some recent literature has looked beyond latent material capabilities to bring attention to the manner in which military force is employed. Steve Biddle provides convincing evidence that force employment—the doctrine and tactics according to which forces are used in combat—mediates the relationship between material strength and victory or defeat in the interstate wars from 1900 to 1992.[25] While Biddle highlights the advantages of militaries that can execute a modern, combined arms strategy in mid- to high-intensity continental warfare, Jason Lyall and Ike Wilson note the drawbacks of the modern army's reliance on mechanization in counterinsurgency operations.[26] Other scholars have critiqued the "American Way of War," arguing that the United States loses limited wars because its strategic culture and organizational interests emphasize conventional warfare strategies that are ineffective against less conventional adversaries.[27]

The most common way of tackling military strategy in a generalizable way within the scholarly literature has been to distinguish among two or three broad strategic approaches. John Mearsheimer developed an "attrition-blitzkrieg" strategy dichotomy in his 1983 book on conventional deterrence.[28] Stam distinguishes among maneuver, attrition, and punishment strategies, arguing that the interaction of two states' military strategies plays an important role in determining war outcomes because of the effect this interaction has on the costs the two sides must bear in the fighting.[29] He concludes that strategy choice, and its interaction with terrain, are the most important factors affecting war outcomes, and his empirical results demonstrate that there are optimal strategy combinations for states to pursue. Robert Pape also makes the case that some military strategies are more effective than others.[30] He examines various strategies for the use of air power and provides evidence that "punishment" strategies, in which the goal is to break the morale of an enemy, are less effective than "denial" strategies, in which the aim is to "thwart the target state's military strategy for controlling the objectives in dispute."[31] Michael Horowitz and Dan Reiter come to the same conclusion based on a quantitative analysis of all instances of air-power coercion from 1917 to 1999.[32]

Ivan Arreguín-Toft develops a theory of asymmetric war outcomes, arguing that strong states lose asymmetric conflicts when they employ the wrong military strategy in relation to their weak opponent's strategy.[33] His typology of strategies is similar to those employed by Pape and Stam. Direct strategies target the adversary's capacity to fight by destroying its armed forces in battle.

In contrast, indirect strategies (barbarism and guerilla warfare) avoid head-to-head military contests and seek primarily to degrade the adversary's will to continue the fight by imposing high costs. He maintains that the stronger actor will prevail in a conflict when both actors employ the same strategy type (direct-direct or indirect-indirect), while the weaker actor will win when the two sides use opposing strategy approaches (direct-indirect or indirect-direct). He reasons that, in an interaction in which the two sides employ opposite strategy types, the strong actor's power advantage is deflected by the weak actor's strategy, leading to a protracted conflict that favors the weaker actor. In contrast, an interaction in which both sides use the same strategy type is likely to be resolved quickly and decisively in the strong actor's favor, because nothing mediates between relative material power and outcomes.

The idea that military strategy is an important determinant of victory and defeat in war fits well with the perspective of military professionals and historians. Poor strategy choice as an explanation for paradoxical war outcomes is particularly prevalent in what has become known as the "Vietnam strategy debate." Andrew Krepinevich, for example, maintains that the United States failed to secure its objectives in South Vietnam because it pursued a conventional attrition strategy rather than engaging in counterinsurgency warfare.[34] He argues that, from 1961 to 1962, U.S. Special Forces, under the direction of the CIA, were successfully employing counterinsurgency doctrine. It was a mistake, he claims, to transfer control to the regular U.S. Army chain of command, because the Army incorrectly viewed the conflict as a traditional war with unconventional sidebars and therefore pursued a strategy of attrition that could not win the war. In stark contrast, Colonel Harry Summers argues that the flaw in U.S. strategy was actually an excessive focus on the Viet Cong insurgents.[35] The United States, he maintains, should have focused more on the conventional aspect of the war: defeating external aggression. Summers blames poor strategic performance on political limitations on the use of force that were imposed by America's civilian leadership, while Krepinevich blames Army doctrine.

Arguments about the importance of military strategy often imply that the war outcome would have been different if the actor who lost with a particular strategy had chosen a different strategy. But we are left to wonder why—if there is an optimal strategy or an optimal strategic response to an adversary's strategy choice—belligerents do not always pursue this strategy? Even if uncertainty about an adversary's capabilities or strategic approach led a state to choose a suboptimal strategy initially, in theory, a losing strategy could be exchanged for a winning one if it becomes clear that the initial strategy is ineffective.[36] Why would strong states initiate wars only to lose because they employ a punishment strategy when a denial strategy would be more effective or a direct strategy when they could win with an indirect strategy? Even more puzzling is one implication of Arreguín-Toft's theory: that weak actors attempt direct defense strategies when they would be more likely to win with a guerilla strategy. By definition, guerilla strategies require fewer resources and can be executed by a relatively small number of lightly armed soldiers. Although lack of technology, training, or troop strength might explain why weak states cannot adopt modern, combined arms warfare strategies—as well as why they might avoid direct strategies requiring head-to-head battle with stronger adversaries—lack of capability cannot explain why weak actors would stand and fight, only to be decimated, when hit-and-run tactics would be more effective.

Although I believe that military strategy and force employment affect war outcomes, I focus on the ways in which each actor's broad strategic approach is constrained by its military capabilities, cost tolerance, and war aims, rather than conceptualizing strategy choice as an exogenous variable. Strategic victory in war is much less likely when an actor's military strategy is not aligned with its war aims. As General Rupert Smith notes in *The Utility of Force*, lack of coherence between "purpose and force" is a primary reason for the failure of many military operations.[37] But limitations on an actor's physical capabilities and tolerance for costs, rather than poor decision-making, frequently account for ill-fated strategic approaches. Physically weak actors employ losing military strategies because they lack the capacity to execute a more effective strategy or are forced by the nature of a stronger adversary's war aims to fight with a strategy for which they are ill-equipped. Strong states with the material resources to adopt almost any strategic approach employ ineffective strategies because they cannot tolerate the human and political costs of using a more effective strategy, or because they have political objectives that render their preferred strategy impotent. Both Krepinevich and Summers are correct to an extent about the uses and limitations of military force. But the root source of the challenge posed by Vietnam was the nature of the United States' political objectives, rather than flawed civilian or military leadership. As Summers argues, military force *is* more effective when it is massively employed to decisively defeat the conventional armed forces of an enemy. But this argument fails to acknowledge that this application of force was not sufficient to achieve the primary *political* objective in Vietnam—which was the creation and maintenance of a stable, independent, and noncommunist South Vietnam.

Resolve

Some scholars have attempted to explain wars in which the materially weak prevail over the materially strong by pointing to the imbalance of "resolve" that frequently exists between actors with disparate levels of military capacity.

For the famous nineteenth- century Prussian general Carl von Clausewitz, moral forces like will, motivation, patriotism, and other intangible factors act as force multipliers *or* force dividers.[38] On a similar note, Rosen maintains that the willingness to absorb costs can play an important role in the ability of a state to prevail in a conflict.[39] A weak actor "may compensate for an opponent's strength, his ability to harm," he argues, "by a greater willingness to be harmed."[40] John Mueller argues that the American strategy in Vietnam was based on the perfectly reasonable assumption that communist forces would reach a "breaking point" after suffering enough punishment.[41] Unfortunately for the United States, the North Vietnamese and Viet Cong were willing to tolerate losses relative to their population that Mueller claims were unprecedented in modern history. Their breaking point, he suggests, may have been at "near extermination limits."[42]

Andrew Mack presents a particularly convincing case for the importance of resolve to asymmetric conflict outcomes.[43] Observing a number of cases of failed major power interventions intended to defeat insurgent movements, Mack notes: "In every case, success for the insurgents arose not from a military victory on the ground . . . but rather from the progressive attrition of their opponents' *political* capability to wage war."[44] He argues that, in conflicts between strong states and foreign insurgencies, conventional military superiority may be useless. Because the insurgents pose no direct threat to the survival of the strong state, full mobilization of the intervening state's military resources is not politically possible, and domestic criticism of the campaign inevitably increases as battle casualties and economic costs rise. For the insurgents, however, the enormity of the threat posed by the intervening state unifies domestic factions behind the cause of defeating the external power.

The "balance of resolve" perspective is intuitively appealing, but the literature on the effect of resolve on war outcomes is problematic. Frequently, lack of resolve is used as a post-hoc explanation for everything about conflict outcomes that could not be predicted with more traditional measures of capabilities and resources. Case studies of individual conflicts often attribute puzzling conflict outcomes to an imbalance of resolve, or "asymmetry of motivation" between the combatants.[45] But the actor with more at stake in a conflict does not always win the war. Few would argue that Kuwait was more important to the United States than to Iraq, or that the United States cared more about who ruled Afghanistan than the Taliban did.

Even if insufficient resolve is to blame in many conflicts in which the weak prevail over the strong, it is not useful as a theoretical concept if there is no way to know if a state *has* "sufficient resolve" to prevail before it initiates a war. Without an ex ante measure of relative resolve, the "balance of resolve" perspective cannot tell us when the militarily strong actor is likely to prevail and when it is likely to abandon its war aims in the face of a militarily weak actor with high tolerance for costs. How can we explain why strong states achieve their objectives vis-à-vis their weak opponents in some instances but not in others, if their targets always have more at stake? When are militarily weak but resolute actors likely to prevail over militarily mighty but irresolute states?

There have been attempts to measure resolve directly. Maoz uses the level of hostility reached by a dispute initiator relative to the level of hostility reached by the target as an indicator of initiator resolve, while Rosen employs casualty ratios.[46] Both higher relative levels of hostility and higher relative casualties are considered indicators of high resolve. But low levels of conflict escalation could indicate that a highly resolved and capable initiator did not have to escalate the dispute because it was able to achieve its objectives with the mere threat of force. Similarly, low casualty rates relative to an opponent's are just as likely to indicate greater military effectiveness as a lack of resolve.

Arguments about political will, motivation, and resolve have typically implied that actors will be most likely to lose when their absolute tolerance for costs is lowest or when the gap between their tolerance for costs and the cost tolerance of their adversary is greatest.[47] But the cost tolerance of materially strong states does not need to exceed or even *match* that of weaker actors, because their strength ensures that the human and material costs of war will be borne much more heavily by the target. *The strong can afford to be less tolerant of costs than their weak adversaries.* Greater resolve on the part of the weak actor is a necessary, but not sufficient, condition for strong state defeat in war.

Rather than focusing on the disparity between two belligerents' tolerance for the human and material costs of war-fighting, I highlight the distance between the *price an actor is willing to pay* and the *true cost* of attaining its political objectives through the use of force. The gap between one actor's tolerance for costs and that of its adversary does not matter nearly as much as the gap between the actor's tolerance for costs and the *actual* cost of attaining its objectives through the use of force. If a state's costs are relatively low because the state has a significant material advantage and a war aim aligned with its strengths, the state can prevail with far lower tolerance for costs than its opponent. If, however, a state *underestimates* the material and human resources required to attain its war aims and costs are unexpectedly high, that state may find itself forced to concede defeat despite a cost-tolerance threshold that is closer to that of its adversary.

In the theory I develop in the next two chapters, states choose to initiate armed conflicts when their prewar estimate of the cost of attaining their objectives through the use of force falls below the threshold of their tolerance for costs. The more the actual costs of victory exceed a state's prewar expectations, the greater the risk that it will be pushed beyond its cost-tolerance threshold and forced to unilaterally withdraw its forces before it attains its war aims. In chapter 3, I build an argument about the conditions under which strong states are most likely to select themselves into an armed conflict only to find that the price of victory will exceed the price they are willing to pay.

My Approach: War Aims and War Outcomes

My approach differs from existing theories of war outcomes in several important ways. I argue that actors do not fail to attain their war aims simply because they have inferior war-fighting capacity or less tolerance for the costs of war than their adversaries. Both the militarily strong and the militarily weak, the highly cost tolerant and the less resolved, select themselves into armed conflicts when they *believe* that the human and material costs they are willing to bear to attain their objective will exceed the cost of attaining the good through the use of force. If they are correct, they have sufficient tolerance for costs to employ force in an effective way for as long as it takes to achieve their objective. If they are incorrect, they lose the war. They may be militarily defeated; more likely, they choose to quit fighting when they become convinced that defeat is inevitable or the cost of attaining their war aims will exceed the price they are willing to pay.

If inaccurate prewar estimates of the risk of military defeat or the cost of victory explain the strategic failures we observe, a complete theory of war outcomes must be able to predict the conditions under which states are most likely to make such miscalculations.[48] I develop a typology that places the political objectives that states pursue through the use of force on a continuum based on the degree to which attainment of the objective is dependent on target compliance. I argue that the nature of a state's primary political objective has both direct and indirect effects on the probability that it can attain that objective through the use of military force. Political objectives directly affect war outcomes because some political objectives are more closely aligned with traditional military objectives, like the attrition of enemy soldiers and destruction of enemy war-fighting materials, than others. The balance of military capabilities between the belligerents is expected to be the most important determinant of outcomes when the objects at stake can be seized and held with physical force alone. The defender's tolerance for costs becomes more significant when the challenger pursues war aims that require a change in target behavior. The more *compliance* dependent an objective, the more difficult it is to translate that political objective into operational military objectives and to establish a link between destructive capacity and the desired end state.

The nature of a state's primary political objective also has an indirect effect on war outcomes, because actors are more likely to misestimate the cost of achieving compliance-dependent objectives before choosing to use military force. When an actor is dependent on a change in target behavior to achieve its war aims, force must be used persuasively, and the target is largely in control of the extent to which victory is costly for the state. The risk posed by underestimating what it will cost to attain one's war aims is particularly significant for strong states that initiate military operations for "limited" objectives with limited tolerance for costs. When a militarily strong state attempts to coerce a target with high tolerance for the costs of war, it is difficult to predict how much force should be used, the manner in which it should be employed, and how long military operations will need to be sustained to reach the enemy's "breaking point." This uncertainty increases the probability that strong states will select themselves into asymmetric wars they cannot sustain to victory.

Outline of the Book

In the next chapter, I present the first part of a theory of war outcomes that posits three possible paths to victory in war. Chapter 2 focuses on the strategic calculus that determines whether or not a conflict escalates to violence. I use two post-Cold War military confrontations between the United States and Iraq to illustrate how the balance of military capabilities, relative tolerance for costs, and each side's beliefs about these distributions influence decisions to initiate and terminate armed conflicts. In chapter three, I develop the argument that a critical characteristic of war aims—the degree to which attaining them requires target compliance—determines whether relative war-fighting capacity or resolve has a greater impact on a war's outcome. Although this theoretical approach is intuitive, the implications of the theory are frequently surprising. A state with greater military capacity than its adversary is more likely to prevail in wars with "total" war aims—the overthrow of a foreign government or annexation of territory—than in wars with more limited objectives. On the other hand, a state's ability to forcibly compel an adversary to change an objectionable foreign or domestic policy is expected to decline as its material strength relative to the adversary increases.

Chapter 4 provides a thorough explanation of the empirical methodology I use to test my argument against the existing explanations of armed conflict outcomes introduced in this chapter. I begin by developing a series of falsifiable hypotheses from my own theory and the competing theories.

I then discuss the historical data I bring to bear on the problem and how I operationalize and measure the concepts in my hypotheses.

In chapter 5, I conduct large-*n* empirical tests of the predictions made by my theory and the rival theories of war outcomes. I employ statistical analyses to test competing hypotheses about the determinants of violent conflict outcomes against the historical record of militarized interstate disputes since 1816. Chapter 6 hones in on a particularly difficult challenge: explaining why states with tremendous capabilities and resources are often unable to attain even limited objectives vis-à-vis much weaker adversaries. I test the empirical implications of my theoretical approach against the most widely accepted alternative explanations of asymmetric war outcomes in an analysis of major power military interventions since 1945. This chapter demonstrates that neither poor strategy choices nor a lack of resolve can fully account for why success eludes powerful states that use military force against weaker state and nonstate adversaries. In the population of major power military interventions since World War II, the major powers prevail more often than their adversaries. But weak actors thwart the objectives of their powerful opponents with increasing frequency as the major powers' war aims become more dependent on target compliance.

In chapter 7, I conclude with a discussion of the theoretical and policy implications of my argument and my empirical results. The theory of armed conflict outcomes that I develop attempts to unify previous theoretical work on the effects of military capability, resolve, and strategic selection on violent conflict outcomes. The policy implications of this approach are not as straightforward or prescriptive as decision-makers might like them to be. Nevertheless, my hope is that recognizing how the utility of military force is dependent on the nature of one's political objectives will help leaders avoid steering their countries into wars that are unlikely to achieve their aims.

CHAPTER 2

Strength and Resolve in the Armed Conflicts We Observe

Predicting the outcome of an international conflict that has escalated to the use of military force by both states is difficult, because conflicts tend to escalate to mutual hostilities in precisely those situations in which it was not easy to predict who would prevail in a war ex ante.[1] There are unlikely to be many wars in which observable indicators of military capabilities *and* resolve suggest an obvious winner; the likely loser of this type of war is expected to negotiate a settlement to avoid escalation of the conflict to war. There are, however, abundant examples of violent conflicts between states that appear grossly mismatched militarily. According to data from the Correlates of War Project, one state had at least a 4:1 advantage in military-industrial capabilities over its adversary in about half of the disputes that escalated to mutual hostilities between 1816 and 2001.[2]

One potential explanation for the asymmetric wars we observe can be found in psychological theories about the limits of human cognition and decision-makers' cognitive biases. When the leaders of weak states initiate violent conflicts against much stronger adversaries, or choose to fight back when targeted by a major power, it is tempting to attribute such a decision to the irrationality of the weak states' leaders. Dominic Johnson argues that there is a human tendency toward overconfidence that is likely to be a particularly common trait among political leaders and an especially acute problem in crisis decision-making. According to Johnson, a "fog of hope and wishful thinking" is often present at the initiation of violent conflicts.[3] This idea is not new. In his 1973 book *The Causes of War*, Geoffrey Blainey asserts that war is "the outcome of a diplomatic crisis which cannot be solved because both sides have conflicting estimates of their bargaining power."[4] Because war results from a disagreement about relative military capabilities, he argues that hierarchical systems, in which differences in power are clear, are the least war-prone. Similarly, Robert Jervis claims that "Excessive military optimism is frequently associated with the outbreak of war," and Stephen Van Evera implicates "false optimism about relative power" as the proximate cause of most wars.[5]

Wishful thinking and false optimism undoubtedly play a role in the escalation of some disputes. But we do not need to invoke the irrationality of leaders to explain why materially weak actors sometimes choose to escalate their conflicts with stronger opponents to war. Because armed conflict outcomes are not determined by war-fighting capacity alone, even actors much physically weaker than their adversaries can reasonably expect that they might achieve their war aims under some conditions.

In this chapter, I develop the first part of a broadly generalizable theory about the utility of organized violence as a policy instrument. The theory incorporates insights from both strategic selection models of war initiation and military doctrine. I begin by establishing a definition of victory in war and positing three paths by which actors can achieve strategic victory in armed conflict. While only states with superior war-fighting capabilities are likely to defeat their adversaries in battle, weak state and non-state actors sometimes prevail over their more powerful foes by exceeding their tolerance for the human and material costs of sustaining a war effort.

The third section of this chapter explains how the process by which state and nonstate actors "select" themselves into violent conflicts helps us to understand the war outcomes we observe. I argue that weak actors have a propensity to select themselves into military contests with much stronger adversaries when they believe that their "cost-tolerance advantage" will allow them to absorb any costs their opponent will impose and inflict enough punishment of their own to convince their opponent that the cost of victory is too high. Stronger actors are inclined to escalate conflicts to war when they believe their advantage in destructive capacity will keep their own costs low and enable them to destroy their opponent's capacity and/or will to fight at an *acceptable price*. When leaders' expectations about the impact of their material or motivational advantage are accurate—or even overly pessimistic—they select themselves into an armed conflict with sufficient tolerance for costs to employ an effective military strategy and achieve their objective. However, when they are overly optimistic about the impact of their strength or resolve, they are at risk of selecting themselves into a war they cannot sustain to victory.

Two brief case studies of post-Cold War military confrontations between the United States and Iraq are used to illustrate these expectations in the fourth section of this chapter. In chapter 3, I develop the second part of my argument, which posits that the nature of the belligerents' war aims determines whether relative war-fighting capacity or tolerance for costs has a greater impact on war-fighting dynamics and, consequently, the risk that a strong state selects itself into a war with insufficient tolerance for costs.

THE UTILITY OF FORCE

I have adopted and use a modified version of the broad definition of war provided by Hedley Bull; war is characterized by two or more opposing political units engaging in the use of organized violence against one another in pursuit of political aims.[6] The definition I employ is consistent with recent scholarly work that views armed conflict as part of a bargaining process.[7] It is also in harmony with the perspective of the nineteenth-century Prussian General and strategist Carl von Clausewitz, who wrote that "war is simply a continuation of political intercourse, with the addition of other means."[8] But my definition is broader than commonly held perceptions of what a "war" is. In this definition, the violence between the opposing sides does not need to reach a particular casualty threshold to be considered war. The unifying characteristic of all the conflicts about which I am concerned is that they have escalated to the deliberate use of armed force by two opposing sides. Although for some purposes it may make sense to separate conflicts with high levels of casualties from less violent conflicts, I believe the outcomes of a wide range of violent conflicts can be explained within the same theoretical framework.

Victory and defeat in armed conflict can be defined in a variety of ways. Classic *military* victory is achieved when one actor degrades the other actor's military capacity to the point where it is no longer able to maintain organized resistance or to continue to pursue its own aims through force of arms. But wars rarely end with the total destruction of an enemy's military capacity.[9] Pursuit of total military victory is enormously costly, even for the victor, and there is generally some negotiated settlement short of one actor's complete annihilation that both sides would prefer over a war fought to the bitter end.[10] More importantly, as Thomas Schelling notes, "[V]ictory inadequately expresses what a nation wants from its military forces."[11]

Because leaders use military force as a policy instrument, military victory is neither a necessary nor a sufficient condition for *strategic victory* in armed conflict. Victory in war is meaningful only if an actor attains the desired political end state for which it decided to use force. Throughout this book, strategic victory is defined as attaining the primary political objectives for which an actor chose to use the costly and risky tool of military force. In theory then, both belligerents in a violent conflict could "win," in that both sides could attain their primary political objectives. More often, however, only one side achieves its objectives—or neither side attains its desired political ends.

The policy aims of the belligerents in an armed conflict are central to my argument. I define a *political objective* as the allocation of a valued good (e.g., territory or political authority) sought by the leaders of a political unit (e.g., a state, terrorist group, or separatist movement). Examples of political objectives typically pursued in military operations include the removal of an incumbent regime (the U.S. intervention to overthrow the New Jewel regime in Grenada in 1983), maintenance of political authority (French military operations in Chad to defend the government against threats from Libya and GUNT/FAP rebels during the 1980s), defense or acquisition of territory (China's seizure of Hainan Island in 1950), and changes in an adversary's foreign or domestic policy (U.S. attempts to gain Iraqi compliance with UN weapons inspections from 1992 to 2003). Table 2.1 displays the primary political objective of the dispute initiator in each of the violent interstate disputes between 1816 and 2001 and of the intervening state in all military interventions by the five permanent members of the UN Security Council between 1946 and 2003.[12]

As several scholars have noted, conflicts over territory are more likely than conflicts over most other issues to escalate to violence or even war.[13] Almost half of the interstate disputes that escalated to violence between 1816 and 2001 were over land. For the strongest states in the international system, however, maintaining a friendly government in another state has been a more common objective since 1945 than either the defense or acquisition of territory. The use of military force to compel an adversary to change objectionable policies is a more common objective in interstate disputes than in military

Table 2.1. INITIATOR'S PRIMARY POLITICAL OBJECTIVE IN ARMED CONFLICTS, 1816–2003

	Violent Interstate Disputes 1816–2001		Major Power Military Interventions 1945–2003	
	N	%	*N*	%
Maintain Political Authority	10	2%	30	24%
Remove Foreign Regime	69	10%	13	10%
Policy Change	198	29%	16	13%
Gain or Defend Territory	319	47%	27	21%
Maintain Empire	n/a		17	14%
Deter Aggression	n/a		13	10%
Peacekeeping	n/a		10	8%
Other/Unidentified	76	11%	n/a	
Total	672		126	

interventions by the major powers, but this is a surprisingly common aim in both sets of cases. In only 10 percent of the violent conflicts and interventions did the initiating state seek to remove an adversarial regime from power.

Political objectives can be contrasted with *military* objectives, which are the operational goals to be accomplished by armed forces as a means of achieving the desired political outcome. Examples include the attrition of enemy combatants, destruction of enemy military capacity, seizure of territory, disruption of enemy lines of command and control, and demoralization of enemy soldiers and/or civilians. Under some circumstances, an actor's primary political and military objectives are the same. A state may, for example, seek only to reclaim a piece of land along its border with another state. In this case, seizure of territory is both the political objective and the military objective—although the state is likely to pursue other military objectives, such as the attrition of enemy combatants or disruption of enemy command and control, as a means to the desired end.

PATHS TO VICTORY

States and other political organizations pursue the vast majority of their political objectives without resorting to the use of force. Occasionally, however, state and nonstate actors do escalate their conflicts to violence. Once a conflict has escalated, an actor can use military force to attain its political objectives in one of three ways.

The actor can:

1. Render her opponent physically incapable of maintaining an organized defense so that she can forcibly seize and/or hold the disputed good (military victory);
2. Convince her opponent that she will eventually render him physically incapable of maintaining an organized offense or defense; or
3. Convince her opponent that the cost of prosecuting the armed conflict to victory will be greater than the value of attaining his political objectives.

The first path to victory is the one for which leaders of modern militaries typically plan and train. From the writings of Clausewitz and Jomini down to contemporary U.S. Army field manuals, military strategists have noted principles for the effective use of force, emphasizing the use of mass, maneuver, and initiative to fight decisive battles and destroy enemy forces.[14] Although Clausewitz is most famous for recognizing the need to use military force as an instrument of policy, he also states unequivocally that "[c]ombat's aim is to destroy enemy forces."[15]

Although modern militaries prepare primarily for defeating enemy forces on the battlefield, the first path to victory exacts the highest toll on both the victor and the vanquished, and only a handful of modern wars between states have ended in the complete destruction of one side's ability to continue fighting.[16] Once one of the belligerents comes to believe that defeat is the most likely outcome if it continues to fight, it makes little sense to continue to expend blood and treasure—further degrading the state's military and making postwar security and recovery even more arduous—simply to postpone making the concessions necessary to end the armed conflict. Given the enormous cost and suffering entailed in war-fighting, the likely victor is also generally happy to accept its opponent's concessions and end the armed conflict without annihilating the opponent. Increasing one's demands or seeking the total destruction of one's enemy is rarely worth the cost of continuing an armed conflict.

In the last path to victory, the opponent is "persuaded" to surrender some portion of the good in contention to avoid suffering further costs in a war effort that it has come to believe is not worth the sacrifice. Even if military victory is attainable, an actor may prefer a negotiated settlement to continuing to fight, because the cost of fighting until its war aims are secured is expected to surpass the value of those objectives. Exceedingly few political objectives are worth unlimited sacrifice, and the price an actor is willing to pay for some objectives may be quite limited. Frequently, a decrease in confidence that one's objectives can be attained coupled with an increase in the anticipated cost of prosecuting an armed conflict to victory work together to encourage an actor to sue for peace.[17]

DESTRUCTIVE CAPACITY AND TOLERANCE FOR COSTS

How do the means available to state and nonstate actors affect their ability to pursue these paths to victory? Because there are multiple paths to strategic victory in armed conflict, military operations generally serve several purposes. Actors may use their military capacity to physically destroy their opponent's capacity to maintain an organized resistance, to change their opponent's beliefs about the eventual outcome of a war fought to the finish, or to change their adversary's beliefs about the cost of continuing to fight. Often, an actor's armed forces pursue all three goals at once. I build my argument on a simple theoretical framework in which each belligerent in an armed conflict has some quantity of two primary determinants of armed conflict outcomes: *destructive capacity* and *tolerance for costs*. An actor's destructive capacity is the physical effect it can produce given the material resources and war-fighting capabilities of its armed forces. Destructive capacity can be used for a wide variety of tasks from the attrition of enemy soldiers and disruption of enemy supply lines to the physical defense of people and territory. Factors like troop strength, training, technology, leadership, firepower, doctrine, and operational capabilities all affect the destructive capacity of an actor's military.[18]

In a violent confrontation between two opposing actors, each side's destructive capacity relative to that of the other side directly affects the probability it will achieve its political objectives by way of its effect on the probability that one side will defeat the other militarily. All else being equal, the greater an actor's destructive capacity relative to that of her opponent, the higher her probability of rendering that opponent physically incapable of defending himself or continuing to pursue his own war aims. At the same time, if a disparity in material resources or war-fighting capabilities makes the eventual outcome of a war fought to the finish more certain, the likely loser may sue for peace even before it is physically incapable of continuing to fight in order to avoid the futility of expending resources and losing lives for a cause that cannot be won.

Relative destructive capacity also determines an actor's physical ability to inflict and deflect the human and material costs of war-fighting. All else equal, the greater an actor's destructive capacity relative to her adversary, the greater are the material and human losses she can impose on that adversary. At the same time, an actor's own vulnerability to her adversary's attempts to impose costs decreases as her destructive capacity relative to that adversary increases. In what the U.S. media has described as one of the deadliest fights of the American intervention in Afghanistan, eight U.S. soldiers were killed in an October 2009 battle that began when three hundred insurgents launched a surprise attack on the fifty-three American troops at Combat Outpost Keating.[19] The loss of eight soldiers was striking for the Americans, but more than *nine* times that many Afghan fighters were killed in this battle that the *insurgents* had initiated. Higher levels of material resources and war-fighting capabilities increase an actor's ability to inflict pain and suffering on her opponent. And better training, technology, leadership, equipment, and operational capabilities decrease an actor's vulnerability to her adversary's attempts to impose costs. Militarily weak actors can expect to suffer a much higher rate of casualties and significantly greater material damages than their militarily strong opponents.

I define *cost tolerance* as the extent to which an actor is *willing* to absorb the human and material costs imposed by an adversary and to bear the human, material, and opportunity costs of using force against that adversary to achieve its objectives in a particular conflict.[20] Although an actor's destructive capacity is a relatively fixed characteristic of that actor at a given point in time, an actor's tolerance for costs varies from conflict to conflict.

Many factors can affect an actor's willingness to bear the costs of fighting. Nation-states may have limited cost tolerance due to competing domestic and international priorities, public war weariness, or citizens' sensitivity to casualties. Some states may have lower cost tolerance than others on average because of variations in the institutional accountability of political leaders or domestic norms.[21] In general, however, I maintain that an actor's cost tolerance in a *specific* conflict is largely a function of how much that actor values the issues at stake in the conflict. The more vital the interests at stake—whether to the security and prosperity of the nation-state or to the survival of the political leadership—the higher are the costs that an actor is willing to bear to secure those interests.

Theoretically, cost tolerance varies along a continuum from unwillingness to absorb any human or material costs in pursuit of an objective to an acceptance of any and all costs that must be borne in order to prevail. Despite President Kennedy's vow to "pay any price" and "bear any burden" in defense of liberty, in reality, there are few conflicts in which the issues at stake will result in a cost-tolerance threshold at either extreme. An actor's cost-tolerance threshold can be thought of as the maximum price it would be willing to pay to achieve its political objectives in a particular conflict.

An actor's cost-tolerance threshold defines the level of pain and loss at which it would prefer terminating the conflict—by making concessions or abandoning its war aims—to continuing to fight. Many wars end not because one side or the other becomes convinced that it will eventually be defeated militarily, but instead because at least one of the belligerents comes to believe that the human and material costs of the war will eventually exceed the value of attaining its war aims. All else equal, the greater an actor's willingness to bear the costs of fighting to secure the interests it has at stake, the longer it can sustain its military operations and the greater are its prospects for achieving its war aims by exceeding the enemy's cost-tolerance threshold.

In addition, an actor's tolerance for costs can affect its ability to defeat an adversary militarily by acting as a constraint on the number of troops and resources that can be committed, military strategy and battlefield tactics, the intensity of operations, and the modes of force employed. On March 20, 1999, the North Atlantic Treaty Organization (NATO) launched a bombing campaign to persuade Slobodan Milošević to halt Yugoslavia's effort to forcibly expel ethnic Albanians from Kosovo. But the coalition's effectiveness in ending atrocities against the Albanians was limited by NATO member countries' reluctance to commit ground troops and the decision to restrict most of their warplanes to flying above 15,000 feet to minimize allied casualties. After seventy-eight days of intensive air strikes, Milošević ultimately agreed to negotiations that resulted in an internationally monitored

Kosovo. But over 90 percent of the Albanians in Kosovo were displaced by the bombing campaign, and the civilian casualty toll—in what was supposed to be a "humanitarian" operation—has been estimated at between ten and twenty thousand.[22] Although an actor's destructive capacity determines its latent potential for imposing losses and destroying enemy war-fighting capabilities, its tolerance for costs determines how much of that latent capacity can be brought to bear in any particular conflict.

CONFLICT ESCALATION: THE ARMED CONFLICTS WE OBSERVE

An actor with greater destructive capacity than its adversary could attain its objectives in armed conflict via any of the paths to victory outlined above. A sufficiently large destructive capacity advantage gives an actor the potential to destroy its enemy's ability to fight, convince the adversary that military defeat is inevitable, or raise costs above that enemy's cost-tolerance threshold. However, materially powerful states can be constrained by relatively low tolerance for the cost of fighting for particular objectives, or frustrated by adversaries that refuse to concede even when the costs inflicted on them are extraordinarily high. An actor that is significantly weaker than its opponent is not likely to achieve its objectives by militarily defeating that opponent. Relatively weak actors typically prevail in armed conflicts by convincing their opponents that the cost of victory will be higher than the price they are willing to pay.

Other scholars, and many military practitioners, have noted the importance of both military capabilities and resolve in determining war outcomes. My approach, however, differs from existing theories of war outcomes in several important ways. I argue that neither inferior war-fighting capacity nor low tolerance for the costs of war is a sufficient explanation for the war losses we observe. Rioting mobs with no military capacity to speak of have managed to attain their objectives in confrontations with superpowers, because they were able to absorb the pain the strong state imposed and raise the cost of the conflict above the price the state was willing to pay. In August 1962, riots broke out in the capital of the Republic of Congo after President Fulbert Youlou declared all opposition parties to be illegal. In response, France, which had been supportive of the Youlou regime since the country gained its independence in 1960, deployed over 1,000 ground troops to reinforce the 3,000 troops they already had stationed in the country in an attempt to quell the rioting and insure the survival of the incumbent government. Over several days, however, the violent demonstrations grew to involve over 10,000 rioters. Fueled by labor unrest and general discontent over the corruption and ineffectiveness of the Youlou regime, the protesters set fire to the homes and cars of government officials and eventually made their way to the presidential palace. Unwilling to commit additional troops or risk their soldiers' lives in defense of the president, France abandoned its effort to maintain Youlou in power on August 17, and he was forced to resign.

Even the strongest states sometimes fail to achieve their objectives when they use military force against much weaker opponents. On the other hand, it is just as important to note that strong states often prevail over weak actors that have much more at stake in a conflict. On December 20, 1989, just days after the Panamanian Defense Forces fatally shot a U.S. Marine lieutenant, the United States intervened with military force to remove General Manuel Noriega from power in Panama. Although some scholars and policymakers expressed concern that American troops could get bogged down after an invasion of Panama, by December 26, resistance to American forces had collapsed. Approximately forty-three American soldiers and 345 Panamanian troops died during the forty-four-day operation. By the end of January, the United States had withdrawn almost all of the troops it had deployed to address the crisis. Strong states frequently succeed in removing foreign regimes from power, despite the fact that, as Horowitz and Reiter note, "[f]or the target government, regime change is the highest price to pay."[23]

My approach makes the process by which state and nonstate actors "select" themselves into violent conflicts an important factor in a complete explanation for the war outcomes we observe. I argue that both the militarily strong and the militarily weak, the highly cost-tolerant and the less resolved, choose to use military force when they *believe* that the human and material costs they are willing to bear to attain their objective will exceed the cost of attaining the good through the use of force. If they are correct, they have sufficient tolerance for costs to employ an effective military strategy and achieve their objective. If they are incorrect, they fail—either because they are militarily defeated or because they become convinced that they are unlikely to prevail at an acceptable cost and they are better off ceding the good than continuing to fight.

When differences in fighting ability between two states are small, there can be considerable uncertainty about which state would prevail in a war fought to the finish. However, as the disparity in destructive capacity between two states increases, uncertainty about the likelihood of military victory or defeat should decline. Nevertheless, we do see armed conflicts in which the two sides are grossly mismatched militarily. In fact, there is mixed evidence about whether a disparity in capabilities between two states significantly decreases the probability that a conflict between them will escalate to violence. Why would actors with clearly inferior military capabilities refuse to make the concessions that would avert an armed conflict, or even initiate the use of force against a strong adversary?

I argue that a physically weaker actor will choose war over any negotiated settlement his adversary is willing to accept only when two conditions are met. First, he must believe that his cost-tolerance advantage is such that he can absorb any punishment his opponent will inflict. In addition, he must believe that his cost tolerance is so much greater than that of his adversary that, despite his relative material weakness, he can impose more costs than she is willing to pay.

Materially weak actors are aware of the devastation that could be wrought by a militarily preponderant state if a conflict between them was to escalate to war. At the same time, weak actors know that, because they cannot defeat a strong opponent militarily, they can only prevail if they can exceed their adversary's cost-tolerance threshold. Consequently, weak actors tend to select themselves into military contests with stronger adversaries only when their value for the issues at stake, and therefore the price they are willing to pay to secure their objectives, is significantly higher than that of their opponent. Materially weak states without a significant cost-tolerance advantage are expected to select themselves out of military contests with materially strong states.

All else being equal, the costs an actor expects to incur in a military confrontation with an adversary should rise with that adversary's destructive capacity. As the anticipated cost of fighting increases, actors with lower cost-tolerance thresholds become less likely to issue a challenge and more likely to make concessions in order to avoid escalation of a conflict. The result of this strategic selection process is that we are unlikely to observe many armed conflicts in which the balance of military capabilities *and* tolerance for costs suggests an obvious winner. In wars in which one actor has an observable military advantage over the other actor, there is likely to be a parallel asymmetry in cost tolerance that favors the physically weaker actor as a result of the mutual selection process behind the escalation of conflicts to violence.

> Proposition 1. Physically weaker actors choose war over any negotiated settlement that their adversary is willing to accept because they believe their cost-tolerance advantage will allow them to (1) absorb any costs their opponent will impose and (2) impose enough costs of their own that they ultimately convince their opponent that the cost of victory will be higher than the price that opponent is willing to pay.

Unlike weak states and substate groups, a state with a considerable capability advantage over her opponent can choose to escalate a conflict to violence with a relatively low cost-tolerance threshold, because the costs that can be imposed on her by a weaker actor are limited by the actor's inferior destructive capacity. Higher levels of material resources and war-fighting capabilities increase a state's ability to inflict pain and suffering on her opponent and decrease that state's vulnerability to her adversary's attempts to impose costs. A target facing a relatively weak challenger is likely to sustain relatively low losses. A target facing a challenger with greater destructive capacity can expect to suffer higher casualties and greater material losses. According to my analysis, weak state and nonstate actors suffered 81 percent of a conflict's battle deaths, on average, when they chose to fight back against major power militaries in the post-WWII period.

Strong states alone have the luxury of choosing to fight wars over marginal interests, secure in the knowledge that they can inflict much more damage than they will sustain and that, even if they fail to attain their objectives, the war will not threaten their survival. Stronger actors tend to escalate conflicts when they believe their advantage in destructive capacity will keep their own costs low and enable them to destroy their opponent's capacity and/or will to fight *at an acceptable price.*

> Proposition 2. Physically stronger actors choose war over any negotiated settlement their adversary is willing to accept because they believe their destructive-capacity advantage will allow them to destroy their opponent's capacity and/or will to fight *at an acceptable price.*

The beliefs that lead actors to choose to use military force parallel their reasons for ending their military operations short of victory. A strong state that selects into an armed conflict with a weak opponent is unlikely to select out of the conflict because it fears *military* defeat. Strong states, I argue, terminate their wars with weaker actors before attaining their war aims because they have come to believe that the *cost* of victory will exceed the value of the good to them. In other words, states "fail to prevail" in armed conflicts with significantly weaker opponents when they select themselves into conflicts that turn out to be more costly than anticipated.[24]

Weak actors, on the other hand, select themselves into armed conflicts with strong adversaries only when they have high cost-tolerance thresholds because they anticipate high costs. Civilian policymakers in militarily powerful states are often optimistic about their ability to use the state's superior destructive capacity to change the cost-benefit calculus of their adversaries.[25] However, after a conflict has escalated to mutual hostilities, we are not likely to see weak actors surrendering to their powerful opponents because the costs imposed on them are too high. When the strong prevail, we should observe that their weak adversaries updated their beliefs about the eventual *outcome* of the war—deciding that, regardless of the importance of the issues at stake for them and the strength of their resolve, they cannot attain their objectives through the use of military force. If they continue to fight, the inevitable outcome will be the complete destruction of their military capacity.

> Proposition 3. Once a conflict has escalated to mutual hostilities, actors with less destructive capacity than their opponents will tend to make concessions only after becoming convinced that resistance is futile (i.e., that they will eventually be rendered physically incapable of maintaining an organized defense if they continue to fight).
>
> Proposition 4. Once a conflict has escalated to mutual hostilities, actors with greater destructive capacity than their opponents will tend to abandon their war aims only after becoming convinced that the human and material cost of victory will be higher than the price they are willing to pay.

Inherent in this explanation of conflict escalation is the assumption that we observe wars only when at least one side has miscalculated. It cannot be simultaneously true that the stronger actor has the ability to destroy its opponent's capacity or willingness to fight at an acceptable price *and* that the weaker actor can impose enough costs to convince the powerful state that the costs will be too high. The conditions under which one side or the other is most likely to make such a miscalculation are the focus of chapter 3. In the remainder of this chapter, I illustrate the selection logic put forth in the propositions above with two examples. The first explores how conflict between the United States and Iraq over the status of Kuwait escalated to war between August 1990 and January 1991 and how that war was terminated. The second example looks at U.S. military operations to overthrow the Iraqi dictator and establish a stable, U.S.-friendly regime in Iraq that began in March of 2003.

THE UNITED STATES VERSUS IRAQ

Crisis over Kuwait

At 2 a.m. on August 2, 1990, Iraq invaded Kuwait, sending 100,000 ground troops and 500 tanks across the border to seize control of the Kuwaiti oil fields and its capital. The 25,000-strong Kuwaiti defense force offered only minimal defense before surrendering the capital just nine hours after the first Iraqi troops had entered the country.

Although the United States had provided Iraq with military aid during its eight-year war with Iran, Iraq's invasion of Kuwait in August 1990 touched off a thirteen-year period of hostile relations between the United States and the Iraqi dictator, Saddam Hussein. Almost immediately, the United States and the UN Security Council began a campaign to coerce the Iraqi leader into withdrawing his troops from the country. Between August

7, 1990 and January 16, 1991, the UN Security Council implemented an embargo and economic sanctions, and the United States repeatedly threatened Saddam with the use of military force. Throughout the fall, the United States assembled an international coalition of states and conducted a massive air, naval, and ground troop buildup in the Gulf to deter an Iraqi invasion of Saudi Arabia and make the threat of military action against Iraq more credible. At the same time, the leaders of France, Jordan, Morocco, Algeria, and Russia all attempted to mediate the crisis, offering proposals that included significant concessions to Iraq's demands. The UN Security Council eventually issued an ultimatum and authorized a U.S.-led coalition of states to use military force if the Iraqi military did not withdraw by January 15. Nevertheless, even though the United States and its coalition allies clearly had the military capacity to reclaim Kuwaiti territory and were mobilizing sufficient force in the region to do so, Saddam refused to withdraw from Kuwait.

Although public support for a war to liberate Kuwait was initially tepid in the United States, by November it was clear that the Pentagon was preparing for offensive operations against Iraq. On January 12, 1991, President Bush made a formal request to Congress for authorization to use military force in the Persian Gulf. Five days later, at 3 a.m. on the morning of January 17, the United States and its coalition partners began an extensive air campaign intended to compel Saddam to withdraw his troops from Kuwait and significantly weaken Iraqi military capacity should coercion fail and a ground campaign become necessary.

Over the next thirty-nine days, coalition forces dropped almost 88,000 tons of munitions on strategic targets in Iraq and Kuwait. The bombing campaign cost the allies close to a trillion dollars and caused severe damage to Iraqi military equipment and transportation and communication infrastructure, as well as the attrition of up to 50 percent of the troops in fifteen Iraqi divisions.[26] Iraq responded by setting fire to hundreds of oil wells in Kuwait, launching SCUD missiles at Israel and Saudi Arabia, and even attempting a small raid into Saudi Arabia. Iraqi ground forces hunkered down, and Iraqi air forces attempted to escape to Iran. However, the situation changed rapidly once coalition ground operations began on February 24. Despite holding out for months under international condemnation, economic sanctions, and finally an intense and extremely damaging bombing campaign, Iraq surrendered and agreed to a complete withdrawal from Kuwait just days after the coalition ground campaign began.

Why did the Iraqi leader resist withdrawing from Kuwait despite all the losses—civilian and military—the country suffered under international economic sanctions and almost six weeks of air strikes, only to capitulate after a few ground battles with coalition troops? The U.S.-Iraqi conflict over

Kuwait contains several critical decision points that are summarized in Table 2.2. At each of these decision points, policymakers had beliefs about the material strength, resolve, and intentions of other actors that influenced the choices they made. They also held beliefs about how their destructive capacity and cost tolerance would interact with the destructive capacity and cost tolerance of their adversary to determine the outcome of the conflict. Sometimes these beliefs reflected reality; at other times decision-makers based their decisions on miscalculations and incorrect assumptions—often with negative consequences. In particular, we see that Saddam Hussein underestimated the United States' strength and resolve, but that this is not sufficient to explain the decision-making that ultimately led to his surrender in Kuwait. The Iraqi dictator's critical miscalculation occurred because he failed to realize the limitations of his cost-tolerance advantage. The United States, on the other hand, actually overestimated the destructive capacity of the Iraqi military forces. The Bush administration was pleasantly surprised to find that the coalition's combined arms campaign to forcibly evict Iraq from Kuwait was shorter and less costly than anyone had predicted. However, some key American decision-makers did overestimate the coercive

Table 2.2. CRISIS OVER KUWAIT

Date	*Action*	*Beliefs*	*Accuracy*
August 2, 1990	Iraq invades Kuwait	Iraq could forcibly annex Kuwait at an acceptable cost	Correct
		The U.S. would not intervene	Incorrect
August 7, 1990–February 23, 1991	U.S. and UN attempt to persuade Saddam to withdraw through coercive diplomacy and air campaign	Saddam would surrender once he was convinced of U.S. destructive capacity and resolve	Incorrect
August 2, 1990–February 28, 1991	Iraq refuses to withdraw	Iraq could prevail by absorbing the costs imposed and exceeding U.S. tolerance for costs	Incorrect
February 24, 1991	U.S. launches ground campaign	Ground combat against the Iraqi army will be moderately costly	Incorrect
		Coalition forces would defeat Iraq	Correct
February 28, 1991	Iraq surrenders and agrees to withdraw from Kuwait	Iraq cannot hold territory in Kuwait against a U.S. ground offensive	Correct

power of their destructive capacity when applied more indirectly in the strategic air campaign that preceded the ground invasion.

The United States did not immediately respond to Iraq's annexation of Kuwait with military force. Although President Bush quickly condemned Iraq's blatant aggression, the administration pursued a strategy of nonviolent coercive diplomacy for five months before escalating to what Alexander George has termed "forceful persuasion" with the use of air strikes.[27] Despite widespread international condemnation, economic sanctions, and thirteen UN Security Council resolutions demanding that Iraq withdraw from Kuwait, Saddam Hussein remained intransigent. Saddam flatly rejected proposals for a negotiated settlement to the crisis by several states in spite of obvious preparations for war by the United States and a large, diverse coalition of other nations. The UN Security Council passed a resolution authorizing the U.S.-led coalition to use "all means necessary" to restore Kuwait's sovereignty if Iraq did not withdraw by January 15. The U.S. Congress gave the Bush administration authority to use military force against Iraq, and the United States sent six of the Navy's sixteen aircraft carrier battle groups to the Gulf. Nevertheless, even after the United States amassed over 500,000 military troops in the theater, Saddam did not back down.

Numerous misperceptions and miscalculations by the Iraqi president appear to have contributed to his uncompromising stance. At first, Saddam refused to believe the United States would go to war to restore Kuwait's sovereignty.[28] Once the United States had amassed a large contingent of combat-ready troops in the region, it appears that Saddam did come to believe the United States would use force—but he saw the United States as lacking the cost tolerance to maintain military operations over time and absorb the losses the Iraqi army could impose on the ground. According to Janice Stein, "Saddam made a series of tactical judgments that led him to question first the likelihood, but then more importantly, the duration and the outcome of war should it occur." He was "confident that Iraq would survive the air and missile attacks and prevail through superior staying power in the ground fighting to follow."[29]

Although there is evidence that the Iraqi leader both underestimated the destructive capacity of the United States and overestimated the Iraqi army's destructive capacity, [30] the key reason for Saddam's refusal to back down appears to be his belief that Iraq could attain its objectives with a strategy based on exceeding America's tolerance for costs. Multiple statements made by Saddam, accounts from his advisors, and his observable behavior all suggest that he firmly believed that (1) his own domestic audience and troops had high cost tolerance and could absorb any losses inflicted by the U.S. military without surrendering, and (2) the United States would withdraw after suffering a politically unacceptable number of deaths in battle.

Prior to his invasion of Kuwait, Saddam famously told the U.S. Ambassador to Iraq April Glaspie, "Yours is a society which cannot accept 10,000 dead in one battle[—]. . . we know that you can harm us although we do not threaten you. But we too can harm you." [31] Speaking to his military commanders before a bold Iraqi offensive into Saudi Arabia, Saddam expressed his belief that the American-led coalition had less "determination" than Iran had had during the Iran-Iraq war and his confidence that "the enemy we are faced with would collapse if we manage to challenge and confront it."[32] The Iraqi president also drew on analogies to U.S. sensitivity to casualties in and eventual withdrawal from Vietnam. In numerous public and private statements he expressed his expectation that the United States would behave as it had in Lebanon in 1983, when it withdrew its troops after 241 American troops were killed in an attack on the barracks housing American and French members of the Multinational Force in Lebanon.[33]

One could argue that Saddam Hussein's statements about the weak political will of the American public and the high cost tolerance of the Iraqis were cheap talk intended for a domestic audience. But the Iraqi dictator's behavior suggests that he believed his own rhetoric. Iraq held out, refusing to withdraw from Kuwait, through weeks of punishing coalition air strikes that degraded his military capacity, weakened his country's economy, and, on several occasions, made the Iraqi leader himself a direct target. Amatzia Baram, professor of history at the University of Haifa, maintains that Saddam believed he could survive both a punishing bombing campaign and a ground war with the United States because his troops, battle-hardened in the Iran–Iraq war, could absorb many times the casualties of the "weak-willed" United States.[34] In their extensive account of the Persian Gulf War, Michael Gordon, chief defense correspondent for the *New York Times*, and General Bernard Trainor, a retired Marine Corps Lieutenant General, also argue that Saddam intended to win a strategic victory—not by militarily defeating the military forces amassed against him—but by exceeding the coalition nations' tolerance for costs.[35] Freedman and Karsh note that "Saddam strongly believed that the United States' Achilles' heel was its extreme sensitivity to casualties, and he was determined to exploit this weakness to the full."[36] Kevin Woods and his co-authors come to the same conclusion based on captured audio tapes of discussions between Saddam and his advisors. As word of the coalition's ground invasion reached them, Saddam's inner circle dismissed media reports that Iraqi troops were surrendering in large numbers as enemy propaganda and focused on their conviction that the coalition would crumble once they began to suffer significant casualties on the ground. In preparation for a coalition invasion of Iraq, Saddam began planning to arm the Iraqi people for a "house to house" fight.[37]

Even as Saddam was planning to defeat a U.S.-led coalition with overwhelming destructive capacity by exploiting his cost-tolerance advantage, some U.S. war planners and military experts were hopeful that the coalition could prevail by exceeding Saddam's tolerance for costs. Both the well-known historian and military strategist Edward Luttwak and former Secretary of State Henry Kissinger were skeptical about engaging in a ground war against Iraq—which they believed would entail high coalition casualty rates—and instead advocated an intensive air campaign to "raise the cost of occupying Kuwait to unacceptable levels."[38] According to Gordon and Trainor, the Desert Storm air campaign was intended by its architects to "persuade Saddam Hussein to pull his troops out of Kuwait and sue for peace—without a ground war."[39] A 1997 U.S. Government Accountability Office (GAO) report provides further evidence, noting that key planners of the air campaign focused on "leadership-related targets deep inside Iraq, with the goal of forcing Iraqi leader Saddam Hussein to 'cry uncle'" and "hoped that the ground offensive would be rendered unnecessary by the effectiveness of coalition air attacks against Iraqi targets."[40]

Although high-ranking military leaders outside the Air Force were critical of relying on air power, President Bush seems to have held out some hope that Saddam would capitulate without a ground war. Bush claimed after the war that he "never considered seriously the possibility of an 'air only' campaign," but he sent his top military advisors to visit the Persian Gulf to "assess whether a ground offensive against President Saddam Hussein's army would be necessary" only after nineteen days of aerial bombardment.[41] The *New York Times* notes that, in a speech on February 5, President Bush was careful to emphasize that he had made no decision about whether a ground war would be necessary. Despite significant civilian casualties in Iraq and Kuwait, as well as fears that a punishing strategic bombing campaign could become unacceptable to the international community, the United States and its coalition allies sustained air operations—flying over a thousand combat sorties a day at a cost of up to $2 million for a single missile strike—for almost six weeks before initiating offensive ground operations.[42] The GAO report evaluating the effectiveness of the air campaign concludes that, "[i]n sum, and not for the first time in armed conflict in this century, it was hoped that the shock and effectiveness of air power would precipitate a collapse of the opponent before a ground campaign."[43]

It does appear that Saddam Hussein became more willing to negotiate an end to the war after twenty-nine days of air strikes. In mid-February, he began bargaining with the United States through a Russian envoy and, by February 22, he had agreed to completely withdraw from Kuwait within twenty-one days.[44] However, the Bush administration responded with a demand that Iraq abandon Kuwait within seven days, and Saddam rejected the ultimatum because the timetable would have required him to leave behind Iraq's heavy military equipment.[45] By this time, the United States and its allies had hundreds of thousands of troops in the theater and were only days away from launching a full-scale ground campaign. American leaders were now committed, not just to the liberation of Kuwait, but also to destroying Iraq's capacity to threaten its neighbors.

Some scholars and military experts have taken Saddam's last-minute scramble to strike a deal with the United States as proof that the strategic air campaign alone succeeded in attaining the United States' primary political objective.[46] The air strikes were incredibly effective at degrading Iraqi military capabilities. The attacks also destroyed many of Saddam's command and control facilities, political headquarters, and residences.[47] But the air strikes did not work by raising the cost of occupying Kuwait to "unacceptable levels," and thereby convincing Saddam to "cry uncle," as envisioned by some of air power's most enthusiastic advocates. Instead, the air campaign—in conjunction with the coalition's obvious preparations for a ground campaign—contributed to Saddam's willingness to withdraw from Kuwait by persuading the leader that military defeat in the coming ground war was inevitable. As Robert Pape observed, air strikes against Iraq's forces in Kuwait "wreaked havoc on Iraq's strategy of waging a protracted war of attrition against a coalition ground offensive by sharply interdicting supply lines, preventing military units from moving on the battlefield, and destroying heavy forces."[48]

Once U.S. and coalition troops began major ground combat operations, it quickly became clear that the Iraqi army and Republican Guard simply could not hold the territory they had seized in Kuwait. Saddam Hussein displayed little concern about the costs to Iraqi civilians or soldiers of continuing to fight—but he did not want his armed forces destroyed in a hopeless bid to hold ground. Freedman and Karsh note:

> From the outset of the Kuwaiti crisis in the summer of 1990, there was an absolute certainty in Saddam's mind of what could not be sacrificed—his political survival. Kuwait, the Palestinian cause, Iraqi lives: all were important so long as they served the perpetuation of Saddam. So was his military strategy and deployment: key units had been held back from the start for this purpose and he was clearly anxious that as many units as possible who had been caught in the Kuwait/Southern Iraq theater would get back to save the regime rather than make a gallant last stand.[49]

Saddam had built up a massive military force in Kuwait and planned to bog the Americans down in a long, bloody war of attrition. However, after just two days of the ground campaign, Saddam publicly announced that Iraq was withdrawing from Kuwait. Iraqi forces began to surrender and flee en masse, and the coalition was able to restore Kuwait's sovereignty after only one hundred hours of ground combat.

Ironically, Saddam was not alone in overestimating how costly a ground campaign to retake Kuwait would be for the United States. In the weeks leading up to Operation Desert Storm, many Western military experts and scholars feared a difficult and costly campaign.[50] The ground campaign phase of Operation Desert Storm was a quick and decisive victory for the United States, and the country suffered far fewer casualties than anyone had predicted. Instead of filling thousands of hospital beds in a protracted conflict, the United States liberated Kuwait after a six-week air campaign and a one-hundred-hour ground war, losing only 148 soldiers in combat.

Both Iraq and the United States misestimated the cost and likelihood of success of the strategies they chose at several points during the conflict. But the Gulf War was not simply a "failure of measurement" of the type Geoffrey Blainey imagined. Military experts in the United States actually grossly overestimated Iraq's military capabilities, even as some air power proponents and political leaders were overly optimistic about their ability to use firepower to break the Iraqi dictator's will to resist.[51] Saddam's fatal mistake was his belief that his troops could make the ground war too costly for the United States. He may have been correct that the U.S. public did not have exceptionally high tolerance for casualties in a war to free Kuwait, but the nature of the United States' political objective and its overwhelming destructive capacity ensured that the ground war was won at low cost to the U.S..

Saddam's Ouster

After more than ten years of frustration with Saddam's intransigence on UN weapons inspections, the September 11, 2001 terrorist attacks on the United States and fears that Iraq had managed to sustain its nuclear weapons program created a domestic climate in which the George W. Bush administration was able to gain political support for a war to remove Saddam from power. The multinational invasion of Iraq, spearheaded by the United States, began on March 20, 2003. By March 27, some observers became nervous about the pace of progress, and there was mounting criticism of Secretary of Defense Donald Rumsfeld.[52] Only eleven days later, central Baghdad fell to U.S. forces. On May 1, the Bush administration declared victory and an end to major combat operations.

However, after the fall of the regime, the United States' primary political objective shifted from regime removal to state-building, and the target became a growing insurgent movement, terrorists, and the population of Iraq. The original war plans had called for a rapid troop draw-down shortly after removal of the regime; instead, more troops were deployed, the Pentagon announced plans to extend tours of duty, each branch of the military issued "stop-loss" orders prohibiting some soldiers and officers from leaving military service at retirement or the expiration of their contracts, and casualties began to mount. Although only 109 U.S. soldiers lost their lives in combat before the United States declared its mission accomplished, the Department of Defense reports that 4,233 American troops were killed in "post-combat" operations between May 1, 2003 and December 31, 2009.

The similarities between Saddam Hussein's beliefs and actions in 1990 and 2003 are remarkable. Despite his experience with the firepower and war-fighting effectiveness of the United States in Operation Desert Storm, Saddam responded to the U.S. threat to forcibly remove him from power just as he had responded to the U.S. threat to forcibly remove him from Kuwait in 1990. In his book about overconfidence in war, Dominic Johnson notes that "assessments regarding the likely outcome of war should have been simple, given that Iraq had lost the 1991 Gulf War, and that it was widely known that in the subsequent decade U.S. military strength had grown extensively while Iraq's had declined."[53] But, once again, Saddam held out hope that the United States was only bluffing and would not really invade, despite obvious war preparations. And again, even if the United States and its coalition allies did invade, the Iraqi leader was optimistic about his prospects for survival.

The United States Joint Forces Command (USFCOM) commissioned the Iraqi Perspectives Project to analyze dozens of interviews with captured Iraqi military and political leaders and thousands of Iraqi government documents seized after Baghdad fell to coalition forces. Principal participants in the project have noted that Saddam was optimistic that France and Russia would prevent the United States from invading Iraq. Moreover, according to Saddam's personal interpreter, if the United States did launch a ground invasion, Saddam believed his "superior" forces would mount "a heroic resistance and . . . inflict such enormous losses on the Americans that they would stop their advance."[54] Saddam even began drawing on analogies to Vietnam again. The United States' failed intervention in Vietnam was seen as undeniable evidence that the Americans could be defeated by a determined enemy willing to both absorb and impose high casualties. In a 2004 PBS interview, Iraqi Lieutenant General Raad al-Hamdani, commander of Saddam's Republican Guard south of Baghdad, admitted that he also expected to be able to "turn Iraq into another Vietnam."

Ironically, the lessons of Vietnam that Saddam wanted to apply to the American invasion of Iraq were much more apt after he was gone, when the U.S. war aim—as in Vietnam—was regime maintenance rather than removal. The United States, it appears, correctly concluded that removing Saddam from power could be accomplished quickly and at an acceptable cost. What the Bush administration failed to predict in its focus on the military task of overthrowing the regime was the possibility that the population would not give them the cooperation they needed to establish a new U.S.-friendly government in Iraq. The destructive-capacity advantage of the United States and its allies became much less important than the strength of insurgent factions' will to resist the imposition of a new regime once the brute-force objective of toppling the Baathist regime was accomplished.

Much has been written about the United States' overconfidence and miscalculations prior to the invasion of Iraq.[55] All evidence suggests that chief advisors and key decision-makers in the Bush administration grossly underestimated the cost of establishing and maintaining a politically viable, U.S.-friendly regime in Iraq. According to Nordhaus, "The only public estimate of the cost of the war by the Bush Administration came in an interview by Larry Lindsey, the economist-in-residence in the West Wing."[56] The *Wall Street Journal* reported Lindsey's "upper bound" estimate of $100 to $200 billion and quoted him as optimistically projecting that "[t]he successful prosecution of the war would be good for the economy."[57] The Democratic Staff of the House Budget Committee did their own study. Based on their assumption that the war would involve just thirty days of combat and a 2.5-month post-combat occupation of Iraq, the report estimated the cost at between $48 and $60 billion.[58] The Congressional Budget Office (CBO) did not make any assumptions about the length of the intervention in its analysis, but their monthly estimates were lower than those in the House study. Neither the House committee nor the CBO attempted to estimate the cost of a protracted war.

In an interview, Frederick Kagan, a professor at the U.S. Military Academy at West Point, observes that war-planners "focused very much on the one thing that we knew we could do, which was destroy the Iraqi military, and didn't think very much about the one thing that was actually going to be very hard to do, which is transition to democracy."[59] Overwhelming firepower was exceptionally effective in the regime-change phase of operations, but there is now widespread agreement that the number of troops was insufficient and that the military was inadequately prepared to manage the transition to peacekeeping and nation-building that followed the overthrow of Saddam Hussein. Few anticipated that the United States would have over 140,000 troops fighting in Iraq six years after Saddam's regime was toppled and the U.S. Commander in Chief declared victory.

Whether key decision-makers in the United States should have foreseen the insurgency that developed after Saddam was removed from power is beyond the scope of the theory of war outcomes that I am presenting.

However, what is notable and in line with predictions of the theory is that policymakers in the Bush administration continued to overestimate the importance of the coalition's destructive-capacity advantage and underestimate the cost of establishing and maintaining the political authority of a new Iraqi government for *years*, even after it became clear that the Iraqi population was not going to be as compliant as anticipated before the invasion. Ali Allawi, minister of trade and minister of defense in the Interim Iraqi Governing Council from September 2003 to June 2004, claims that the Bush administration and the Coalition Provisional Authority (CPA) ignored the evolving insurgency, maintaining a "blindly optimistic interpretation of events."[60] Even as the insurgency gained momentum through the end of 2003 and 2004, "the CPA and the Pentagon continued to deny publicly that what they had on their hands in Iraq was the germination of a full-scale insurrection of the Sunni Arabs of Iraq."[61]

It is too early to tell what the United States has achieved in Iraq. Political violence declined and the stability of the Iraqi government improved after the U.S. troop surge in 2007. In June 2009, U.S. forces began to withdraw from urban areas in Iraq, including Baghdad, under a security pact with Iraq that calls for a full withdrawal by the end of 2011. In an address from the Oval Office in August 2010, President Obama declared an end to the American combat mission in Iraq.

On the other hand, as of May 2011, almost 50,000 U.S. soldiers remained in Iraq to advise, assist, and train Iraqi Security Forces. Leon Panetta, President Obama's choice to replace Robert Gates as secretary of defense, has said he expects Iraq to ask the United States to keep its troops in the country beyond the 2011 withdrawal deadline. Sunni Islamist insurgents maintain a steady flow of attacks, and Panetta warned members of the Senate Armed Services Committee of a continuing threat from al Qaeda in Iraq during his confirmation hearing.[62]

Military defeat was never a possibility for U.S. forces in Iraq. Tragically, the military has lost more soldiers to suicide than combat in Iraq and Afghanistan. However, there has always been a substantial risk that the United States would quit before the desired end state was attained, because the cost of sustaining operations until there is a politically viable government could exceed the cost-tolerance threshold of the American people. Battling the sectarian strife that broke out after Saddam was removed from power has claimed the lives of more than 4,000 American soldiers. But the loss rate has been many times higher for Iraqi insurgents. In 2007, the U.S. military released data indicating that more than 19,000 militants had been killed in fighting with coalition forces since the insurgency began in 2003.[63] This is compared to just over 3,000 U.S. troops killed in combat at the time the data were released—a loss ratio of six insurgents for every American soldier who died. On a per-capita basis, the Iraqi death toll has been sixty times that of the United States, *excluding civilian deaths.*[64]

Nevertheless, according to a CBS News poll, by August 2010, only one in five Americans thought the war had been worth the loss of life and other costs. When the war began, two-thirds of the public agreed that the military intervention in Iraq was the right thing to do. A year later, 60 percent of Americans believed efforts to stabilize Iraq were going badly, and 58 percent of respondents thought that the fighting in Iraq had not been worth the cost. In a CBS News/*New York Times* poll published in 2004, 44 percent of Americans said that the fighting in Iraq was more difficult than they had personally expected, and 67 percent thought the war was harder than the Bush Administration had expected.

Like the conflict over Kuwait, the case of Saddam's overthrow illustrates the importance of leaders' beliefs about relative destructive capacity and resolve for understanding both the escalation of conflicts to violence and the termination of violent conflicts. In both cases, Saddam Hussein chose war over capitulating to the United States' demands because he believed that (1) his state's cost-tolerance advantage would allow it to absorb any costs the United States could impose, and (2) the Iraqis could impose enough costs of their own that they would ultimately convince the United States that the cost of victory would be higher than the price the American public was willing to pay. The United States chose war over continuing to negotiate with Iraq because American decision-makers believed the U.S. military's destructive-capacity advantage would enable the United States to destroy Iraq's capacity and will to fight at an acceptable price. Saddam was wrong, and the United States won both the first Gulf War and the first phase of Operation Iraqi Freedom because, as I will argue in the next chapter, the United States had objectives—expelling the Iraqi military from Kuwait and removing Saddam from power—that could be achieved with brute force alone. The United States' destructive-capacity advantage was easily translated into the ability to destroy Iraq's physical capacity to resist, and Saddam was surprised to find his cost-tolerance advantage to be of little use.

Circumstances changed significantly, however, as violent domestic opposition to the CPA and the establishment of a new U.S.-friendly Iraqi government grew in Iraq. Leaving aside whether the American war-planners should have predicted this type of domestic response to the U.S. invasion, it is important to note that decision-makers continued to underestimate the cost of maintaining the political authority of a new Iraqi government for years, as political violence against coalition troops and Iraqi political leaders and security forces grew. In part because there were domestic political incentives not to acknowledge the extent of the predicament they had gotten the country into, and in part because anticipating how military force should be used to secure a government against violent domestic opposition is inherently difficult, the Bush administration had difficulty finding a military strategy that could win the war. Materially weak but highly resolved Iraqi insurgents were able to push the U.S. public closer to its cost-tolerance threshold by inflicting costs intended to convince its strong adversary that the price of victory was too high.

CONCLUSION

Case studies of individual conflicts often attribute otherwise puzzling conflict outcomes to an imbalance of resolve or "asymmetry of motivation" between the combatants. But these explanations cannot predict when a militarily strong actor is likely to prevail and when it is likely to abandon its war aims in the face of a militarily weak but highly resolute actor. In the next chapter, I build an argument about the specific conditions under which strong and weak actors are most likely to select themselves into wars they cannot win. In wars between unevenly matched opponents, the stronger side is less at risk of selecting into a war it cannot sustain to victory when pursuing what I call "brute force" objectives. The nature of these objectives provides ideal conditions for strong states to employ their destructive-capacity advantage and forces weak targets to adopt direct defense strategies for which they are ill-equipped. The weak, on the other hand, are more likely to prevail when a strong adversary pursues an objective that requires their active compliance. The nature of these objectives—which turn wars into competitions in pain tolerance—enables a weaker actor to avoid direct combat and take full advantage of its superior ability to tolerate costs. When their objectives are dependent on target compliance, states have more difficulty estimating what it will cost to achieve their objectives ex ante and are consequently at greater risk of selecting into a war with a cost-tolerance threshold below the price of victory.

CHAPTER 3

War Aims and War Outcomes

War outcomes are not determined by destructive capacity alone. Although actors with greater destructive capacity than their opponents are better able to impose costs and degrade their opponent's ability to continue fighting, they can be constrained by relatively low tolerance for costs or stymied by an opponent that is willing to absorb extremely high levels of punishment. Weak states are sometimes able to prevail over much stronger adversaries by convincing them that the cost of victory will be higher than the price they are willing to pay. Even a state that has no expectation that it could achieve a military victory could reasonably expect that it might prevail by exceeding its adversary's cost-tolerance threshold—*if it can avoid a decisive defeat.*

Both scholars and military practitioners have suggested poor strategy choices, domestic political constraints, and insufficient commitment as explanations for strong state defeat in war. I argue that the key to understanding strategic success and failure in armed conflict lies in a better understanding of the nature of the political objectives that states pursue through the use of military force beyond their borders. In this chapter, I argue that the nature of a strong state's war aim has a significant effect on its risk for selecting itself into an armed conflict that it cannot sustain to victory. The more "compliance-dependent" an objective, the more difficult it is to translate that political objective into operational military objectives and to establish a link between destructive capacity and the desired end state. When an actor is dependent on a change in target behavior to achieve its war aims, force must be used persuasively, and the target has greater control over the extent to which victory is costly for the state. It is difficult to predict how much force should be used, the manner in which it should be employed, and how long military operations will need to be sustained to reach the enemy's threshold for pain. As a result, states are more likely to misestimate the cost of achieving compliance-dependent objectives before choosing to use military force. This uncertainty increases the risk that states with limited resolve will select themselves into wars they cannot sustain to victory.

THE NATURE OF WAR AIMS

The literature on the effect of resolve on conflict outcomes implies a straightforward, linear relationship between the extent of the asymmetry in "interests at stake," "motivation," or "tolerance for costs" between two belligerents and the probability that one side will prevail over the other. However, as an actor's advantage in military capabilities grows, the human and material costs that actor can expect to bear in the fighting decline, so that stronger actors can afford to have lower tolerance for costs than their weaker adversaries. The key metric, therefore, is not the distance between an actor's cost-tolerance threshold and the cost-tolerance threshold of its adversary, but the distance between the *price* an actor is *willing to pay* and the *actual cost* of attaining that objective through the use of force.

Powerful states do not lose small wars simply because they have less cost tolerance than their weak adversaries. The extent to which a physically weaker actor's cost-tolerance advantage can affect armed conflict outcomes is largely a function of the degree to which the stronger actor has war aims that *require the weak actor to change its behavior*. The balance of military capabilities between the belligerents is expected to be the most important determinant of outcomes when the objects at stake can be seized and held with physical force alone. The defender's tolerance for costs becomes more significant when a challenger pursues political objectives that require a change in target behavior.

A TYPOLOGY OF WAR AIMS

I define a *political objective* as the allocation of a valued good sought by the leaders of a political unit. When a political objective is pursued through the use of organized violence, I use the terms *war aim* and *political objective* interchangeably. Although there are often myriad personal, domestic political, and grand strategic *motivations* for using military force, the political end state that each belligerent in an armed conflict desires is typically fairly transparent.[1] For example, despite persistent criticism that the objectives of the U.S. intervention in Indochina were ambiguous, the primary, immediate-term political objective the United States sought through the application of force was clear: an independent, noncommunist South Vietnam.

In Figure 3.1, I place the political objectives that actors frequently pursue through the use of military force on a continuum based on the *degree of target compliance* required to attain the objective. In order to place a political objective along the continuum, I consider two questions: (1) Is the object at stake something that *could* be forcibly seized and held, or would attaining the objective *require* the target's cooperation? (2) If the objective were attained, would a reversal require the actor to forcibly change the status quo or simply stop complying?[2]

The political objectives at the left end of the continuum in Figure 3.1—acquiring and defending territory, removing a foreign regime, repelling an invasion—are what I call "brute force" war aims. A state with a significant destructive-capacity advantage can attain brute-force war aims with minimal target compliance, because these objectives can be seized and held with overwhelming force. As Schelling observes, "Forcibly a country can repel and expel, penetrate and occupy, seize, exterminate, disarm and disable, confine, deny access, and directly frustrate intrusion or attack."[3] Prior to World War II, the Soviets overran Latvia, Lithuania, Estonia, and part of Finland. Germany absorbed Czechoslovakia, conquered Poland in less than three weeks, and, after only one year of fighting, occupied Denmark, Norway, Belgium, the Netherlands, and France as well. In the spring of 1950, China invaded Tibet and reasserted its authority over the autonomous province in just eighteen days. And on August 2, 1990, Iraq annexed the neighboring state of Kuwait. Resistance from the victims of these attacks was futile.

Of course, a weak adversary's resistance can make seizing territory, removing a regime from power, or annexing an entire country more costly for a strong state. But a state that is strong enough can effectively *impose* a solution to an armed conflict over brute-force objectives. If necessary, the target's armed forces can be completely destroyed or disarmed, making the strength of the target's will to resist and its tolerance for costs largely immaterial. As a result, despite the fact that Estonia, Poland, and Tibet faced the ultimate threat to vital

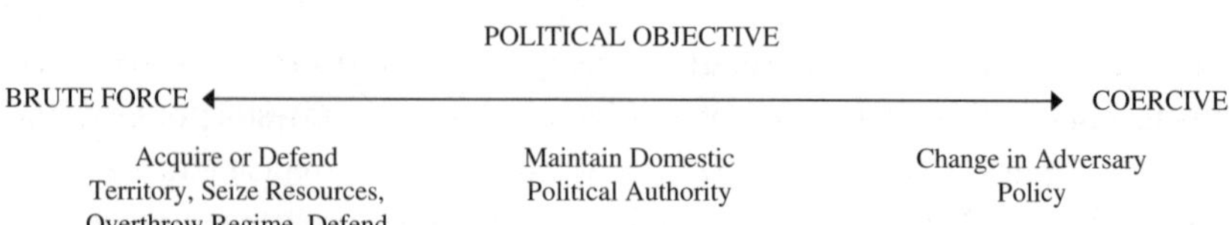

Figure 3.1. Typology of Political Objectives

state interests, all surrendered long before they were rendered incapable of defending themselves.

In contrast, no matter how great its destructive-capacity advantage, an actor can only achieve *coercive* objectives if it can gain target compliance. A regime cannot be physically forced to change its foreign or domestic policies; a foreign power cannot forcibly seize compliance from a native population; and a dissatisfied ethnic minority group within a state cannot be physically forced to abandon its aspirations for statehood. The basic principle underlying this distinction is generalizable to all types of conflicts—between states, substate organizations, and even individuals. If Actor A seeks a change in Actor B's behavior (rather than simply his demise), Actor A must *persuade* Actor B to comply by manipulating the costs and benefits of compliance versus noncompliance. A criminal suspect, for example, can be detained, deprived of physical comforts, threatened, and even tortured, but an interrogator cannot forcibly elicit words—much less "the truth"—from the prisoner's mouth. The same constraint exists when policy change is the objective of military operations. Military force can raise the cost to an adversary of refusing to comply with a state's demands, but military force cannot change a regime's policy toward ethnic minorities within its borders or compel a government to stop sponsoring international terrorism. The target government must be convinced that compliance is less costly than resistance.[4] Compliance-dependent objectives enhance a weak target's ability to *avoid decisive defeat* and determine the cost of victory for a strong state.

Brute-force and coercive objectives are ideal types. Almost all strategic victories in war involve at least passive compliance from some group. Although only brute-force objectives can be seized and held without target compliance, even they are typically attained through a combination of the direct application of force to take or hold the objective and attempts to convince the adversary to voluntarily relinquish the object at stake. The primary reason for this is that leaders typically seek to attain their objectives at the lowest possible cost. Completely destroying an adversary's capacity to sustain an organized offense or defense is an inefficient and tragic waste of human and material resources if the adversary can be persuaded to concede well short of annihilation.

At the same time, many war aims are not located at the extremes of the brute force–coercive continuum. When a state seeks to maintain its own political authority over a population or that of an ally facing a domestic insurgency, the objective falls somewhere in the middle of the continuum. The state can use brute force in an attempt to erode an opposition movement's capacity for resistance, but the population of that territory must eventually be *persuaded* to withhold or terminate its support for the resistance, because elimination of an insurgent threat is not possible as long as popular support for the opposition is sufficiently strong.

Finally, a state with a brute-force war aim could be forced to adopt a more coercive war aim after attaining its original objective, or it could decide to abandon a coercive objective to pursue a brute-force war aim. The most prominent example of the former is a state that is compelled to sustain its military operations in an attempt to maintain its political authority in a territory it has seized or after removing a foreign government. A government that abandons its efforts to influence an adversary's policy choices and initiates military operations intended to forcibly remove the regime from power provides an example of the latter.

Although war aims can change during the course of a single war, I believe it is still useful to think about strategic victory in war in terms of the conditions under which an actor can achieve a particular political objective. If an objective is abandoned because an actor decides that it is too costly or difficult to achieve, I consider this a strategic failure—regardless of whether or not a substitute objective is then adopted. If an objective is attained and maintained for at least one year after a war ends, I consider the military operation a success, even if achieving that objective creates conditions that make the state worse off in the long run. The larger, grand strategic consequences of achieving a war aim are clearly important, but they involve a multitude of political, social, and economic factors beyond the scope of my model. Whether a domestic insurgency develops (as it did after the United States overthrew authoritarian regimes in Iraq and Afghanistan) or peace prevails (as it did after the United States removed dictators in Germany, Panama, and Grenada) clearly matters for the well-being of populations in both the intervening and the target state.[5] Nevertheless, my task in this analysis is to explore the factors that determine whether a state is likely to achieve a specific political objective—its primary war aim—through the use of force. Although the long-term effects of attaining a war aim are arguably more significant than the immediate victory or defeat, I leave predictions about how the short-term gains of war are likely to affect an actor's broader interests to future studies.

WAR AIMS AND THE RELATIVE IMPACT OF DESTRUCTIVE CAPACITY AND COST TOLERANCE

The nature of an actor's primary political objective has both direct and indirect effects on the probability that it can attain that objective through the use of military force.

The nature of an actor's war aims directly affects armed conflict outcomes because there is a much tighter relationship between the military's ability to kill people and destroy things and attainment of brute-force war aims than between an actor's destructive capacity and the attainment of coercive war aims. Mack critiques "the prevalent military belief that if an opponent's military capability to wage war can be destroyed, his 'will' to continue the struggle is irrelevant."[6] But this belief is warranted in campaigns in which a strong state has brute-force political objectives. When an actor pursues war aims that can be seized and held with physical force, its material resources and war-fighting capacity relative to that of the adversary are the primary determinants of success and failure.

The more compliance dependent an objective, however, the more difficult it is to translate that political objective into operational military objectives and to establish a link between battlefield military effectiveness and overall strategic success. Stephen Cimbala notes, "Planners frequently approach the problem of targeting as a question of the destruction of so many physical things: bridges, air defenses, depots, and so forth. This is a legitimate concern, but from the perspective of the relationship between force and policy, not the most important issue."[7] Whereas destructive capacity is most naturally aligned to the attainment of brute-force war aims, a cost-tolerance advantage is most easily translated into strategic victory when political objectives are coercive in nature. Materially weak but resolute targets can thwart a strong state's ability to achieve *coercive* objectives by refusing to comply no matter how high the cost.

Figure 3.2 illustrates the nature of the relationship between military force and political objectives. Actors with inferior destructive capacity will find their cost-tolerance advantage of little use against a strong adversary willing to employ the military force necessary to seize or hold a brute-force objective. But a destructive-capacity advantage is more difficult to translate into the ability to convince an enemy to alter policy. The use of overwhelming force can raise the cost of resistance for the target of the attacks, but greater military effectiveness will not necessarily convince that adversary to change its behavior.

It is not that coercive political objectives are inherently more difficult to achieve than brute-force objectives. Brute-force objectives like conquest and territorial acquisition generally require enormous resources and cost many lives, whereas states often achieve coercive political objectives like

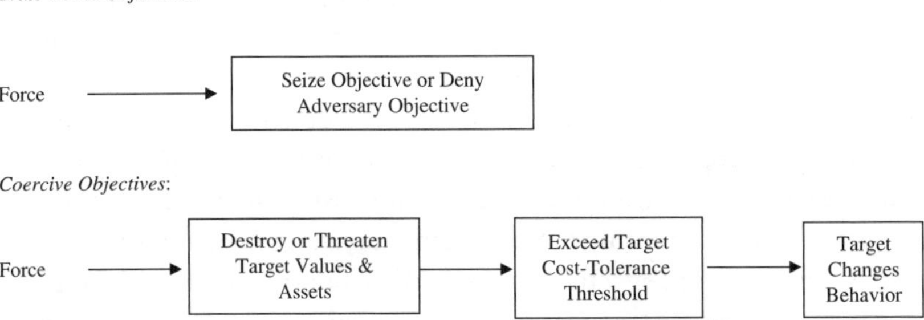

Figure 3.2. The Relationship between Military Force and Political Objectives

policy change without even invoking the use of military force. In general, brute-force objectives are more ambitious than coercive objectives. The stakes are extremely high for a target faced with an enemy seeking to claim territory or change the composition of the target's government. Actors with less destructive capacity than their adversaries have little chance of attaining brute-force objectives. Even militarily strong states must have sufficient tolerance for costs to commit the human and material resources they are capable of bringing to bear if they hope to prevail in a violent conflict over brute-force objectives. But an actor with preponderant capabilities can seize brute-force objectives in spite of an opponent's determination to resist, as long as it is willing to use enough physical force. As Art and Jervis note in their classic text, "If you can take what you want, you do not need your adversary's cooperation and do not have to bargain with him."[8]

States can attempt to coerce an adversary into surrendering any type of objective, but they only have the option of pursuing compulsive settlement by force—of physically imposing their will on the adversary—when they have a brute-force war aim. No matter how great its military advantage over an opponent, an actor that is dependent on target acquiescence to achieve its objectives must use force persuasively, employing its destructive capacity in an effort to gain target compliance by raising the current and anticipated costs of resistance.

WAR AIMS AND UNCERTAINTY

In addition to the direct effects of the nature of an actor's war aims, the type of political objective an actor is pursuing has an indirect effect on armed conflict outcomes through the selection process that generates the armed conflicts we observe. The amount of coercive leverage an actor can derive from a fixed amount of destructive capacity is contingent upon the target's willingness to absorb the costs imposed. The target, therefore, is largely in control of the extent to which achieving a compliance-dependent objective is costly for its opponent and can thwart a strong state's ability to attain a coercive objective simply by refusing to comply, regardless of the level of destruction visited upon it. Because it does not need to win, or even fight, battles against enemy forces to accomplish this, it can avoid direct combat and frustrate a strong state's efforts to achieve a decisive military victory.

Although there can be considerable uncertainty about an adversary's destructive capacity, an adversary's tolerance for costs is inherently less observable than the size of its army, the type of military equipment it possesses, and even its armed force's effectiveness in battle. Modern military organizations are reasonably adept at estimating force requirements and even forecasting casualties for conventional campaigns involving direct combat to destroy enemy military forces. Battles and operations can be war-gamed, intelligence estimates of enemy capabilities can be analyzed, and complex strategies to seize tangible objectives can be planned out in minute detail. There is much greater inherent uncertainty about how much military force will be required, the manner in which force should be employed, and how long a campaign will need to be sustained when attainment of the primary political objective of an operation is dependent on changing target behavior.

Although chance and what Clausewitz calls "friction" are always factors in war, the limits of an enemy's war-fighting capabilities are easier to determine than the bounds of its resolve. After observing a battle, a state can update its beliefs about an enemy's firepower, training, tactics, technology, and leadership. However, upon observing that an enemy chooses not to concede after incurring significant casualties in a battle, a state can only conclude that its enemy has not yet reached its cost-tolerance threshold. Just how much higher that threshold is, the outside observer cannot say. It is difficult to predict future costs or plan military strategies with any type of precision when success is dependent upon reaching an enemy's inherently unknowable "breaking point."[9]

Of course, before opting to use military force, an actor's cost estimates could be *higher* or *lower* than the actual cost of attaining its objectives by force. However, because war is more likely to occur when a state is overly optimistic about the cost, we observe more cases in which costs were initially underestimated than cases in which prewar cost estimates were too high.

Figure 3.3 illustrates my assumptions about the distribution of a state's prewar cost estimates and the probability of war. In this figure, two probability density functions—one for each type of political objective—are graphed to illustrate the theoretical distribution of the challenger's cost estimate errors in a dyadic dispute. The horizontal axis represents the size of the error: Moving along the x axis to the right of zero error, prewar cost estimates are higher than the "true" cost of a war; moving along the axis to the left of zero error, the estimates are too low. The y axis shows the probability that an error of that size will be observed.

Regardless of the nature of the challenger's primary political objective, its cost estimate errors are distributed normally with a mean of zero. On average, its cost estimates are correct. However, the distribution of cost estimate errors for a state pursuing brute-force objectives (solid line) is expected to be less dispersed than the cost estimate errors of a challenger with coercive objectives (dashed line). The probability that a challenger's prewar cost estimate is correct is higher for brute-force objectives than for coercive objectives, and the probability of cost estimates that are way too high (++) or way too low (- -) is greater when the challenger has a coercive objective.

The solid line sloping downward from left to right represents the probability of observing war as the challenger's cost estimate error goes from

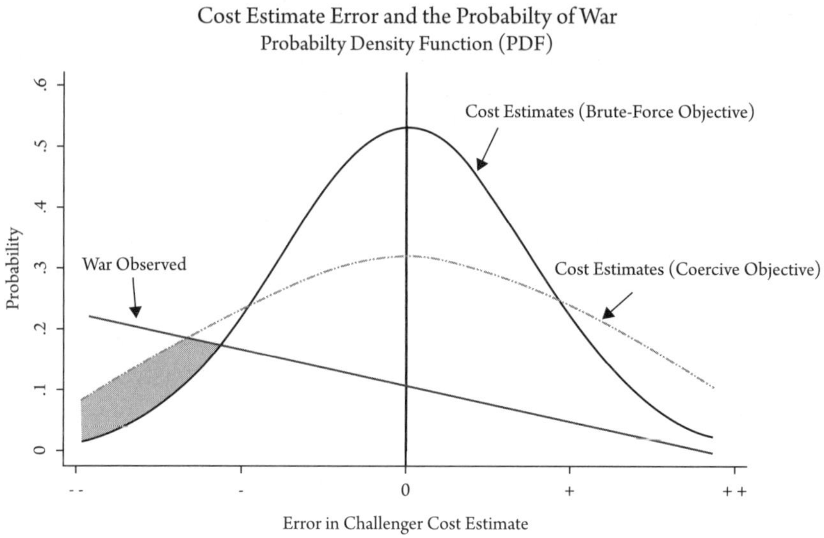

Figure 3.3. Cost Estimate Error and the Probability of War

negative to positive. When all else is equal, the probability that the challenger will choose to escalate a conflict declines as the challenger's prewar cost estimate relative to the true cost increases. When a challenger's prewar cost estimates are lower than the "true" cost of victory, the challenger is more likely to use force, because its cost estimates are more likely to be lower than the price it is willing to pay to attain its objectives (i.e., the challenger expects costs to be lower than its cost-tolerance threshold). At the same time, the target of an overly optimistic challenger has reason to believe it can improve its bargaining position by fighting to correct the challenger's beliefs. A challenger that has underestimated the cost of war is more likely to demand more than the target is willing to concede without a fight.[10]

The probability of war is higher for all of the cost estimates to the left of the vertical line indicating zero error, because the challenger is more likely to escalate, and the target is more likely to resist, when the challenger's cost estimates are too low. The cost estimates that are higher than the "true" cost (i.e., the overestimates to the right of the line) are less likely to result in escalation. The consequence is that, although both overestimation and underestimation of costs are equally likely ex ante, we observe more wars in which costs were initially underestimated. At the same time, because challengers with coercive objectives are more likely than challengers with brute-force objectives to have cost estimates that are far too low, all else being equal, we are more likely to observe wars due to optimistic expectations about costs when states have coercive objectives. The shaded area under the coercive objective cost estimate distribution shows the increased probability of observing a war in which the challenger initially underestimated costs when the challenger's objectives are coercive versus brute force in nature.

Both strong and weak actors can underestimate the cost of fighting a war. It appears, for example, that Slobodan Milošević underestimated the costs that NATO would inflict in its bid to convince the authoritarian leader of Yugoslavia to halt attacks on ethnic Albanians and withdraw his military forces from Kosovo. Although he knew NATO's destructive capacity was far superior to his own, he believed that it lacked the political will to carry out extended military operations.[11] However, after a punishing seventy-eight-day bombing campaign, Milošević conceded to NATO's demands. Susan Allen and Tiffiny Vincent argue that his capitulation finally came because "the intensifying bombing campaign by NATO clearly demonstrated that Milošević had guessed wrong about the Alliance's resolve and cohesion."[12]

But uncertainty about the cost of victory is expected to be especially problematic for powerful states. The consequences of underestimating a strong enemy's capacity to impose costs can threaten the survival of weak actors. Choosing to fight back against a much more powerful state risks not only high human and material losses, but also potential annihilation. Powerful states have much less to lose when they contemplate employing a fraction of their overwhelming destructive capacity in an attempt to change a weak opponent's behavior. The strong can choose to use force with much lower tolerance for costs because they anticipate significantly lower costs and because the consequences of miscalculation are a good deal less dire. As a result, they are at greater risk for selecting into an armed conflict they do not have the cost tolerance to sustain to victory.

The militarily strong cannot be physically defeated by significantly weaker adversaries, but they can fail to prevail in wars with weak state and nonstate actors if, during the course of the armed conflict, they decide that the cost of victory will exceed the price they are willing to pay and choose to terminate military operations before attaining their war aims. Even if strong and weak actors are equally likely to misestimate costs ex ante—and prewar cost estimates are just as likely to be too high than too low—we are more likely to observe wars when prewar estimates are too low and strong actors are more likely to *lose* wars because they have selected themselves in with insufficient tolerance for costs.

MILITARY STRATEGY: CONNECTING MEANS AND ENDS

Both scholars and Western military professionals emphasize the effectiveness of war-fighting strategies that seek to destroy an enemy's *capacity* to fight over strategies in which the primary goal is to degrade the enemy's *will* to fight.[13] Since WWI, U.S. armed forces field manuals have emphasized the use of rapid maneuver and overwhelming firepower to defeat opponents in decisive battles.[14] Scholar and military strategy expert Stephen Biddle describes what he calls the "modern system" of force employment—a war-fighting doctrine centered on the use of combined arms firepower, cover and concealment, and small-unit independent maneuver to allow soldiers to close with and destroy enemy soldiers in direct battle. He argues that "[b]y 1918, a process of convergent evolution under harsh wartime conditions had produced a stable and essentially transnational body of ideas on how to operate effectively in the face of radically lethal modern weapons."[15] At the same time, a number of contemporary scholars provide empirical evidence that direct counterforce strategies are more effective than strategies focused on eroding an adversary's will to resist. Robert Pape, for example, examines various strategies for the use of air power and maintains that "punishment" strategies—in which the goal is to break the morale of an enemy—are less effective than "denial" strategies—in which the aim is to "thwart the target state's military strategy for controlling the objectives in dispute."[16]

Although I agree that military strategy affects war outcomes, I argue that actors' strategies are often constrained by their military capabilities, cost tolerance thresholds, and war aims. As a result, strategy choice has less explanatory power than the conditions that determine the strategic options available to an actor. Strategic victory in war is much less likely when an actor's strategic approach is not aligned with its goals and resources. However, limitations on an actor's physical capabilities and tolerance for costs, and constraints inherent in the nature of its goals, rather than poor decision-making, frequently determine an actor's strategic approach. For example, whenever possible, the target of an overwhelmingly stronger challenger is unlikely to attempt a direct defense strategy, relying instead on an indirect strategy of imposing costs while evading enemy firepower. But weak state and nonstate actors must adopt direct defense strategies if they want to hold territory or maintain their access to the central facilities of command and control within a country.

When Germany invaded Poland on September 1, 1939, Polish forces withdrew to established lines of defense, prepared to hold their ground, despite early battlefield losses, until France and Britain came to the country's defense. However, after the Soviet Union invaded from the east on September 17, it became clear to the Polish government that their military forces could not defend the territory, and Polish troops were ordered to evacuate to Romania.[17] On October 6, 1939, the Polish state ceased to exist when it was annexed and divided among Germany, the Soviet Union, Lithuania, and Slovakia.

The Poles clearly valued their sovereignty—the defensive operations of their armed forces resulted in heavy German losses, and a robust Polish resistance movement persisted under German occupation. But the cost tolerance of the Polish government and people could not change the fact that resistance became futile after the Soviets opened a second front. Relatively weak actors are unlikely to prevail in direct combat with stronger adversaries. Weak actors cannot defend territory or maintain their sovereignty in the face of an invading army by employing a punishment strategy that avoids direct combat. If the object at stake can be seized and held with physical force alone and a stronger opponent is resolved to use a denial strategy to attain that objective, a weak actor cannot prevail by simply avoiding pitched battles, imposing costs, and waiting for the strong state to lose the political capacity to maintain the fight.

Unlike scholars who maintain that some military strategies are inherently superior to others or that there is always an optimal strategic response to an adversary's strategy, I argue that a state's military strategy must match its means and the nature of its objectives. A state with a destructive-capacity advantage over its adversary and a brute-force war aim is likely to prevail if it employs a denial strategy—regardless of the strategy employed by the target. A state can acquire territory, remove a foreign leader from power, or defend its own sovereignty against an invading army by rendering its opponent physically incapable of maintaining an organized offense or defense so that the state can forcibly seize and hold the disputed good. In fact, if a strong state with a brute-force objective has sufficient cost tolerance to employ a denial strategy, that state is likely to prevail even before its adversary is rendered incapable of continuing to fight, because the adversary is likely to sue for peace as soon as it is convinced that the inevitable outcome of continuing to fight will be military defeat.

On the other hand, an actor with a destructive-capacity advantage over its opponent is unlikely to prevail if it has insufficient cost tolerance to employ a denial military strategy—regardless of its war aim. In a 1978 article, Richard Schultz critiques the model of counterinsurgency (COIN) warfare that the United States adopted in Vietnam after the assassination of South Vietnam's President Ngo Dinh Diem. In an attempt to prevent the government from falling to the North Vietnamese Army and the communist guerillas of the National Liberation Front, the United States implemented what Schultz labels a "cost-benefit" model of COIN warfare predicated on the use of coercive techniques intended to defeat the insurgents by modifying the behavior of the larger population. The model, Schultz argues, assumes that "if force and coercion are applied in large enough doses the will of both the populace and insurgents will be broken and the war won. Costs will outweigh the benefits, resulting in the decline of the insurgency."[18]

An actor that employs a punishment strategy is attempting to convince her adversary that the cost of prosecuting the armed conflict to victory will be greater than the price he is willing to pay to attain his political objectives. Such strategies are often tempting for strong states because high costs can be imposed on a weak target without exposing the strong state's soldiers to much physical risk. But the relatively weak state and nonstate actors that select themselves into military contests with powerful states tend to have extraordinarily high tolerances for costs—making it exceptionally difficult to exceed these adversaries' cost-tolerance thresholds.

Moreover, the use of overwhelming force—whether directed against enemy military capacity or civilians—can actually decrease an actor's ability to attain coercive objectives. Crushing an enemy's armed forces is not only costly and inefficient, it is also counterproductive if the desired outcome is a policy change that can be enforced and guaranteed by the existing regime, rather than a collapse of that regime. At the same time, military operations that inflict pain and suffering on a civilian population are likely to do more harm than good if the goal is to increase long-term popular support for a political regime. What Robert Jackman observes regarding a regime's use of force domestically applies equally well to foreign military operations: "[F]orce may not induce compliance, and is unlikely to engender active support."[19] In fact, Andrew Mack maintains that French military repression directed against the insurgents in Indochina "achieved for the militants what they had been unable to achieve for themselves—namely, the political mobilization of the masses against the French."[20]

Punishment strategies are not inherently less effective than denial strategies under all conditions. It is unquestionably the case that punishment attacks sometimes provoke resentment and stiffen resolve rather than inducing a population to demand surrender. Nevertheless, the weak can—and often do—prevail over stronger opponents with a punishment strategy when they could not have prevailed with a denial strategy. The United States did not end its military operations in Vietnam until it had lost almost 60,000 troops, but it was undeniably the costs of fighting their much weaker adversaries, rather than impending military collapse, that led to American withdrawal. A smaller toll imposed by insurgents and terrorists fighting for independence drove France to grant independence to its most prized colony, Algeria. Britain abandoned Aden in 1967, and the United States withdrew from Somalia in 1993, after weak, disorganized armed movements dragged their soldiers' mutilated bodies through the streets.

I argue that punishment strategies are most effective for actors facing an adversary with lower tolerance for costs and an objective that cannot be seized and held with brute force alone. Denial strategies are superior when an actor has an adversary with less destructive capacity and an objective that does not require target compliance. Inflicting sufficient costs to erode a state's political will takes time. If a stronger actor has a brute- force objective and employs sufficient force in a decisive manner, a weak adversary will not survive long enough for its coercive campaign to succeed.

Table 3.1 summarizes the broad expectations of the theory of armed conflict outcomes I have presented in this chapter.

We should not see many wars in which one actor has both greater destructive capacity and greater tolerance for costs. The actor with less war-fighting capacity should anticipate high costs in an armed conflict with a stronger opponent and, unless that actor has high tolerance for costs, it should make whatever concessions are necessary to avoid a fight. A strong state pursuing a coercive war aim will find it difficult to translate that destructive capacity into strategic success against opponents with high cost-tolerance thresholds. Weak but highly resolved actors are expected to prevail when their strong adversaries have political objectives that are dependent on their compliance. But a materially weak actor's cost-tolerance advantage is unlikely to blunt the effectiveness of a strong actor's destructive capacity when the strong actor pursues an objective it can obtain with brute force alone. If the object at stake can be seized and held with physical force alone and a stronger actor has sufficient resolve to use the force necessary to do so, the target cannot simply avoid pitched battles, impose costs, and hold out until the costs of fighting have exceeded the strong state's cost-tolerance threshold. If, however, the strong state does not have

Table 3.1. ARMED CONFLICT PREDICTIONS MADE BY THE THEORY

		Challenger's Destructive Capacity	
		Lower than Target	***Higher than Target***
Challenger's Cost Tolerance	*Lower than Target*	No challenge/No war observed	Win with a brute-force war aim and denial strategy Lose with a coercive war aim or punishment strategy
	Higher than Target	Win with a coercive war aim Lose with a brute-force war aim	Target makes concessions/No war observed

sufficient cost tolerance to employ a direct denial strategy, it is unlikely to prevail, regardless of its war aim.

In chapter 4, I lay out the empirical implications of the theory I have developed and discuss how I use statistical analyses and two different sources of historical data on armed conflict to test my hypotheses. The final section of the current chapter uses a brief case study of confrontations between the United States and Iraq following the first Gulf War to illustrate how the nature of a strong state's war aims affects the utility of preponderant military capacity.

FULL-SPECTRUM FRUSTRATION

The United States' experience in Operation Desert Storm stands in sharp contrast to the years of Iraqi intransigence that followed. After the first Gulf War, political and military leaders in the United States hailed the military victory as a model for the future of warfare. Both President Bush and Chairman of the Joint Chiefs of Staff Colin Powell claimed that the war in the Gulf had exorcised the ghosts of the Vietnam War.[21] And the Joint Chiefs subsequently began developing military doctrine that would allow the United States to attain "full-spectrum dominance"—the ability "to defeat any adversary and control any situation across the full range of military operations."[22]

In retrospect, claims that the Gulf War had exorcised the ghosts of Vietnam and that the United States could develop the military capacity to prevail in any form of conflict were far too optimistic. The most capable military in the world prevailed over the poorly trained, poorly equipped, and poorly motivated military of a developing country in precisely the scenario that we would expect it to—when pursuing a brute-force war aim with a denial strategy. In the coercive diplomacy and air campaign phases of the conflict, however, the United States underestimated the importance of Iraq's tolerance for costs. The United States may have demonstrated its tremendous military capacity in Desert Storm, but its performance in the ground campaign did not change the nature of war or increase the utility of military force. As the United States would learn over the next twelve years, high tolerance for costs can trump superior destructive capacity when a strong state has a coercive political objective or is unwilling to employ a denial strategy against a weak target.

Following Operation Desert Storm, the United States pushed the United Nations to monitor Iraq's nuclear, chemical, and biological weapons facilities to ensure that Hussein's regime was not able to develop weapons of mass destruction. UN Security Council Resolution 687, adopted on April 3, 1991, required the Iraqi government to destroy all stockpiles of chemical and biological weapons, along with all related facilities, to abandon all attempts to acquire or develop nuclear weapons, to destroy any ballistic missiles with a range greater than 150 kilometers, and to submit to ongoing international supervision and inspection of all suspected WMD-related facilities.[23] The United States, Britain, and France also set up two no-fly zones to protect Iraqi Kurds in the north and Shiite Muslim civilians in the south. Iraqi aircraft were not permitted to fly over Iraqi territory north of the 36th parallel or south of the 32nd (later extended northward to the 33rd) parallel.[24]

In the decade that followed the coalition campaign to oust Iraq from Kuwait, the United States and Britain had primarily coercive political objectives—they wanted to change Iraqi behavior from noncompliance to compliance with the no-fly zones, arms embargo, and weapons monitoring. And they pursued these objectives with a mixture of punishment and denial strategies. The allies employed air patrols to shoot down Iraqi planes that violated the no-fly zone and take out any ground forces that advanced toward the protected areas—a denial military strategy—as well as punitive air strikes and economic sanctions in an attempt to change the Iraqi leader's behavior. Although the air patrols succeeded in achieving their operational objective while they were active, the United States never reached a point at which it had secured a lasting change in Saddam's intentions that would enable the allies to withdraw their military forces from the region with the expectation that the protected populations would be safe. Saddam continuously demonstrated his desire to challenge the no-fly zones—even risking the serious damage inflicted by U.S. air strikes in attempts to take down U.S. and British planes.

Maintaining the containment regime was expensive for the United States because it required a major U.S. military presence in the region. Before the troop buildup for Operation Iraqi Freedom, the United States had approximately 28,000 troops, two hundred aircraft, and thirty ships directly deployed in support of containment efforts. Economists from the National Bureau of Economic Research and the University of Chicago attempted to calculate the cost of the effort to the United States in a 2006 paper. Their estimates ranged from $11.3 to $19.4 billion per year, including approximately $200 million in expended munitions alone.[25]

Despite his decisive defeat in 1991, punishing economic sanctions, and the continued presence of coalition military forces, Saddam repeatedly refused to comply with UN weapons inspections and frequently violated the no-fly zones. On multiple occasions, Saddam denied UN weapons inspectors access to suspected chemical, biological, or nuclear weapons production facilities or detained UN weapons inspectors who found evidence of weapons programs.[26] Ali Allawi notes that "[t]he UN weapons monitoring effort in Iraq entailed a running battle of wits between the inspectors of the United Nations Special Commission (UNSCOM) team and the Iraqi authorities who had fiercely resisted the UN's programme."[27] Iraqi planes crossed into the no-fly zones and the military attempted to shoot down patrolling aircraft on an almost daily basis. There were even Iraqi military incursions into the demilitarized zone on the Iraq–Kuwait border. In October 1994, the Iraqi leader deployed 20,000 Republican Guard troops to the border with Kuwait, triggering fears of another invasion.[28]

The United States responded by condemning Iraqi behavior in the United Nations, threatening Iraq with military action, increasing aerial patrols in the no-fly zones, and conducting air and missile strikes against Iraqi targets. U.S. and British air forces repeatedly chased and occasionally shot down Iraqi aircraft that crossed into the no-fly zones.[29] For three days in January of 1992, the United States, Britain, and France bombed 114 targets in five Iraqi cities. Days later, they conducted missile and air raids on a factory suspected of being involved in nuclear weapons development in Baghdad and four targets in the southern no-fly zone. The Rashid Hotel in central Baghdad was hit, and the Iraqis reported twenty-one civilian deaths from the air strikes in the south. Later that year, the United States dropped cluster bombs in the northern no-fly zone in response to Iraqi anti-aircraft fire. After a U.S. government report documenting Saddam's violations of UN resolutions was released late in 1998, the United States and Britain launched Operation Desert Fox—four days of aerial assaults on approximately eighty-five targets within Iraq. The result was that Saddam announced that his government would not let UN weapons inspectors return to Iraq and would no longer recognize the northern and southern no-fly zones.

The containment of Iraq was by no means a complete failure. In a 2004 article in *Foreign Affairs*, George Lopez and David Cortright make an especially strong case for the effectiveness of economic sanctions, maintaining that "[s]anctions compelled Iraq to accept inspections and monitoring and won concessions from Baghdad on political issues such as the border dispute with Kuwait. They also drastically reduced the revenue available to Saddam, prevented the rebuilding of Iraqi defenses after the Persian Gulf War, and blocked the import of vital materials and technologies for producing WMD."[30] After the United States removed Saddam Hussein from power in 2003, the Pentagon and the U.S. Central Intelligence Agency sent a team of 1,400 American, British, and Australian inspectors to Iraq to determine the scope of the leader's remaining weapons program. The Iraq Survey Group's (ISG) final report, commonly referred to as the Duelfer report, was released in September 2004. The team concluded that Saddam had dismantled his nuclear program in 1991, that there was no evidence of a concerted effort to restart the program, and that the combination of international sanctions, inspections, and embargoes had devastated Iraq's chemical and biological weapons programs.

Less publicized, however, was the ISG's conclusion that "[t]he Regime made a token effort to comply with the disarmament process, but the Iraqis never intended to meet the spirit of the UNSC's resolutions. Outward acts of compliance belied a covert desire to resume WMD activities."[31] The ISG uncovered evidence of efforts by the regime to evade sanctions in order to improve its long-range missile and unmanned aerial vehicle capabilities. Numerous times, the report notes that senior officials from Saddam's regime told inspectors that Saddam always intended to restart his nuclear and chemical weapons programs after sanctions were lifted.[32] The report concludes that "Saddam directed the Regime's key ministries and governmental agencies to devise and implement strategies, policies, and techniques to discredit the UN sanctions, harass UN personnel in Iraq, and discredit the U.S. At the same time . . ., he also wanted to obfuscate Iraq's refusal to reveal the nature of its WMD and WMD-related programs, their capabilities, and his intentions."[33] Finally, it appears that even Saddam's efforts to maintain the appearance that he was cooperating eroded after 1995. From 1995 onward, the report concludes, the regime shifted its focus to minimizing the impact of the inspections on Iraq's military-industrial capabilities, obstructing the work of UNSCOM inspectors "through site sanitization, warning inspection sites prior to the inspectors' arrival, concealment of sensitive documentation, and intelligence collection on the UN mission."[34]

The frustration that U.S. policymakers experienced during this period in their relations with the Iraqi dictator is strikingly dissimilar to the experience of decision-makers in the military operations that bracket it. In the conflict over Kuwaiti sovereignty that followed Iraq's invasion and annexation of the state in 1990, the United States and its allies established an objective that could be attained with brute force—the return of all Kuwaiti territory to Kuwait. Although they initially pursued this objective with a coercive punishment strategy involving economic sanctions, military threats, and limited air strikes, when this approach failed to attain the objective, the coalition launched a combined arms denial campaign that rapidly brought about Iraq's surrender. The final phase of the United States' engagement with Saddam Hussein's regime ended with a dramatic change in American political objectives. The terrorist attacks on American soil in September of 2001 established domestic political conditions that allowed the second Bush administration to end the threat posed by the Iraqi dictator irreversibly. Tired of trying to coerce the regime into compliance and convinced that Iraq posed a threat to U.S. security, the administration decided to adopt a brute-force war aim—the removal of the regime—and committed to achieving it with a denial military strategy. Central Baghdad fell to a U.S.-led coalition just eighteen days after it invaded on March 20, 2003.

When strong states pursue brute-force objectives and employ denial strategies, their emphasis on relative destructive capacity will serve them well, because the outcome of the armed conflict will be primarily determined on the battlefield. Brute-force war aims can be seized and held with physical force alone and can only be defended with a direct defense strategy. The strong are less likely to underestimate the force that must be brought to bear to win militarily, and battles between the two adversaries will eventually convince the weaker actor that continuing to fight would be a futile waste of lives and resources—regardless of the strength of their resolve.

When Iraq invaded and annexed neighboring Kuwait, Saddam Hussein succeeded in attaining a brute-force war aim because a weaker adversary became convinced—not that the costs of fighting back would be greater than the value of the objective (presumably survival would be worth an extremely high price to the Kuwaiti people and government)—but that the inevitable outcome of fighting back would be military defeat by the Iraqi army. Although the government of Kuwait undoubtedly valued its sovereignty, territory, and oil resources highly, Iraq had much greater destructive capacity and trying to hold out against the invading army would have been futile. The inevitable result of sustaining a direct defense against the invading army would have been a massive loss of life and equipment, leading ultimately to the complete destruction of Kuwait's armed forces.

As their political objectives become more dependent on target compliance, leaders of strong states are likely to find themselves frustrated by their inability to translate their military advantages into influence over their adversary. We are more likely to observe the strong terminating their military operations short of victory when they have coercive war aims, because (1) the weak can prevent the strong from achieving coercive objectives by avoiding pitched battles and refusing to concede despite the cost, and (2) the strong are more likely to underestimate the true cost of attaining coercive objectives before choosing to use military force.

In the case of Iraq, the United States did not simply withdraw from Iraq without attaining its objectives. The terrorist attacks of September 11, 2001 gave American decision-makers the domestic support they needed to switch to a brute-force objective—the overthrow of Saddam's regime—and to pursue it with a denial strategy. However, the United States failed to achieve its primary political objectives in approximately 30 percent of its major military operations between 1946 and 2002. In almost every one of these failures, the United States chose to terminate its military intervention short of victory despite the fact that it retained an overwhelming *physical* capacity to sustain military operations. The U.S. withdrawal from Somalia after the death of sixteen Army Rangers may appear to be an extreme case, but it is consistent with a pattern in which the United States experienced higher-than-expected costs and withdrew its troops short of attaining intervention objectives, despite the fact that its military was, at most, only marginally degraded in the conflict. The United States' unsuccessful intervention in Vietnam is, of course, the quintessential example.

In early 1962, President Kennedy began to increase military assistance to South Vietnam in the hopes of maintaining the country as an independent, noncommunist state. Initially, the United States sought to bolster the South Vietnamese military with an influx of assistance, training, and advisors, but gradually it increased its troop presence. In March of 1965, President Johnson sent 3,500 marines to the south, marking the beginning of the U.S. ground war. The number of U.S. troops reached 200,000 by the end of 1965 and 500,000 by the end of 1968. However, the intervention failed to achieve the objective of maintaining an independent South Vietnam. After the Tet Offensive in January of 1968, American public opinion turned more decisively against the war effort. In 1969, newly elected President Nixon began the "Vietnamization" of the war, which called for building up the South Vietnamese armed forces to take over the defense effort. The United States signed the Paris Peace Accords on January 27, 1973, ending direct U.S. military involvement. In April 1975, South Vietnam surrendered to the North, and Vietnam became united.

Saddam could not prevail over the United States by turning the war over Kuwait into another Lebanon or Vietnam because the objective—Kuwaiti territory—could be seized and held with physical force alone if necessary. If Iraq had not surrendered, the coalition could have completely destroyed the Iraqi army's ability to maintain an organized defense of the ground they held. In Vietnam and Lebanon, in contrast, the United States was trying to maintain the domestic political authority of regimes that faced substantial domestic opposition—a moderately coercive objective that can only be attained with some degree of compliance from the population. Although individuals who took up arms against the governments in South Vietnam and Lebanon could be physically eliminated, maintaining a regime's governing authority is incredibly difficult if there is widespread noncompliance within the society. In fact, the core conclusion of Field Manual 3–24, the "counterinsurgency" field manual adopted in 2006 by the U.S. Army and Marines, is that, regardless of how effective direct strikes on enemy combatants are, insurgencies cannot be defeated unless the government can earn the support of the general population. On the appropriate level of force in counterinsurgency operations, the manual notes: "An operation that kills five insurgents is counterproductive if collateral damage leads to the recruitment of fifty more insurgents."[35]

Weak actors select themselves into armed conflicts with strong adversaries when they have high cost-tolerance thresholds because they anticipate high costs. After a conflict has escalated to mutual hostilities, we are not likely to see weak actors surrendering to their powerful opponents because the *costs* imposed on them are too high. When the strong prevail, we should observe that their weak adversaries updated their beliefs about the eventual *outcome* of the war—deciding that, regardless of the importance of the issues at stake for them and the strength of their resolve, they could not attain their objectives through the use of military force. If they continued to fight, the eventual, inevitable outcome would be the complete destruction of their military capacity.

Saddam believed that he could prevail in his confrontation with the United States over Kuwait by refusing to comply regardless of the cost and by imposing costs on U.S. forces that would be politically unacceptable to the American public. Regardless of the coalition's destructive capacity, a strategy that relied on raising costs above Saddam's cost-tolerance threshold was unlikely to succeed. Demolishing Saddam's residences, leadership facilities, and military headquarters; punishing the Iraqi population with the destruction of power plants, transportation infrastructure, and industrial targets; and targeting Saddam's Republican Guard units was not enough to convince the leader to withdraw from Kuwait. Although the air campaign was extremely damaging, air power alone could not physically remove Iraq from Kuwait unless the coalition was willing to annihilate every living thing in the territory the Iraqi army occupied. Only after the air campaign began to focus more heavily on targeting in preparation for a ground campaign, and the coalition ground offensive was imminent, did Saddam begin his first moves toward making concessions to end the conflict. When it became apparent that Iraqi ground forces would not be able to draw the Americans into a long, bloody war of attrition, Saddam Hussein realized that his strategy for holding Kuwait was fundamentally flawed. Saddam did not surrender because he became convinced that holding Kuwait would be too costly or because he realized how much damage and suffering the coalition could inflict. He surrendered when it became clear that the United States was committed to a ground offensive to remove Iraq from Kuwait, and the Iraqi army could not physically hold the territory of Kuwait against the far superior war-fighting capacity of coalition troops.

CONCLUSION

Could an alternative theory explain the pattern of decision-making and armed conflict outcomes in the series of post-Cold War military confrontations between the United States and Iraq just as well as the war aims approach? An exclusive focus on relative military capabilities seems to have little explanatory power for this set of cases—where we see variation in conflict outcomes as the balance of material power between the belligerents remains overwhelmingly skewed in favor of one of the actors. Tolerance for costs certainly played a role in actors' escalation decisions, strategy choices, and willingness to concede, but the balance of resolve is not able to fully account for the pattern of outcomes we observe either. The United States was most successful, at the lowest cost, when it pursued regime change in Iraq—an objective that clearly threatened Saddam Hussein's highest value.

Although the cases I explore in this chapter and the one that preceded it are consistent with my expectations, I cannot make any broad claims about the explanatory power of my approach or any of the rival theories based on this exploration. My core hypotheses are probabilistic rather than deterministic—the strong are expected to be more likely to prevail when they have brute-force objectives and employ denial strategies, and the weak are more likely to prevail when their adversaries have coercive war aims or employ punishment strategies. But there will surely be historical cases in which the strong prevail with coercive objectives or fail to attain brute-force objectives despite employing a denial strategy. Violent conflicts are complex, and their outcomes are determined by a multitude of factors. Probabilistic expectations are best tested with comparative statistical methods. In the following chapter, I present specific hypotheses from my own theory and three of the most prominent alternative theories of war outcomes. Chapter 4 also describes the empirical analyses I conduct to evaluate these hypotheses. In chapters 5 and 6, I use statistical methods and two separate sources of data to systematically test my arguments about the conditions under which states are able to attain their war aims against alternative explanations for war outcomes.

CHAPTER 4

Testing the Argument

In this chapter, I explain how I employ historical data to evaluate how well the theory I have developed—which I refer to as the war aims model—stacks up against alternative explanations of violent conflict outcomes. I begin by asking what we would expect to observe if the model accurately represents the primary determinants of war outcomes. I derive specific, falsifiable hypotheses from my own theory and the competing theories described in chapter 1. I then discuss the data I bring to bear on the problem and how I operationalize and measure the concepts in my hypotheses. In the following chapter, I establish the broad generalizability of the theory by testing its predictions against the empirical evidence provided by the history of violent international disputes since 1919. Chapter 6 tests the expectations of the war aims model for armed conflicts between strong states and their weaker state and nonstate adversaries.

As is the case with most phenomena in international relations, I cannot design experiments that would allow me to manipulate the variables of interest and observe their effects on outcomes. Nor are there so many cases of war in modern history that it is easy to isolate the effects of only the key explanatory variables by holding constant all of the other factors that could determine war outcomes. Fortunately, war is relatively rare. Stuart Bremer calculates the probability of war between a random pair of states in the international system to be under one-half of 1 percent a year between 1816 and 1965.[1]

The complexity and subjectivity of both the dependent variable—war outcomes—and the explanatory variables of interest also make testing the argument more difficult. Although it is a fairly straightforward prospect to quantify the number of soldiers in a state's armed forces, the quality of those soldiers, the nature of a state's war aims, and a nation's tolerance for the costs of war are all considerably more difficult to pin down.

Despite these challenges, one major aim is to avoid testing the competing arguments in a way that introduces a bias that favors some models over others. My strategy for avoiding this is twofold: First, I select a set of violent conflict cases that is both manageable and relevant to my question and collect original data on the conflict outcomes and a wide range of factors hypothesized to determine those outcomes. In collecting these data, I make every effort to develop rigorous coding procedures to guard against the introduction of bias. I describe this dataset and the way the data were collected and coded in the data subsection of this chapter. The second part of my approach is to conduct tests of the theory on an entirely different dataset, collected by other scholars for a different purpose.

Although neither dataset is perfect for testing my argument, their strengths and weaknesses compensate for each other in many ways. My original dataset on major power military interventions is small enough to allow for careful, detailed research and coding of the variables of interest in my own and competing theories of war outcomes. The flip side is that using a limited number of cases calls into question the generalizability of the findings. The second dataset has much greater breadth, but there is limited information for each case, and I am forced to rely on rudimentary proxy measures of the variables in which I am most interested. Nevertheless, results of tests with these two disparate datasets are remarkably consistent, allowing for greater confidence that the results are substantively meaningful rather than simply an artifact of case selection or the way that the variables are measured.

HYPOTHESES

Because the theory I develop builds on existing theories, I briefly present hypotheses derived from these existing theories first and then lay out the hypotheses developed from my own argument.

Relative Power

Michael Desch reflects a widely held view when he maintains that "the most important, powerful and consistent predictor of whether a state will win or lose a war is its share of the material indicators of national power."[2] Realist theories of war outcomes have always emphasized relative military capabilities as a primary determinant of outcomes for all types of international conflict. In fact, the expectation that the militarily strong will prevail over the militarily weak in war makes the very existence of asymmetric wars puzzling. Recent theories about the determinants of victory and defeat in war incorporate a wide range of factors in addition to conventional measures of military-industrial power—soldiering skill, force employment doctrine, civil-military relations, and leadership.[3] But even these factors tend to be highly correlated with an actor's material resources. The basic expectation remains that the probability that a state will prevail over its opponent increases with the magnitude of that state's war-fighting capabilities relative to those of its opponent.

Hypothesis 1 presents the straightforward expectation that states become more likely to attain their war aims as their military capabilities and war-fighting effectiveness increase relative to those of their adversary. If war outcomes are largely determined by battlefield outcomes, the state with the greatest war-fighting capacity should be most likely to prevail in war. At the same time, if the balance of military capabilities is the primary determinant of war outcomes, a state's ability to gain concessions in conflicts short of full-scale war should rise with its destructive-capacity advantage over an adversary.

> H1 (relative power): The probability of strategic victory will increase as a state's war-fighting capacity and military effectiveness increase relative to those of the its opponent.

Political Will

In addition to the military balance, some scholars have argued that the importance of the issues at stake to each party and the willingness of each side to bear the burdens of war are primary determinants of conflict outcomes.[4] My second set of competing hypotheses is based on what I call "balance of resolve" or "political will" arguments. According to this perspective, the salience of the issues at stake for each side can be just as critical as military capabilities for explaining war outcomes.[5] Because strong states frequently have relatively little at stake in conflicts with weaker adversaries, they are at risk of exhausting the domestic political will necessary to sustain a military campaign before achieving their war aims.[6] Even relatively weak states should be unlikely to back down when vital interests are threatened, and states that are strongly motivated by what is at stake in a dispute may be able to prevail over stronger, but less resolved, opponents. Weak states can even the playing field against stronger opponents by balancing their greater willingness to be hurt against their adversary's greater ability to hurt.[7]

Hypothesis 2 anticipates that states should be more likely to escalate disputes that threaten regime survival or the territorial integrity of the state than conflicts in which they are faced with a demand for policy change or seek policy change from an adversary. Hypothesis 3 predicts that, all else being equal, states become more likely to attain their objectives when they have greater interests at stake than their adversary.

H2 (political will): Disputes over territory and governance should be more likely to escalate to war than disputes over policy.
H3 (political will): The probability of strategic victory will increase the more salient the issues at stake in the conflict for the state relative to those of its opponent.

Strategy

My final set of rival hypotheses is drawn from theories suggesting that the manner in which force is employed by a state is a critical determinant of war outcomes.[8] A number of scholars and military practitioners argue that denial (also called direct or counterforce) strategies, which seek to destroy an enemy's capacity to fight, are more effective than punishment strategies, which target an enemy's will to fight.[9] Although Thomas Schelling observes that the power to hurt is bargaining power, other scholars maintain that the decision-making of belligerents in wartime is influenced primarily by the ability of their armed forces to continue to offer a coherent military challenge to their adversaries on the battlefield. Efforts to coerce political leaders into conceding by inflicting pain and suffering are likely to backfire by inducing civilians to rally around the political leadership and increasing their resolve to resist the enemy.[10]

In the first military strategy hypothesis, I distinguish between two broad approaches to the use of military force by states. Denial strategies are employed to win wars by degrading the enemy's capacity to fight, whereas punishment strategies attempt to raise the human and material costs of the conflict above the adversary's ability or willingness to tolerate these costs. Punishment strategies may be targeted at enemy civilians or combatants—but rather than concentrating attacks on denying the enemy the means to continue fighting, the goal is to coerce the adversary's political leadership into making concessions in order to avoid incurring further costs.

H4 (military strategy): States will be more likely to experience strategic success when they employ denial strategies and less likely to achieve strategic victory when they employ punishment strategies.

An alternative theory, which Ivan Arreguín-Toft calls the "strategic interaction" thesis, maintains that strong states are more likely to prevail against weak targets if they use the same strategic approach as the target (i.e., direct vs. direct or indirect vs. indirect). When both actors use the same strategic approach, he argues, there is nothing to mediate or deflect a strong actor's power advantage and ". . . these interactions should therefore be resolved in proportion to the force applied."[11]

> H5 (military strategy): Strong states will be more likely to experience strategic success when belligerents on both sides employ the same strategic approach.

War Aims

The war aims model does not deny the importance of material strength, military strategy, or resolve, but it makes several unique predictions about the effects of these factors on war outcomes.

Due to the mutual selection process behind the escalation of conflicts to war, a destructive-capacity advantage that favors one actor tends to be balanced by a cost-tolerance advantage that favors the other actor in the wars we observe. I argue that a critical characteristic of war aims—the degree to which attaining them requires target compliance—determines whether relative destructive capacity or tolerance for costs has a greater impact on the dynamics of a war.

The balance of military capabilities between the belligerents is expected to be more important when the object at stake can be seized and held with physical force alone. The nature of these objectives provides ideal conditions for strong states to employ their destructive-capacity advantage and forces weak targets to adopt direct defense strategies for which they are ill-equipped. A materially weak actor's cost-tolerance advantage is unlikely to blunt the effectiveness of a strong actor's destructive capacity when the strong actor pursues an objective it can obtain with brute force alone.

The weak, on the other hand, are more likely to prevail when a strong adversary pursues an objective that requires their active compliance. The nature of these objectives—which turn wars into competitions in pain tolerance—enables a weaker actor to avoid direct combat and take full advantage of its superior ability to tolerate costs. The greater the target's cost-tolerance advantage, the more difficult it will be for even the strongest state to exceed the target's cost-tolerance threshold, and the longer the target can prolong a war over objectives that require its compliance.

The more compliance dependent the objective, the more difficult it is to translate destructive capacity into strategic success. The use of overwhelming force can raise the cost of resistance, but it will not necessarily convince a highly resolved target to change its behavior. When a state is dependent on a change in target behavior to achieve its war aims, force must be used persuasively, and the target is largely in control of the extent to which victory is costly. When a militarily strong state attempts to coerce a target with high tolerance for the costs of war, it is difficult to predict how much force should be used, the manner in which it should be employed, and how long military operations will need to be sustained. This uncertainty increases the probability that strong states will select themselves into asymmetric wars that they cannot sustain to victory. The military operations of powerful states are most likely to fail when they choose to use force based on an expectation that they can achieve their objectives at a reasonable cost, but later come to believe that the cost of attaining their war aims is going to exceed the price they are willing to pay.

Hypothesis 6 anticipates that a state's destructive-capacity advantage will be positively correlated with the probability of victory in violent conflicts with brute-force objectives but negatively correlated with the probability of victory in armed conflicts with coercive objectives.

> H6 (war aims): A state's destructive-capacity advantage should be positively correlated with the probability of victory in armed conflicts with brute-force objectives but negatively correlated with the probability of victory in armed conflicts with coercive objectives.

My second broad expectation follows directly from the first. Because the nature of states' war aims affects war outcomes, it will also affect the probability that a state attains its objectives short of war and the likelihood that a conflict will escalate to war. When all else is equal, I expect disputes over territory and governance to be more likely to escalate to the use of military force by both sides, because both states are more likely to see these issues as worth fighting over. Few conflicts over policy will have stakes that both sides see as salient enough to risk the use of military force. However, I also expect that states will become less likely to escalate a dispute over territory or governance as the disparity in military capabilities between the disputants increases. The distribution of destructive capacity between two belligerents should have a greater effect on the likelihood of escalation in disputes over brute-force objectives—like territory—than in disputes with objectives that require target compliance—like policy change. If the balance of military capabilities between two states is the primary determinant of outcomes in wars over brute-force objectives, but the defender's tolerance for costs becomes more important in violent conflicts over coercive objectives, the distribution of military capabilities should provide more information about who would prevail in a war over brute-force objectives than about who would prevail in a war with coercive objectives. As the disparity in two states' capabilities increases, uncertainty about the outcome of a potential war between them decreases, but uncertainty should decrease *most* in disputes with brute-force objectives. It should be more difficult for the weaker state in a dyad to be optimistic about the outcome of a military contest over territory or governance than over policy. And decreasing uncertainty about the outcome of a potential war between two states increases the probability that the states can negotiate a distribution of the object at stake without actually going to war.[12]

Hypothesis 7 anticipates that the balance of military capabilities between disputants will exert a stronger effect on the likelihood of escalation in disputes over brute-force objectives than in disputes over coercive objectives.

> H7 (war aims): The balance of military capabilities between two actors should exert a stronger effect on the likelihood of escalation in disputes over brute-force objectives than in disputes over coercive objectives.

My final hypothesis anticipates that strong states will be more likely to attain brute-force political objectives, unless they lack the cost tolerance to employ a denial strategy. A strong state that seeks to win cheaply by employing a punishment strategy surrenders its primary advantage—the ability to use battlefield results to convince its target that resistance is futile—and provides its target with an opportunity to employ its preferred strategy—imposing costs, avoiding pitched battles, and prolonging the fight until the strong state decides that the costs of continuing its military operations will exceed the value of attaining its objectives.

Brute-force war aims allow strong states to take full advantage of their destructive-capacity advantage to seize their objective and destroy an opponent's military capabilities, thereby minimizing the impact of target cost tolerance. If the object at stake can be seized and held with physical force alone, and a stronger opponent has sufficient resolve to use the force necessary to do so, the target cannot simply avoid pitched battles, impose costs on the state, and hold out until the costs of fighting have exceeded the strong state's cost-tolerance threshold. Objects that can be seized and held with physical force alone must be defended with a direct denial strategy. If, however, the strong state does not have sufficient cost tolerance to employ a denial strategy, it is unlikely to prevail, regardless of its war aim. A strong state that employs a punishment strategy cedes the primary benefit of its destructive-capacity advantage—the ability to convince its target that resistance is futile. At the same time, a strong state that seeks to win cheaply by avoiding a denial strategy signals its low tolerance for costs to the adversary and provides an opportunity for a weak target to prevail with its preferred strategy—imposing costs, avoiding pitched battles, and prolonging the fight until the strong state decides that the costs of continuing its military operations will exceed the value of attaining its objectives.

> H8 (war aims): Employing a punishment strategy will reduce the likelihood of strategic success for strong states pursuing brute-force objectives. Adopting a punishment strategy should have no effect on the probability of strategic success for weak states or states with coercive political objectives.

Table 4.1 summarizes expectations about dispute escalation and conflict outcomes from the relative power, political will, and military strategy perspectives and provides competing hypotheses from the war aims theory presented in chapters 2 and 3.

Table 4.1. SUMMARY OF HYPOTHESES

Theory	Prediction
Relative power	Hypothesis 1: The probability of strategic victory will increase as a state's war-fighting capacity and military effectiveness increase relative to those of its opponent.
Political will	Hypothesis 2: Disputes over territory and governance should be more likely to escalate to war than disputes over policy.
	Hypothesis 3: The probability of strategic victory will increase the more salient the issues at stake in the conflict for the state relative to those of its opponent.
Military strategy	Hypothesis 4: States will be more likely to experience strategic success when they employ denial strategies and less likely to achieve strategic victory when they employ primarily punishment strategies.
	Hypothesis 5: Strong states will be more likely to experience strategic success when belligerents on both sides employ the same strategic approach.
War aims	Hypothesis 6: A state's destructive-capacity advantage should be positively correlated with the probability of victory in armed conflicts with brute-force objectives but negatively correlated with the probability of victory in armed conflicts with coercive objectives.
	Hypothesis 7: The balance of military capabilities between two actors should exert a stronger effect on the likelihood of escalation in disputes over brute-force objectives than in disputes over coercive objectives.
	Hypothesis 8: Employing a punishment strategy will reduce the likelihood of strategic success for strong states pursuing brute-force objectives. Adopting a punishment strategy should have no effect on the probability of strategic success for weak states or states with coercive political objectives.

DATA, CONCEPTS, AND MEASURES

In chapter 5, I test the hypotheses laid out above by examining the historical record of militarized interstate disputes and wars from 1919 to 2001. I identify all disputes between two states in the Correlates of War Militarized Interstate Disputes dataset.[13] In chapter 6, I test the hypotheses developed in this chapter on an original dataset consisting of all foreign military interventions conducted by five major powers since the termination of World War II.

Militarized Interstate Disputes (MIDs) are defined as conflicts in which at least one state threatens, displays, or uses force against one or more other states. Although the MID dataset has its limitations, using it to test my theory has several important advantages: First, because it includes conflicts that escalate to the use of force and conflicts that are settled without violence, it allows me to test the selection argument I am making directly and to control for possible selection bias introduced by states' decisions to escalate a conflict to violence. Second, the MID dataset includes a very wide range of conflicts over a long period of time. Testing my argument with this dataset demonstrates the theory's broad applicability. Finally, the cases were identified, the data were collected, and all of the variables were coded by other scholars. The dataset does not include all of the information in which I am interested; there are no data on the military strategies that states employed, and I must code dispute outcomes and states' political objectives based on variables in the dataset that only partially capture these factors as they are conceptualized in my theory. Nevertheless, because the data were collected and coded by other scholars for other purposes, I can be confident that my own biases did not influence case selection or measurement.

One potential critique of using this dataset to test my argument is that most of the disputes involve uses of force that fall short of standard definitions of war. The Correlates of War Project, for example, defines war as sustained combat between military organizations that results in at least 1,000 battle-related deaths.[14] The Uppsala Conflict Data Program (UCDP), on the other hand, defines an armed conflict as "a contested incompatibility that concerns government and/or territory where the use of armed force between two parties . . . results in at least 25 battle-related deaths in one calendar year."[15] Although for some purposes it may make sense to separate conflicts with high levels of casualties from less violent conflicts, I believe the outcomes of relatively low-level armed conflicts can be explained within the same theoretical framework as major wars. Moreover, it is an explicit expectation of my theoretical argument that the factors that determine war outcomes will also influence the outcomes of conflicts that fall short of war. As Wittman noted in 1979, nations bargain in the shadow of total war.[16]

Each actor's anticipation of the likely cost and outcome of a war fought to the finish drives its decisions about making concessions and continuing to fight. Therefore, any factor that has an effect on war outcomes (and is observable to the participants) should have an effect on leaders' expectations about the ultimate outcome of a war and, consequently, the probability that a minor armed conflict escalates to high levels of violence. The unifying characteristic of all the armed conflicts I analyze is that they involve two or more political units using organized violence in pursuit of their political aims. In the statistical analyses of violent conflict outcomes in chapter 5, I include only those militarized disputes that escalate to the use of military force by both sides, last more than one day, and involve at least one battle-related fatality.

The Military Intervention by Powerful States (MIPS) dataset, which I use to test hypotheses in chapter 6, is much smaller than the MID dataset, but it contains more precise measures of both my dependent and independent variables. The MIPS dataset provides detailed data on American, British, Chinese, French, and Russian uses of military force against both state and nonstate targets between 1946 and 2003.[17] I began this data collection effort with the express goal of developing a rigorous, generalizable measure of the effectiveness of military force as a policy instrument. In particular, I wanted to identify the political objectives that strong states pursue through the use of force and evaluate conflict outcomes relative to the states' goals. The dataset also includes extensive data on the human and material costs of military operations, as well as factors commonly hypothesized to be associated with war outcomes, like the military strategies employed and military aid and assistance provided to each side.

Major powers are much more likely than less capable states to resort to the use of military force in an attempt to obtain their political objectives.[18] Patrick Regan finds that a handful of major power states were responsible for approximately 40 percent of all third-party interventions into civil conflicts between 1944 and 1994.[19] According to a study by Barry Blechman and Stephen Kaplan, in the first three decades after the end of World War II, the United States alone employed military force in an attempt to achieve specific foreign policy objectives on more than 200 occasions.[20] The frequency with which powerful states invoke a "military option" and the far-reaching consequences of their decisions to intervene abroad make determining the circumstances under which military force can be used to achieve foreign policy objectives, and the factors that limit the effectiveness of this policy instrument, a crucial task.

It is also important to focus particular attention on the class of events I define as major power military interventions because relatively little scholarly attention has been focused on the determinants of unconventional war outcomes. Studies of violent conflict outcomes tend to focus exclusively on wars between states. But many national security experts believe that nonstate actors constitute a significant and growing threat to states. The primary target is a nonstate actor in almost half of the major power military interventions in the post-World War II period. Of these, thirty-one operations are conducted against insurgents, sixteen against civilian rioters, and four against terrorist organizations. In addition, ten military operations target an insurgent movement and state military forces concurrently. Employing these data, I can conduct a direct test of the common assumption that military force is less effective as a policy instrument when the adversary is a nonstate actor like the Mujahideen that fought the Soviet occupation of Afghanistan or the Algerian National Liberation Front that struggled for independence from France.

I define a foreign military intervention as a use of armed force that involves the official deployment of at least 500 regular military personnel (ground, air, and/or naval) to attain immediate-term political objectives through action against a foreign adversary.[21] To qualify as a "use of armed force," the military personnel deployed must either use force or be prepared to use force if they encounter resistance.[22] For a deployment to be "official," a state's political leaders must authorize it,[23] and it must be intended to attain immediate-term political objectives through military action, or the imminent threat of military action, against another actor.

Britain, China, France, Russia/USSR, and the United States conducted 126 military interventions between 1945 and 2003. Table A1 in the appendix to this chapter lists the intervening state, target, location, initiation date, and termination date of each of these operations. The United States undertook thirty-four military interventions, about 27 percent of the total. France was the second most militarily active major power, with thirty operations (24 percent). It is significant to note that the number of French and British interventions declined sharply after about 1975, while the number of U.S. operations increased. Both France and the United Kingdom were most active in the 1940s, 1950s, and 1960s, while the United States was responsible for more than half of the interventions after 1979. China conducted the fewest military interventions, only seventeen in the six decades covered by the dataset. Russia engaged in twenty significant uses of armed force abroad during this time period.

The unique characteristics of major power military interventions present an exceptional opportunity to explore the utility and limitations of military force as a policy instrument. Major power military interventions provide a population of cases with extreme values on two variables that feature prominently in theories of war outcomes—relative military capabilities and relative resolve. These military interventions are characterized by striking asymmetries of power between the intervening state and the primary target of the military intervention. The average military-industrial capabilities of a major power state in the years between 1945 and 2003 accounted for approximately 11 percent of global capabilities. The targets of major power military interventions, in contrast, tended to possess less than 1 percent of global capabilities. In the average intervention, the major power had a nine-to-one advantage in military-industrial capabilities and thirteen times the military personnel of the intervention target. In almost half of the cases, the intervention targeted a nonstate actor lacking a regular military force, industrial production capabilities, the ability to tax the population, and other sources of military might.

The limited variation in relative power in the MIPS data could be a liability. Because the dataset is comprised entirely of asymmetric conflicts, it is less useful than the MID dataset for exploring how material capabilities affect war outcomes. On the other hand, this particular set of cases has a number of advantages that complement the strengths and limitations of the MID data. The striking imbalance of power in these cases means that they should constitute an "easy" test for realist theories of war outcomes.[24] If relative military capacity is the most important determinant of war outcomes, military operations that pit the world's most powerful states against some of the weakest states in the international system should have overwhelmingly favorable outcomes for the major powers. Poor measures of relative warfighting capacity might account for some "surprising" results in wars between more closely matched opponents, but measurement error is implausible as an explanation for outcomes in which "David" defeats "Goliath." Although thousands of idiosyncratic factors—low troop morale, poor decision-making by individuals, or "accidents that nobody could have foreseen"[25]—might exert enough of an impact to sway the outcome of some wars, their effects on the margins should not be enough to change the end result of military contests between such mismatched opponents.

These cases are also likely to be characterized by striking asymmetries in cost tolerance that favor the intervention targets due to the process of mutual selection that drives the escalation of conflicts to war. Although the major powers have the destructive capacity to completely disarm their weak adversaries, weak actors do not threaten the physical survival of major power states. In fact, the weak targets of major power military interventions only rarely present a significant threat to truly vital interests. Even if they are optimistic about their ability to achieve their objectives in a war with a strong opponent, weak actors are unlikely to underestimate the devastation that could be wrought by a major power provoked to war. As a result, weak actors refuse to make the concessions that would avert an armed confrontation only when their value for the issues at stake, and therefore their tolerance for costs, is extraordinarily high. Major powers, on the other hand, invoke the use of military force over marginal interests relatively frequently—knowing that they can inflict much more damage than they will sustain and that, even if they fail to attain their objectives, a limited war will not threaten their survival.

Finally, these cases can provide insight into the importance of military strategy. While the armed forces of weak state and nonstate actors frequently do not have the technology, training, leadership, or troop strength to employ the most effective military strategies, the major powers have a wide range of strategic options. Compared to their targets, major powers face few material constraints on the military capabilities and resources they can bring to bear in a conflict. Major powers possess superior technology, more numerous and better trained troops, higher quality leadership, better tactical capabilities, and a wider range of options for delivering firepower than almost all of their adversaries. Unlike the majority of their targets, major power states have the skills necessary to coordinate movement with suppressive fire in order to "operate effectively in the face of radically lethal modern weapons."[26] If ineffective military strategies are to blame for major power military intervention failures, we cannot simply attribute the failure to resource constraints. Instead, we need to ask why the major powers were unable to adopt more effective strategies in their conflicts with weaker opponents. At the same time, if weak actors can defeat strong states by adopting indirect, guerilla warfare strategies, we need to explain why all weak targets do not adopt these tactics when confronting a militarily superior power.

Although major power military interventions are not representative of the "typical" war, they provide a population of cases well suited to test a theory that predicts that the relative magnitude of the effect of destructive capacity versus cost tolerance varies with the nature of the stronger actor's war aims.

Measuring War Outcomes

Due to a lack of reliable data, the handful of rigorous, systematic studies of the determinants of war outcomes that do exist often employ overly restrictive measures of the dependent variable. Empirical analyses frequently make the assumption that all wars are fought for the same objective. For example, Regan defines the success of third-party intervention as the achievement of a cessation in fighting and intentionally avoids consideration of other objectives on the part of the intervening state.[27] Although this simplification makes the analysis more tractable, it also means that the results of his study cannot tell us much about the utility of military force as a policy instrument, because conflict termination is not always the primary goal of military interventions. Frequently, in fact, states intervene to *sustain* fighting until the dispute can be settled on terms they consider more favorable to their own interests. Other studies code belligerents as winners or losers only relative to each other, without any regard for the extent to which they attained their war aims.[28] In reality, however, both sides can lose more than they gain in a war. Although leaving the other guy worse off may boost a state's image abroad or make citizens proud, my concern in this book is with the utility of military force as a *policy* instrument. Losing less than your enemy is not winning if you do not achieve the political objectives for which you chose the costly instrument of war.

I define success and failure in Clausewitzian terms—measuring war outcomes against a state's war aims. When using the Correlates of War MID data, my dispute outcome measure is a dichotomous variable indicating whether or not the dispute initiator attained its primary objective in the dispute. I use the MID dataset "revisionist state" and "outcome" variables to code the outcome of each dyadic dispute. The revisionist variable indicates whether a state is attempting to maintain the status quo or demanding a change in it (e.g., a revision of its borders with the target or a change in the target state's foreign policy). Dispute initiators seeking a revision of the status quo are considered to have achieved this goal if the MID dataset's outcome variable indicates that (1) the initiator was victorious, (2) the target yielded, or (3) a compromise agreement was reached. Initiators demanding a revision of the status quo are coded as failing to achieve their objective when (1) the target is victorious, (2) the initiator yields, or (3) the dispute ends in a stalemate or release. Dispute initiators seeking to maintain the status quo are coded as attaining their objective if the MID dataset indicates that (1) the initiator was victorious, (2) the target yielded, or (3) the prewar status quo did not change (stalemate and release). Dispute initiators making status quo demands are coded as failing to maintain the status quo when (1) the target was victorious, (2) the initiator yielded, or (3) a compromise was negotiated.[29] Disputes in which the MID outcome is missing or coded as "unclear" and cases in which the dyad joins an ongoing war are coded as "missing" in my dataset. Out of 2,105 dyadic disputes between 1919 and 2001, 80 (3.8 percent) are missing the dispute outcome code. The initiator attained its primary objective (prevailed) in 418 (21 percent) of all militarized disputes and in 144 (28 percent) of the disputes that escalated to the use of violence by both sides.

In the MIPS dataset, intervention success and failure are measured with respect to whether the major power was able to achieve its primary political objective. A key focus of the MIPS data project has been identifying the primary political objective for which a state employed military force and evaluating whether that objective was attained. David Baldwin maintains that "neither the costs nor the benefits of military statecraft have received the scholarly attention they deserve" and notes that a critical issue is the challenge of defining "success."[30] For each case in the MIPS dataset, trained student coders used a decision algorithm to code whether or not the intervening state attained its primary political objective (PPO) and, if so, how long that objective was sustained after military operations ended. The variable used in the statistical analyses in chapter 6 is dichotomous and has a value of one when the intervening state attains its primary political objective and that objective is maintained for at least one year after the military intervention is terminated; otherwise it is zero.[31] This coding rule was adopted so that only interventions that resulted in a meaningful foreign policy achievement were considered "successful." The intervention outcome equals one (objective attained) in 60 percent of the cases.

Although it happens less frequently than one might expect, the primary political objective of a military intervention can change dramatically during the course of an intervention. When the original objective is attained and the major power decides to pursue another objective, as the United States did, for example, during its involvement in Korea during the 1950s, the intervention is treated as two operations, and the first is coded as a success. In the Korean case, the U.S. military intervention to maintain the South Korean regime is one operation. The push north to the Yalu river to "liberate" North Korea (i.e., to remove and replace the North Korean regime) is considered a second operation. Without such a distinction, whether the United States achieved strategic success or failure is ambiguous, and factors contributing to the success of the first operation cannot be distinguished from factors contributing to the failure of the second. When, on the other hand, the major power changes its objective because it decides it cannot attain its original objective, the intervention is retained as one case, and the outcome is coded as a failure if it terminates and the original political objective was not attained. This occurs most frequently in the case of British and French interventions to maintain colonial rule. As it became apparent that the original objective of retaining colonial authority was too costly, either strategically or domestically, the colonial powers changed their objectives, agreeing to grant some degree of independence while continuing to fight for control over the makeup of the new government or over that government's policies. Of course, in either case, if the major power terminates an intervention through either a formal agreement or withdrawal of 70 percent of its combat troops, and then reintroduces troops, the two operations are coded as separate interventions regardless of the objectives being pursued in each one.

The major power terminates its military operations without ever attaining its primary political objective in 29 percent of MIPS cases. In 69 percent of the cases, the major power attains and maintains the objectives for at least six months. The intervening state maintains its PPO for at least one year after intervention termination in approximately 63 percent of cases and maintains its objective for three or more years in only 52 percent of the cases. Our data indicate that intervention outcomes have remained remarkably stable over the last sixty years with the probability of success (defined as attaining the primary objective and maintaining it for at least one year after intervention) hovering around 60 percent. Although there appears to be a slight increase in success rates in the 1960s and 1970s, the difference does not approach statistical significance. These results are important because they cast some doubt on claims about revolutionary changes in warfare or in civilian sensitivity to the costs of war. At the same time, the data provide no evidence that the Cold War significantly affected the ability of the major power states to attain their foreign policy objectives through the use of military force abroad. Neither success rates nor the frequency of interventions varies significantly across Cold War and non-Cold War years.

Defining War Aims

The key explanatory variable in my theory of war outcomes is the degree to which a state's primary political objective is dependent on target compliance. One way to code this variable would be to examine historical records and secondary sources and assign some value for each case based on my subjective evaluation of the extent to which the war aims were dependent on target compliance. Obviously, the risk of introducing bias into the analysis via this approach is significant. I wanted to adopt a procedure that would, to the extent possible, remove the influence of my own subjective understanding of the nature of actors' objectives and avoid the danger of assigning values based on ex post knowledge about the way in which objectives were pursued or the outcome of a particular conflict. To that end, I assign *categories* of political objectives, rather than individual objectives, to values along the continuum from most compliance dependent to least compliance dependent. For the MIPS dataset, the intervening state's primary political objective is assigned to a category by independent coders. For the MID dataset, I use the categories coded by the Correlates of War Project. The result is a less nuanced, but more objective, measure of the nature of a state's war aims.

The MIPS project defines a *political objective* as the allocation of a valued good sought by the political leaders of a state or a nonstate organization. The good may be tangible—a piece of land, oil wells, a river—or intangible—political authority over a population, social protections for an ethnic group in another state, or containment of an enemy's expansionist ambitions.

Examples of political objectives commonly pursued in military operations include the defense of territory, seizure of political authority, and maintenance of political authority. Political objectives contrast with *military objectives,* which I define as the operational goals to be accomplished by the armed forces of a state or opposition movement as a means to achieve the desired political outcome. Examples of military objectives include the attrition of enemy combatants, destruction of enemy military capacity, disruption of enemy lines of command and control, and demoralization of enemy soldiers and/or civilians. Occasionally, an actor's political and military objectives align perfectly. For a state trying to defend its border with another state in the face of an armed invasion, holding territory is both the primary political objective and the principal military objective.

Similar to the study conducted by Blechman and Kaplan, I focus on the political objectives of each military intervention, rather than policymakers' personal, domestic political, or grand strategic motivations for employing force.[32] Domestic political and personal motivations include a leader's desire to maintain office or increase personal power. Grand strategic objectives are goals such as maintaining the credibility of a country's commitments to allies, preventing the global spread of an ideology, sending a message about foreign aggression, and similar overarching, long-term foreign policy aims. In contrast, the primary political objective of a military operation is a concrete, observable outcome to be attained through the employment of military force. Blechman and Kaplan note that "[m]otivation is extremely difficult, if not impossible, to determine in any situation,"[33] but ". . . operational objectives tend to be expressed in relatively tangible and specific terms and their satisfaction or non-satisfaction can be judged much more easily. There is much greater agreement among public documents, memoirs, and scholarly studies of incidents as to what the decision-makers' operational objectives were than as to either fundamental strategic objectives or personal motives."[34]

While larger strategic goals and personal political agendas often motivate the use of force, once national leaders decide to employ force, they must operationalize these goals by giving their armed forces a directive. Following the Iraqi invasion of Kuwait in 1990, President Bush and other decision-makers had a multitude of motives and rationales for responding to the invasion. Nevertheless, each military operation had a primary political objective: Operation Desert Shield was intended to deter an invasion of Saudi Arabia, and Operation Desert Storm was intended to restore Kuwait's sovereignty over its territory. The removal of Saddam Hussein's regime, destruction of the Republican Guard, and elimination of the Scud missile threat to Israel were only secondary objectives, as evidenced by the lack of consensus that existed among civilian and military leaders on the time and resources to devote to them.[35]

Common wisdom, particularly within professional military circles, holds that ambiguous civilian war aims are a common cause of defeat for otherwise capable states.[36] I have found, however, that although there are myriad personal, domestic political, and grand strategic motivations for using force, the desired political outcome of a military operation is unambiguous more often than not. What is more frequently unclear is the connection between the *military* objectives of an operation and attainment of the desired *political* outcomes. During the U.S. intervention in Indochina, for example, the political objective was explicit: The United States fought to maintain an independent, noncommunist South Vietnam. The relationship between achieving military objectives, such as the attrition of Viet Cong, and attaining that political outcome was much less clear. The question for the United States was not "What is the desired outcome?" but rather "How do we use our military capability to achieve the desired outcome?"

Based on a preliminary historical analysis of approximately 30 percent of the cases, I identified six broad political objective categories: Maintain Foreign Regime Authority, Remove/Replace Foreign Regime, Policy Change, Acquire/Defend Territory, Maintain Empire, and Social Protection/Order. Table A2 in the appendix to this chapter provides operational definitions for each category. To facilitate rigorous coding of the political objective of each intervention, my colleague Michael Koch and I assigned two independent student coders to each intervention case. These coders worked separately to identify the primary political objective (PPO) for which the intervening state employed military force, using a Boolean logic decision procedure and a codebook with operational definitions of the political objective categories. Each coder consulted at least three approved sources for each case, including scholarly studies, newspapers, chronologies of international events, and government and military records. To assess the reliability of data coded with this procedure, we assigned a random sample of 25 percent of the cases to two sets of student coders: a first set at the University of Georgia and a second set at Texas A&M University. A third coder was assigned whenever the primary political objective category assigned by the first coder did not match the category assigned by the second coder.[37]

In order to place a political objective category along the continuum from least compliance dependent to most compliance dependent, I consider two questions: (1) Is the object at stake something that *could* be forcibly seized and/or held, or would attaining the objective *require* the target's cooperation? (2) If the objective were attained, would a reversal require the actor to forcibly change the status quo or simply to stop complying? My first measure codes three types of war aims from the six original PPO categories. The intervening state's objective is considered to be "brute force" if its primary war aim is the acquisition or defense of territory or the removal of a foreign regime. Attempting to maintain the political authority of either a foreign government or of its own colonial government in the face of internal opposition is considered a "moderately coercive" objective. I code the major power's PPO as "coercive" if the state is seeking a policy change from a foreign government or is engaged in an operation to suppress violence or restore order in a situation of unrest.

For the analysis in chapter 5, which employs the Correlates of War MID data, I construct a similar variable that distinguishes between brute-force and coercive objectives based on the MID dataset's "revision type" variables. For each state in a dyadic dispute, the revision type variables indicate whether the state sought a revision of the status quo and, if so, whether the state sought territory, a policy change, or a regime change. According to the originators of the dataset, revision type is coded based on "operational demands made prior to the onset of a MID that were directly related to a challenge of the pre-existing status quo."[38] Argentina's claim on the Falkland/Malvinas Islands and American attempts to overthrow Fidel Castro are examples of MIDs with territorial and regime change objectives respectively. The British are coded as having a policy change objective in their disputes with Brazil over its slave trade.

Following the typology of war aims presented in chapter 3, I create a dichotomous variable indicating that the dispute initiator had a *brute-force* war aim if the dispute was over territory or governance and a *coercive* war aim if the dispute was over policy. An adversary's resistance can make seizing territory or removing the governing regime from power costly for even the strongest states. But a state that is strong enough can achieve these objectives with brute force alone, even if it would prefer to attain them without having to physically destroy their adversary. In contrast, an opponent cannot be physically forced to change its foreign or domestic policies.

Relative Power: War-fighting Capacity and Military Effectiveness

In order to test whether war-fighting capabilities and military effectiveness affect strategic success and failure in asymmetric wars, we need good measures of these factors. Traditionally, scholars have used the military-industrial capacity variable from the Correlates of War project (the Composite Index of National Capabilities, or CINC score) as a measure of states' power. A country's CINC score records the proportion of total system capabilities the state holds in six areas: iron and steel production, urban population, total population, military expenditures, military personnel, and energy production. I use this variable as well. But I also employ several other measures of war-fighting capacity and military effectiveness in an attempt to overcome some of the limitations of the CINC measure and give theories that expect military strength to matter a fair trial. In particular, I want to develop variables that capture the military strength a state applies in a particular conflict (rather than simply a state's latent capacity), measure military effectiveness in addition to raw strength, and allow for comparisons between the military capacity of states and that of nonstates.

My first measure of war-fighting capacity is simply the widely used variable that calculates the ratio of one state's proportion of system military-industrial capabilities to the proportion held by both states in the dispute dyad. As an alternative measure, I use the ratio of military personnel in each state prior to the dispute. For militarized disputes that escalate to violence and the major power interventions, I also create indicators of military effectiveness and the assistance provided to each side by allies. Military effectiveness is measured by a variable that divides the proportion of the dispute initiator's military personnel lost in battle by the proportion of the target's military personnel lost in battle. Two additional variables count the number of allies that join the fight on each side.

Because the quality of its troops is likely to matter as much, if not more, than the size of its military, I use a state's military expenditures per soldier as a rough indicator of the state's investment in training, equipping, and supporting its troops. For the major power military interventions, I create a measure of the quality of the troops actually *committed* to a military intervention by multiplying the number of troops deployed by the troop quality variable.

Political Will

In the literature on international relations and military history, as well as among military practitioners, "resolve" has been used synonymously with motivation, political will, morale, commitment, and the value of the issues at stake in a conflict. In the vast international relations literature on the causes of war, resolve often simply means that a state is willing to use force if the adversary refuses to back down. At the political and strategic levels of analysis, resolve could refer to a civilian population's willingness to sacrifice lives and resources to the war effort. Or, depending on the accountability of the political leadership of a nation, resolve could reflect the extent to which leaders are able to sink blood and treasure into military operations without threatening their tenures in office. At the tactical and operational levels of analysis, resolve often refers to the morale of the troops—their willingness to fight and die for their country, a cause, an ideology, or their fellow soldiers.

All of these factors are likely to be important to the outcome of wars—particularly when the war-fighting capabilities of the two sides are relatively balanced or there is a great disparity in the value of the issues at stake for each belligerent. Unfortunately, it is extremely difficult to develop direct measures of resolve. At both the individual and the national levels of analysis, motivation, willingness to sacrifice, and morale are all unobservable—although they might be inferred on the basis of observable evidence.

Zeev Maoz uses the level of hostility reached by a dispute initiator relative to the level of hostility reached by the target as an indicator of initiator resolve.[39] Steve Rosen takes the lives lost in battle by each belligerent as a measure of each side's cost tolerance.[40] Both escalating a conflict to higher levels of hostility and suffering more casualties than one's opponent are considered indicators of greater resolve, but both these measures are problematic. Using greater levels of violence than an opponent is not necessarily an indicator of higher resolve. Presumably, both sides would prefer to achieve their objectives at the lowest possible cost. Although escalating to higher levels of violence does indicate a willingness to use that level of violence, we cannot infer that actors that did not escalate were not also willing to bear those costs if necessary. Low levels of conflict escalation relative to an opponent could simply indicate that a highly resolved and capable actor was able achieve its objectives without escalating to greater levels of force. Similarly, low casualty rates relative to an opponent are just as likely to indicate greater military effectiveness as they are a lack of resolve.[41]

The broader issue is the problem of partial observability that plagues much of social science research. Although we can observe the human and material losses an actor actually suffered in a conflict ex post—and possibly even infer the limits of an actor's tolerance for costs in cases in which the actor sued for peace because the costs were deemed too high—there is no way to know the level of suffering that actors would have tolerated in cases in which they prevail over their opponents before reaching that limit, are rendered incapable of sustaining military operations, or surrender because they anticipate military defeat.

Despite these limitations, lack of resolve is an intuitively appealing explanation for war outcomes that cannot be explained on the basis of hard power alone, and it is especially important to incorporate this factor into any predictive model of asymmetric war outcomes. I attempt to create a number of proxy measures for resolve so that I can test conventional expectations about the effects of observable indicators of cost tolerance, as well as the general expectation that states are more likely to prevail in armed conflict when they have higher resolve.

Issue Salience

Using the revision type variables in the Correlates of War MID dataset and the primary political objective variable in the MIPS dataset, I construct ordinal measures that rank how important the issues at stake are likely to be for each side, as shown in Table 4.2. In general, leaders are expected to be willing to tolerate the greatest costs to defend the sovereignty of their state or to stay in power. I assume that defending territory and removing an enemy regime from power in another state are second only to sovereignty and regime survival in importance. Maintaining control over foreign colonies, gaining territory, and defending an ally fall below these objectives, but are expected to be more salient than maintaining particular domestic or foreign policies. All else being equal, states should be least motivated to fight to change an adversary's policies.

I also create a measure of the relative importance of the issues at stake to each disputant by subtracting the target's issue salience measure from the variable indicating how high the stakes are for the dispute initiator or intervening state. Finally, I create a set of dummy variables to indicate that the dispute target is facing a demand of *critical* salience (category 5), *medium* salience (category 3 or 4), or *low* salience (category 1 or 2).

Distance

The issues in contention are likely to be seen as more important if the dispute is over a good, or with an enemy, close to a state's capital. Therefore, I also construct measures of how far each state is from where the dispute originated by taking the natural log of the distance from the state to the location of either the militarized dispute or the military intervention.[42] Although quantitative studies of dispute escalation often control for the distance between the disputants, this distance is the same for each state in a dyadic dispute. Using a measure of each state's distance from the fighting, rather than from each other, allows for the possibility that, for example, the territory in contention borders the target state but is thousands of kilometers

Table 4.2. ISSUE SALIENCE RANK

5	Defend sovereignty and/or governing authority
4	Defend territorial integrity or remove adversarial regime from power
3	Gain territory, maintain empire, or defend an ally
2	Maintain own domestic or foreign policies
1	Change adversary's policies

from the initiator. In this case, I would expect the territory to be of greater importance to the target. The assumption is that, when all else is equal, the stakes of a conflict and a state's willingness to bear costs to attain its objectives in that conflict decrease the farther from the homeland that conflict takes place.

Troop Commitment

This variable is only available for the military intervention dataset. The troop commitment variable measures the maximum number of major power ground troops deployed to the combat zone at any one time during an intervention. The assumption is that troop commitment levels—and in particular ground troop levels—could indicate the extent of a state's resolve. That said, we have to recognize that a state may have been willing to commit more of its capacity in some of the military interventions that were successful at lower levels of commitment.

Military Strategy

Testing arguments about the effects of military strategy on war outcomes is more complicated than it might first appear. Although the distinction between punishment and denial strategies seems relatively clear, in practice, states often use military force to simultaneously impose costs and degrade an enemy's military capacity. Distinguishing attrition strategies from maneuver strategies is even trickier. According to historian Carter Malkasian, "[A]ttrition is a gradual and piecemeal process of destroying an enemy's military capability" and "few examples of attrition were taken as models to be replicated or developed."[43] Attrition strategies are most often adopted by default, when a military is unable to execute a successful maneuver strategy due to limited capabilities or the constraints imposed by geographical conditions or enemy characteristics.[44]

Despite these caveats, it is important to try to uncover whether military strategies have any independent effects on war outcomes. In the analyses of major power intervention outcomes, I use several variables as proxy measures of the military strategy employed by the intervening state and another variable to indicate the interaction between initiator and target strategies. My first measure attempts to replicate Allan Stam's maneuver-attrition-punishment typology. According to Stam, "Maneuver strategies are those in which states focus on the use of speed and mobility to disarm the opponent by disrupting the opponent's ability to effectively organize its force"; "Attrition strategies seek to destroy or capture opposing forces, making them incapable of continuing to fight, without necessarily using mobility to achieve this. Typically an attrition strategy seeks large confrontations with the enemy"; and "Punishment strategies attempt to inflict such high costs on an opponent that they either cease an attack or surrender even though their military forces may not actually be defeated in battle."[45] When a case from my dataset is also in Stam's dataset, I employ his coding. In the remaining cases, I use his description of the strategy types to code my own cases.

The second measure collapses attrition and maneuver strategies into a denial strategy category and contrasts that strategy with punishment strategies. Following Biddle, the third measure employs country dummies, dichotomous variables that simply indicate which major power is the intervening state, in order to capture the possibility that the major powers have different force employment doctrines that would impact their military effectiveness.[46] A common distinction is made, for example, between the "American Way of War" emphasizing superior firepower and movement and the Chinese military's emphasis on mass.[47] Military analysts and historians frequently suggest that American-style war-fighting is particularly ill-suited to fighting "small wars" or insurgencies and point to the British Army's superiority in this regard.[48]

A final variable is created by interacting the dichotomous denial/punishment strategy indicator for intervening states with a dichotomous variable indicating whether the target adopted a primarily punishment or primarily denial strategy. This allows me to test Arreguín-Toft's thesis that strong states are more likely to prevail against weak targets if they use the same strategic approach as the target.

Unfortunately, the MID dataset does not contain data that could be used to code the states' military strategies. For the statistical tests in chapter 5, I create a force employment variable that simply indicates whether the dispute initiator engaged ground troops in combat.[49] While air strikes and long-range missile fire can degrade an enemy's military-industrial capabilities and inflict suffering on enemy populations, states cannot seize territory or exercise political authority without putting boots on the ground. Reliance on standoff uses of firepower may be akin to utilizing a punishment military strategy. Rather than directly denying an enemy the means to continue fighting, often the goal is to coerce the adversary's political leadership into making concessions in order to avoid incurring further costs. If the decision-making of belligerents in wartime is influenced primarily by the ability of their armed forces to continue to offer a coherent military challenge, and inflicting pain and suffering on enemy populations can backfire by inducing civilians to rally around the political leadership, ground combat should be a more effective means of utilizing military force.[50] However, the effects of employing ground troops must be interpreted with caution. Although ground combat may be more effective, states that commit ground troops to combat may also have greater cost tolerance than states that restrict their involvement to air strikes or naval bombardment. Ground combat typically involves higher costs and a greater risk of casualties than standoff uses of firepower. At the same time, states may deploy ground combat troops when their war aims are most difficult to attain.

CONCLUSION

This chapter laid out testable hypotheses for my own theory, as well as several alternative theories of war outcomes. In addition, I described the data I use to test the hypotheses and explained how I measure key dependent and independent variables. In the next chapter, I test the hypotheses with historical data on violent international disputes since 1919. Chapter 6 tests the hypotheses with data on military interventions by five major powers in the post-World War II era.

CHAPTER 5

Interstate Dispute Outcomes, 1919–2001

In the preceding chapter, I presented a set of testable hypotheses derived from the war aims model and several rival theories of armed conflict outcomes. In this chapter, I conduct large-*n* empirical tests of some of these predictions. In a series of statistical analyses, I explore the effects of relative military capabilities, the balance of interests, and the nature of states' war aims on the escalation and outcome of disputes between states. To evaluate hypotheses about the probability of conflict escalation, I examine all dispute dyads in the Correlates of War Militarized Interstate Disputes (MID) dataset between 1919 and 2001.[1] I test hypotheses about the outcomes of conflicts that have escalated to mutual hostilities on those disputes in which both sides use military force and the fighting lasts for more than one day.

If the relative power perspective reflects the way the world works, I expect to observe a strong correlation between the distribution of destructive capacity within a dyad and dispute outcomes. If the political will school is a more accurate model of reality, the probability of dispute escalation and strategic victory should vary with the importance of the issues at stake to each belligerent. Even relatively weak states should be unlikely to back down when vital interests are threatened, and states that are strongly motivated by what is at stake in a dispute may be able to prevail over stronger, but less resolved, opponents. All else being equal, states should be most likely to escalate disputes that threaten regime survival or the territorial integrity of the state. They should be much less likely to escalate conflicts in which they are faced with a demand for policy change or seek policy change from an adversary. Moreover, states should be more likely to prevail when they have greater interests at stake than their adversary. When an outside power uses military force with the aim of removing a weak state's leaders from power, for example, we may be especially likely to see "surprising" war outcomes, because leaders fighting for their own survival should have much higher resolve than the leaders of a foreign state seeking to replace them. States using military force to compel an adversary to change objectionable foreign or domestic policies should have greater success rates than states demanding territory or a change in who governs in another state.

I anticipate, however, that the effects of both material capabilities and resolve are conditioned by the nature of the political objectives for which an actor employs military force. The balance of military capabilities should be positively correlated with the probability of strategic victory when the object at stake can be seized and held with brute force alone. Even if a weak target has much higher resolve, the stronger state is expected to prevail in conflicts over brute-force objectives. When the challenger seeks a change in the target's foreign policy or behavior, on the other hand, actors with a significant cost-tolerance advantage may be able to convince a more powerful state that the cost of fighting will exceed the price that state is willing to pay.

I evaluate the hypotheses presented in chapter 4 in two steps. First, I test for bivariate relationships between the key explanatory variables from each theoretical argument and three different dispute outcome variables. My first dependent variable, dispute escalation, simply indicates whether or not a militarized dispute lasted for more than one day and escalated to the point where both the initiator and target used military force. About 25 percent of dyadic militarized disputes escalate to the use of organized violence by both sides. A second analysis examines how the distribution of military capabilities and the dispute initiator's primary political objective affect the probability that the initiator attains its primary political objective without a fight. The dependent variable in this test, dispute resolution, is a dichotomous indicator that the dispute target backed down—making concessions to the initiator or dropping its own demands—rather than escalating the dispute by fighting back. Dispute resolution equals one when the target does not use military force and the initiator attains its objective.[2] My final dependent variable, violent conflict outcome, codes whether the dispute initiator attained its primary objective in a dispute that escalated to mutual hostilities. I code disputes as "violent conflicts" when both sides use military force and hostilities last for more than one day. There are 533 violent conflicts in the dataset. The initiator prevailed in 144 (28 percent) of the violent conflicts between 1919 and 2001. Because all of the dependent variables are dichotomous measures, I use logit models to estimate the effects of the explanatory variables.[3]

After exploring the bivariate relationships between these dependent variables and the key explanatory variables from the competing theoretical perspectives, I estimate more sophisticated multivariate models. The more complex models allow me to do several things that I cannot do in simple bivariate analyses. I can estimate the effects of key independent variables while controlling for a number of other factors expected to be correlated with dispute outcomes. I can compare the explanatory power of variables from my own theory with the explanatory power of alternative theories. And I can employ two-stage statistical models to account for the selection process that my theory predicts will influence both dispute escalation and violent conflict outcomes.

BIVARIATE RESULTS

Dispute Escalation

In examining the escalation of international disputes to the use of force, I find some evidence for both the relative power and the political will perspectives. The salience of the issues at stake to each side clearly influences the likelihood of dispute escalation. Not surprisingly, as the interests at stake for either the dispute initiator or the dispute target become more salient, the probability of dispute escalation increases. Although less than 20 percent of the disputes involving policy change demands escalate to mutual hostilities, over 40 percent of the disputes over territory escalate to violence, and almost 57 percent of the disputes in which the initiator is seeking regime change from the target become violent conflicts. Disputes over policy are much less likely to escalate to violence than disputes over who controls territory or who governs, because an adversary's foreign and domestic policies are less likely to threaten vital interests and policy change demands are less threatening to the target of the demand than demands for changes in borders or regime composition. As a result, both the state demanding a policy change and the target of such a demand are less likely to be willing to use military force to attain their objectives. These disputes tend to be resolved (or simply dropped) before they escalate to violence.

The distribution of material capabilities also influences dispute escalation in a predictable way. The greater the disparity in military capabilities between two states in a conflict, the less likely it is that the conflict will escalate to mutual hostilities.[4] If war outcomes are largely determined by battlefield outcomes, the state with the greatest war-fighting capacity should be most likely to prevail. The greater its military disadvantage, the less likely a state is to be victorious in a war and the more likely it should be to make concessions to its stronger opponent to avoid escalation to war. Approximately 25 percent of all MIDs escalate to violent conflicts, but only 20 percent of the disputes in which one side or the other possesses at least a nine-to-one advantage in military capabilities escalate to mutual hostilities. Presumably, disputes between states with a significant imbalance of power are not as likely to escalate as disputes between more closely matched states because the weaker actor makes concessions to avoid escalation to a military contest it has little chance of winning. The difference is small, but statically significant.

Although both relative strength and the salience of the issues at stake have predictable effects on dispute escalation, the war aims approach has more explanatory power than either the relative power or political will approaches alone. As the war aims model anticipates, the balance of military capabilities between two states exerts a much stronger influence on the likelihood of escalation in disputes over territory and governance (brute-force war aims) than in disputes over policy. Figure 5.1 shows how the probability of dispute escalation changes as the disparity between the disputants' military capabilities increases. Disputes over land and political authority are significantly more likely to escalate to violence than disputes over policy.[5] But territorial and governance disputes become less likely to escalate as the gap between the two sides' military capabilities increases, while the probability that a dispute over policy will escalate is unaffected by the balance of material power. As the balance of capabilities moves from perfectly equal (1:1) on the far left side of the graph to a distribution in which one state possesses

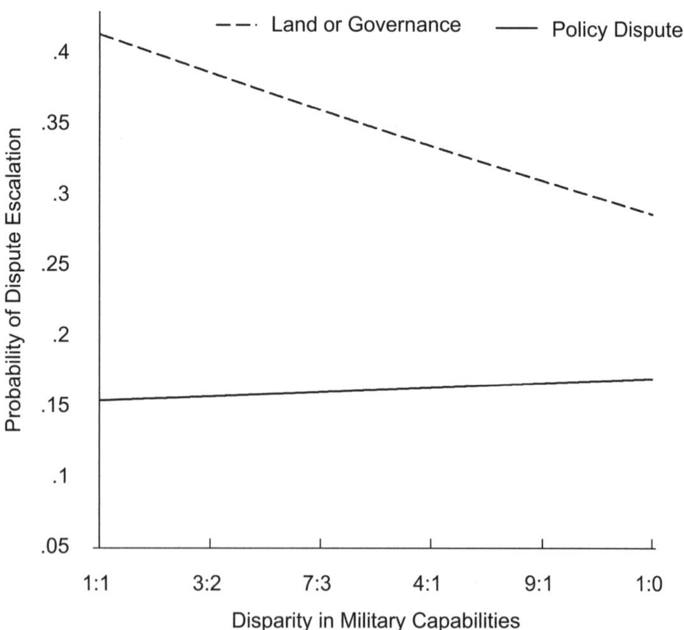

Figure 5.1. Change in the Predicted Probability of Dispute Escalation as the Disparity in Military Capabilities Increases

all of the dyad's military capacity (1:0), the probability of dispute escalation decreases from slightly over 40 percent to under 30 percent in disputes over territory or governance. The probability that a dispute over policy will escalate to mutual hostilities, on the other hand, stays relatively constant at about 15 percent throughout the range of capability distributions.

The significant decline in the risk of escalation for disputes over territory and governance as the balance of military capabilities shifts suggests that states' uncertainty about the outcome of a war over these stakes decreases as the disparity in their material power increases. However, the material balance of power does not appear to have the same effect on uncertainty about who would prevail if a dispute over policy escalated to the use of military force by both sides. This is precisely what we would expect to see if relative destructive capacity is a better predictor of outcomes in wars to control territory or seize power than in wars with coercive aims like policy change.

Dispute Resolution

Militarized interstate disputes can terminate without escalating to violence because one side or the other makes concessions to prevent escalation or because one or both states choose not to use force, even though no settlement has been reached. The political will argument anticipates a higher probability of target concessions over policy demands, whereas the relative power school predicts an increasing likelihood of target concessions as the dispute initiator's military advantage increases. The war aims model's predictions are consistent with these expectations, but they introduce a slight twist. I expect relative war-fighting capacity to exert a stronger influence on the probability of target concessions when the dispute initiator has brute-force objectives.

Figure 5.2 graphs the predicted probability that the target of a threat or use of military force will back down—making concessions to the initiator or dropping its own demands—rather than fight back to defend its interests. Regardless of the nature of the initiator's demand, targets become more likely to acquiesce as the initiator's destructive-capacity advantage increases. But, as expected, the effect of the military capability balance is much greater when the initiator has threatened to use force to seize territory or change who governs in the target state. The probability that the target of a regime change or territorial demand will make concessions increases by 62 percent as the dispute initiator's capabilities increase from one-fourth to three-fourths of the dyad's combined military-industrial capabilities. The difference is statistically significant at $p < 0.05$. The same increase in the initiator's proportion of dyad capabilities has a statistically

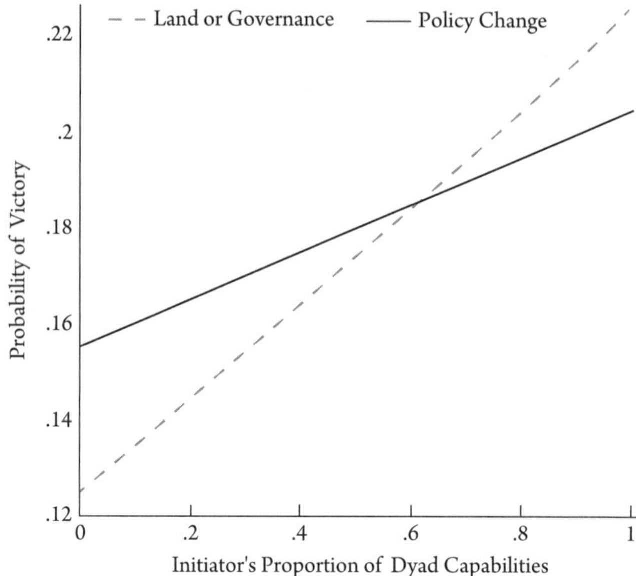

Figure 5.2. Change in the Predicted Probability that the Target Backs Down as Initiator Military Capacity Relative to Target Increases

insignificant effect on the probability that the target will make policy concessions. Although the line showing the predicted probability of initiator victory in a dispute with policy objectives slopes upward as initiator capability share increases, the 95 percent confidence interval around those predicted probabilities indicates that we cannot reject the null hypothesis that the effect of capabilities is zero (i.e., the line is flat).

Violent Conflict Outcomes

The difference between the determinants of outcomes in disputes over brute-force versus coercive objectives becomes even starker when we look at who wins in conflicts that have escalated to mutual hostilities. Weak states that are not willing to tolerate the high costs of a war with a much stronger adversary are likely to select themselves out of a dispute before it escalates by making concessions to their adversary. Those weak states that resist making concessions are likely to have significantly higher cost-tolerance thresholds, on average, than their strong state adversaries. In other words, relative cost tolerance should be inversely correlated with relative destructive capacity in conflicts that both sides have selected into by initiating or reciprocating the use of military force. The war aims theory of war outcomes predicts that a state's destructive capacity relative to its adversary will be positively correlated with the probability of victory in violent conflicts over brute-force objectives. But the probability of victory should be negatively correlated with relative destructive capacity—and positively correlated with the target's tolerance for costs—in violent conflicts with coercive objectives.

Table 5.1 displays the proportion of violent conflicts between 1919 and 2001 in which the state that initiated the use of military force attained its primary political objective. As the power preponderance school would expect, strong states (defined here as states that possess at least 85 percent of the military-industrial capabilities of the dispute dyad) are more likely to prevail when they seek territory or regime change, or when they use force to defend their territory or government. Dispute initiators with preponderant destructive capacity have been approximately 1.7 times as likely as weak states to succeed in defending or seizing territory from their adversaries. Strong states have also been 2.6 times more likely to maintain their own political authority in the face of an external threat to the ruling regime and five times more likely to succeed in removing a foreign regime from power. Although targeted states are likely to be highly resolved to maintain their own political authority, the incumbent regime in a weak state only rarely survives a military attack by a strong state that opts to use military force to remove the regime from power. It is also telling that weak states initiate only nine of the eighty-one violent MIDs in which the initiator seeks to force regime change in the target state, and they are successful in only one case. Clearly, destructive capacity trumps cost tolerance when states use military force to overthrow foreign regimes.

More surprisingly—at least from a realist perspective—weak states appear to be *more* likely than strong states to prevail in violent conflicts over policy change demands. Overall, initiators that use force to compel their

Table 5.1. SUCCESS RATE FOR MILITARIZED INTERSTATE DISPUTE INITIATORS, 1919–2001

		Initiator's Share of Dyadic Destructive Capacity		
		Weak (<15% of dyad capabilities)	***Strong (>85% of dyad capabilities)***	***Overall Success Rate***
Initiator's Objective	Defend or seize territory	27%	44%	34%
	Remove foreign regime	11%	56%	38%
	Maintain political authority	17%	44%	33%
	Policy change	53%	45%	46%

adversaries to change an objectionable foreign or domestic policy are more likely to be successful than initiators that seek territory or try to overthrow a foreign regime. But military capabilities are inversely correlated with the probability of prevailing in violent conflicts over an adversary's foreign or domestic policies. Weak states are almost 20 percent more likely to achieve their policy change demands through force of arms than strong states.

MULTIVARIATE RESULTS

The results presented in Table 5.1 are simply descriptive, but Table 5.2 presents maximum-likelihood regression estimates for four violent dispute outcome models. I use two-stage Heckman selection models, because I anticipate that the factors that determine the outcomes of disputes that have escalated to violence are correlated with the factors that determine whether a dispute escalates to mutual hostilities. In the first stage, an equation predicts whether a militarized dispute will escalate to the use of force by both sides using measures of the distribution of military capabilities, each state's distance from the dispute, the salience of the issues at stake for each side, and a dummy variable indicating that the dispute is between two democracies.[6] The second stage equation estimates the effects of the explanatory variables from the hypotheses presented in chapter 4 on the probability that the dispute initiator will attain its primary political objective (i.e., prevail) if the dispute has escalated to mutual hostilities. Out of 1,964 dyadic disputes, 508 are uncensored, meaning that they escalate to the use of military force by both sides and last more than one day. The dependent variable for the second stage equation is coded according to the procedure described in chapter 4.

The effects of the variables in the dispute escalation equation are generally consistent across all four specifications of the model. Contrary to the bivariate results presented earlier, in a model with additional independent variables, dispute escalation becomes slightly more likely as the disparity between the states' military-industrial capabilities increases. The effect is small, however, and the variable becomes insignificant in model 4. Dispute escalation also becomes more likely as the issue at stake becomes more salient to the initiator. The probability of escalation to mutual hostilities varies from less than 15 percent when the dispute initiator has a policy change demand (lowest salience) to over 70 percent when the initiating state is defending its sovereignty (highest salience). After controlling for issue salience for the initiator, target issue salience has a small negative effect on the probability of dispute escalation across all four models. However, we cannot conclude that disputes are less likely to escalate when the

Table 5.2. COMBINED MODEL OF ESCALATION TO VIOLENCE AND VIOLENT CONFLICT OUTCOME

Violent Conflict Outcome	Model 1 Relative Power	Model 2 Political Will	Model 3 War Aims	Model 4 War Aims
Relative Military Capacity	0.377*	0.439*	0.741***	0.652**
	0.217	0.240	0.265	0.305
Initiator Allies	0.072***	0.069**	0.078**	-0.070
	0.028	0.030	0.033	0.085
Target Allies	-0.066	-0.038	-0.039	-0.094
	0.060	0.056	0.055	0.130
Initiator vs. Target Distance	0.028	0.099*	0.118**	0.145**
	0.042	0.051	0.051	0.063
Initiator vs. Target Issue Salience		0.360***	0.364***	0.394***
		0.105	0.107	0.133
Policy Objective			0.816***	0.984***
			0.279	0.314
Policy Military Capacity			-1.244***	-1.624***
			0.405	0.482
Initiator Democracy Level				0.029***
				0.010
Target Democracy Level				-0.006
				0.010
Ground Combat				-0.657***
				0.221
Constant	-0.198	-0.512	-0.664	0.405
	0.207	0.245	0.275	0.384
		Escalation to Violent Conflict		
Disparity	0.492**	0.470**	0.473**	0.250
	0.224	0.228	0.228	0.239
Initiator Distance to Dispute	-0.077***	-0.083***	-0.083***	-0.090***
	0.026	0.026	0.026	0.027
Target Distance to Dispute	-0.129***	-0.130***	-0.130***	-0.111***
	0.024	0.024	0.024	0.026
Issue Salience for Initiator	0.501***	0.468***	0.468***	0.447***
	0.047	0.049	0.049	0.051

(continued)

Table 5.2. (continued)

	Model 1 Relative Power	Model 2 Political Wil	Model 3 War Aims	Model 4 War Aims
Issue Salience for	-0.138***	-0.100*	-0.100*	-0.121**
Target	0.051	0.052	0.052	0.056
Democratic Dyad	-0.099	-0.134	-0.143	-0.031
	0.157	0.161	0.161	0.161
Constant	0.142	0.154	0.151	0.046
	0.255	0.260	0.260	0.272
$p > \|z\|$: Equations are independent	0.0001	0.1006	0.1132	0.0772
Observations	1963	1963	1963	1857
Uncensored Observations	508	508	508	403

Note: SE displayed under estimated coefficient.
* significant at $p < 0.10$. ** significant at $p < 0.05$. *** significant at $p < 0.01$.

dispute target has more at stake, because the stakes for the belligerents are highly correlated. If the initiator is seeking to gain territory, the target is seeking to defend territory; if the initiator is defending its regime, the target must be seeking to overthrow it. When the variable indicating issue salience for the initiator is dropped, target issue salience is significant and positively correlated with the probability of dispute escalation. An additional measure of the degree to which a dispute is likely to be important to a state—the distance between the state's capital and the location of dispute onset—has the predicted effect. Dispute escalation becomes less likely the farther either disputant is from the locus of the dispute. Somewhat surprisingly, democratic dispute dyads do not appear to be any less likely to escalate their disputes to mutual hostilities—although further investigation reveals that they are less likely to escalate their conflicts all the way to a level of violence that involves more than a handful of battle deaths.[7]

Unlike the dispute escalation equation, the violent conflict outcome equation has four different specifications in Table 5.2. Model 1 includes measures of relative destructive capacity, the number of allies that joined the fight on each side of the dispute, and the dispute initiator's distance from where the dispute began relative to the target's distance from the dispute onset location.[8] In this model, the dispute initiator's destructive capacity relative to the target state has a statistically significant, but small, positive effect on the probability that the initiator will attain its primary political objective. The probability of strategic victory increases from 18 percent to 23 percent when the destructive capacity of the dispute initiator increases from one-fourth of the combined capabilities of the two belligerents to three-fourths of combined capabilities.[9] But knowing the distribution of destructive capacity between the disputants improves our ability to predict violent conflict outcomes by less than 1 percent over simply guessing the modal dispute outcome (initiator fails to attain its objective). The variable indicating that the dispute initiator has allies is also statistically significant and positive in model 1. The predicted probability of success is 27 percent for initiators fighting with an ally, but only 21 percent for initiators fighting alone.

In model 2, I add a variable that measures the difference between the salience of the issue at stake for the initiator and the salience of the issue at stake for the target. This variable has a robustly significant effect on dispute outcomes in all of the models that include it. In model 2, the predicted probability of strategic victory for the initiator is 28 percent when the issues at stake are roughly equally salient to the belligerents. When the balance of interests tips in favor of the target, the predicted probability of initiator success drops to 22 percent. The probability that the dispute initiator attains its primary objective in a violent conflict increases to 43 percent when the initiator has more salient issues at stake than the target. The relative destructive capacity and allied assistance measures have about the same effect on violent conflict outcomes in models 1 and 2.

In order to test whether the effects of destructive capacity vary with the nature of the interests at stake, model 3 adds a dichotomous variable indicating that the states were fighting over a coercive objective and an interaction term created by multiplying relative military capabilities by the coercive objective indicator. Model 4 also includes the regime type of each state and the ground combat control variable. The statistical estimates from both models provide strong evidence that the effect of relative destructive capacity on violent conflict outcomes varies with the nature of the issue at stake. Figure 5.3 uses the coefficients from model 4 to calculate the predicted probability of initiator success as the initiator's proportion of destructive capacity increases from 0 to 100 percent of the dyad's military-industrial capacity.

Figure 5.3 demonstrates that a core hypothesis from the war aims model is supported by this analysis. The dispute initiator's destructive capacity advantage is positively correlated with the probability of victory in violent conflicts with brute-force objectives, but negatively correlated with the probability of victory in violent conflicts with coercive objectives. As the initiator's destructive capacity increases from one-tenth to nine-tenths of the combined military capabilities of the two states, the probability it will attain territory or regime change objectives almost triples—increasing from 15 percent to 43 percent. However, the same increase in the initiator's destructive capacity *decreases* the probability of attaining policy concessions

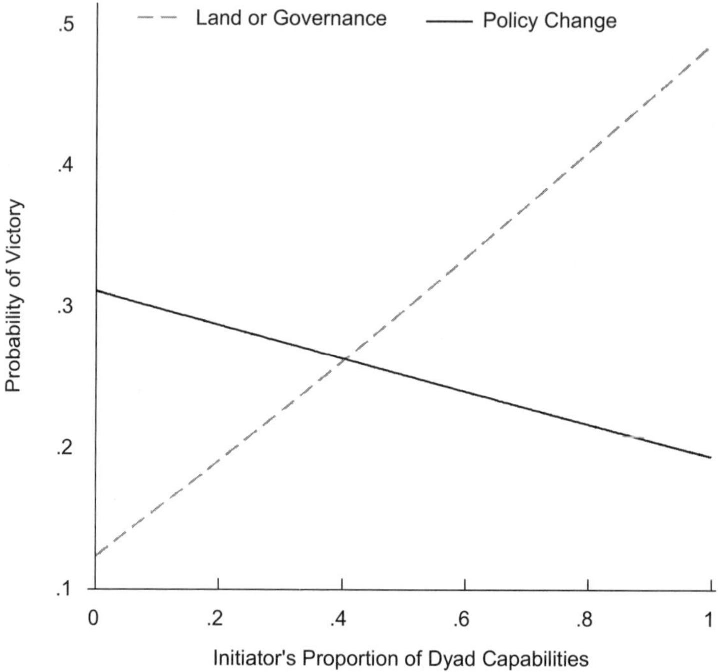

Figure 5.3. Change in the Predicted Probability Initiator Prevails as Initiator Military Capacity Relative to Target Increases (Violent Conflicts)

from 29 percent to 22 percent.[10] Although it is not surprising that states become more likely to succeed in gaining territory or removing a foreign adversary from power as their destructive-capacity advantage increases, the predicted probabilities plotted in Figure 5.3 have two counterintuitive implications. Physically weak states may be more likely than strong states to prevail in violent conflicts over policy. And very strong states are more likely to win wars with expansive (i.e., "total") war aims than wars with much more limited aims.[11]

In addition to destructive capacity and the nature of the issue at stake in the conflict, the regime type of the dispute initiator has a statistically significant effect on violent conflict outcomes in model 4. All else being equal, a completely democratic country is 22 percent more likely than an entirely autocratic country to attain its war aims. Two alternative models, one including an interaction between the initiator's regime type and distance from the fighting and another including an interaction between initiator regime type and target capabilities, are tested but not shown in the table. Although some scholars have argued that democracies are less likely to prevail in wars against distant, weak opponents, because domestic cost tolerance should be lower when adversaries are weak and far from the homeland, the effect of initiator regime type does not vary with the dispute initiator's distance from the target or the target's military-industrial capabilities. In fact, in models 2 through 4, all initiators appear to become slightly *more* likely to attain their objectives in a violent conflict as their relative distance from the dispute increases.

Finally, the variable indicating that the dispute initiator committed ground troops to combat is statistically significant, but the direction of the effect runs contrary to my expectations. Dispute initiators that engage in ground combat are approximately 24 percent *less* likely to prevail than dispute initiators that rely on air strikes, sea power, or long-range missiles. An alternative model, not shown in the table, includes an interaction between strategy and objective, but there is no evidence that the effect of ground combat varies across political objective categories. It is unlikely that ground combat is a less effective way of utilizing military force in general, or that committing ground combat troops would decreases the likelihood that a state prevails in any particular armed conflict. The negative coefficient is, in all probability, a result of the fact that states are more likely to engage in ground combat in the most "difficult" conflicts. If states commit ground troops when they face the most intransigent adversaries, ground combat can be correlated with failure, even if committing ground troops does not actually cause failure. We cannot conclude that states lose armed conflicts because they commit ground troops to combat, but neither can we conclude that reliance on air power and other standoff firepower is a significant predictor of failure in armed conflicts.

To explore the utility of the war aims model for predicting violent conflict outcomes, I generate predicted probabilities and compare them to actual success rates in six scenarios representing plausible combinations of the key independent variables. Table 5.3 displays the results. Column 1 shows the balance of military capabilities within the dyad. In three of the scenarios, the balance of capabilities between the belligerents reflects at least a four-to-one advantage for the dispute initiator. In the other three, there is at least a four-to-one advantage for the dispute target. Column 2 notes the initiator's primary political objective. Column 3 displays the mean predicted probability of success across the cases in that set. I calculate the predicted probability that the dispute initiator will achieve its primary political objective, given that the dispute has escalated to violence, using the coefficient estimates from the equation for model 4. Finally, column 4 shows the actual success rate as the number of cases in which the initiator prevailed out of all cases in the dataset with parameter values matching those in the scenario.

The model predicts that, if a dispute has escalated to mutual hostilities, a dispute initiator with at least four times the destructive capacity of the target state has only a 17 percent probability of coercing the target government

Table 5.3. MODEL SUCCESS RATE PREDICTIONS

Balance of Capabilities	Initiator's Political Objective	Predicted Success Rate (pr)	Actual Success Rate
> 4:1	Policy change	17%	6 of 39 (15%)
> 4:1	Regime change	45%	4 of 8 (50%)
> 4:1	Territory	33%	11 of 35 (31%)
< 1:4	Policy change	29%	5 of 14 (36%)
< 1:4	Regime change	3%	0 of 4 (0%)
< 1:4	Territory	17%	6 of 43 (14%)

into making a policy change. Among the cases in the dataset that match this scenario, the initiator achieved its objective in only six of thirty-nine violent conflicts. In contrast, the predicted probability of success for dispute initiators with this much of a military advantage is 45 percent when the initiator seeks a change in who governs in the target state and 33 percent when the initiator is demanding a revision of the territorial status quo. In the dataset, an initiator with a four-to-one military advantage achieves its objectives in four of eight disputes over regime change and eleven out of thirty-five violent conflicts over land. Weak dispute initiators, on the other hand, have only a 3 percent predicted probability of success when they seek regime change and are unsuccessful in all four of the attempts in the dataset. Their likelihood of gaining territory is also low—with a 17 percent predicted probability of success and an actual success rate of 14 percent. Perhaps most notably, weak dispute initiators are 70 percent more likely than strong dispute initiators to achieve a policy change objective in a dispute that has escalated to mutual hostilities. In the dataset, the weakest dispute initiators are successful in five of fourteen violent conflicts in which they are seeking a policy change and are able to resist a policy change demand from a strong dispute initiator in thirty-three of thirty-nine cases.

CONCLUSION

The results of the empirical analyses conducted in this chapter provide strong evidence that the utility of military force depends on the nature of the issues at stake. Both military capabilities and resolve are important determinants of conflict outcomes. But I argue that relative destructive capacity should be more important than relative tolerance for costs when states use military force to attain political objectives that can be seized and held with physical force, while target cost tolerance may compensate for material weakness when a state pursues objectives that require target compliance.

In this chapter, I find that when states have "brute force" political objectives, their military threats become significantly more likely to result in target concessions as their destructive capacity advantage increases. Although the targets of territorial and regime change demands are likely to be highly motivated to resist, they also appear to recognize that they have little chance of prevailing if a much stronger state uses military force to seize territory or remove them from power. As a result, as the gap between two states' military capabilities increases, the weaker side becomes more likely to acquiesce to demands for regime change or land and these disputes become less likely to escalate to violence. When disputes over brute-force objectives do escalate to violence, the stronger state is much more likely to prevail.

In contrast, the balance of material capacity between two states has no effect on the likelihood that one state will make policy concessions in response to a threat. Moreover, if a dispute over policy escalates to the use of military force by both sides, relatively weak states have a higher probability of achieving their policy aims than strong states. States that refuse to make concessions to significantly stronger opponents are likely to have significantly higher cost-tolerance thresholds than those opponents. When the object at stake can be seized and held with brute force alone, a weak state's cost-tolerance advantage does not appear to matter. However, in violent conflicts over policy, materially weak but highly resolved states appear to have an edge.

In chapter 6, I explore the effects of military strategy with better data on the strategies employed by both sides. For now, it is most important to note that the nature of the dispute initiator's primary political objective continues to have a strong effect on armed conflict outcomes after controlling for the way force is utilized by the dispute initiator. Whether a state relies on air power or puts boots on the ground, the likelihood of attaining a brute-force objective rises while the probability of attaining a policy change from an adversary declines as a state's destructive capacity relative to that adversary increases.

These results are important because they demonstrate that the model has predictive power for a wide range of cases—spanning over eight decades and encompassing all violent conflicts between states within the international system. But there are limitations as well. The universe of cases used in these analyses does not include wars in which one of the belligerents was a nonstate actor. At the same time, because of the large number of cases, measures of key concepts are less precise than I would like. In the following chapter, I focus on a smaller number of cases for which I could obtain more detailed data on political objectives, force employment strategies, and war outcomes.

CHAPTER 6

Military Interventions by Powerful States:

At What Price Victory?

This chapter hones in on a particularly difficult challenge: explaining why states with tremendous capabilities and resources—the most powerful states in the world—are often unable to attain even limited objectives through the use of military force against much weaker adversaries. The primary goal of this chapter is to identify the conditions under which powerful states achieve their political objectives when they use military force against weak targets and the factors that limit their ability to use force as a policy instrument. I am particularly interested in how the nature of a strong state's political objectives affects the likelihood that the state will attain its war aims. Do even the great powers become less likely to prevail over their opponents when their objectives require the adversary to positively comply, as the theory anticipates?

Chapters 2 and 3 developed a broad theoretical argument about the determinants of armed conflict outcomes. Chapter 4 presented hypotheses from my own theory and several competing theories, and chapter 5 tested those hypotheses with data on almost two thousand militarized disputes between pairs of states. In this chapter, I test two hypotheses from the war aims model and four hypotheses from the alternative approaches on a distinct set of cases—all foreign military interventions conducted by the five permanent members of the UN Security Council (hereinafter the "major powers") since 1945.

The empirical analyses in this chapter examine a diverse range of cases—from wars between states over claims to territory to counterinsurgency operations against guerilla armies. The results challenge both existing theories and conventional wisdom about the impact of factors like military strength, resolve, troop commitment levels, and war-fighting strategies on asymmetric war outcomes. Scholars and military leaders have argued that domestic political constraints on democratic governments, failure to commit sufficient resources to a war effort, or poor strategy choices could explain why strong states lose small wars. But differences between the requirements of wars in pursuit of brute-force objectives and military operations with coercive aims suggest a more fundamental limitation on the utility of military force. In the population of all major power military interventions since World War II, the major powers prevail more often than their weak state and nonstate adversaries. But weak actors thwart the objectives of their powerful opponents almost two-thirds of the time when the major powers pursue coercive war aims.

This chapter is organized into two main sections. In the first section, I briefly describe the dependent, explanatory, and control variables I use in the quantitative analyses in this chapter. The second section presents a series of statistical models exploring the effects of these factors on the outcomes of major military operations by five of the most powerful states in the international system.

DETERMINANTS OF ASYMMETRIC WAR OUTCOMES

The dependent variable in this chapter is military intervention outcome. Chapter 4 contains more detailed information about how this variable was measured. In the statistical analyses below, the variable is dichotomous and takes a value of one when the intervening state attains its primary political objective and that objective is maintained for at least one year after the military intervention is terminated; otherwise it is zero. Intervention outcome equals one (objective attained) in 60 percent of the cases. Because the dependent variable is a dichotomous measure of success, I use logit models to estimate the effects of the explanatory variables.

The key explanatory factor in all of the models in this chapter is the degree to which the intervening state's primary political objective is dependent on target compliance. The theory I develop in this book predicts that even an overwhelming preponderance of military capacity will not always result in strategic victory in war. Although states with greater destructive capacity than their opponent are better able to impose costs and degrade their opponent's ability to continue fighting, they can be constrained by relatively low tolerance for costs or stymied by an opponent willing to absorb extremely high levels of punishment. That said, even an extreme imbalance of resolve or cost tolerance does not necessarily result in a militarily strong state's defeat. The extent to which a physically weaker actor's cost-tolerance advantage can impact war outcomes is largely a function of the degree to which the stronger actor has war aims that require the weak actor to change its behavior. In this chapter, I test my expectation that materially strong states become less likely to prevail over materially weaker adversaries as the political objectives they pursue become more dependent on target compliance.

To avoid introducing any subjective bias into the coding of this critical variable, I employed independent coders and developed a rigorous coding procedure. These procedures are described in more detail in chapter 4. I test the explanatory power of several different measures of the intervening state's primary political objective in this chapter. As a preliminary step, I simply assess whether there are statistically significant differences among success rates by primary objective category. There are six broad political objective categories: Maintain Foreign Regime Authority, Remove/Replace Foreign Regime, Policy Change, Acquire/Defend Territory, Maintain Empire, and Social Protection/Order. Next, I conduct multivariate analyses with two indicators of the nature of the major power state's political objective in each intervention. For this analysis, I code three types of war aims from the six original primary political objective categories. The intervening state's objective is considered to be "brute force" if its primary war aim is the acquisition or defense of territory or the removal of a foreign regime. Attempting to maintain the political authority of either a foreign government or of the state's own colonial government in the face of internal opposition is considered a "moderately coercive" objective. I code the major power's primary political objective as "coercive" if the state is seeking a policy change from a foreign government or is engaged in an operation to suppress violence or restore order in a situation of unrest. This measure is included in the statistical models as two dummy variables and one excluded category. Finally, I create a dichotomous measure by dividing the political objectives that states pursue through the use of force into two categories—those that can be seized and held with military force alone (brute-force objectives) and those that can only be attained if the target chooses to comply (coercive objectives). The variable is produced by collapsing the "moderately coercive" and "coercive" categories from the first measure.

ALTERNATIVE EXPLANATORY VARIABLES

Military Capabilities and War-fighting Effectiveness

The vast majority of international relations theory assumes that relative military capacity is the most important determinant of war outcomes and that the probability of victory in war rises with increases in a state's destructive capacity relative to its opponent. If so, military operations that pit the world's most powerful states against some of the weakest actors in the international system should have overwhelmingly favorable outcomes for the major powers. The striking imbalance of power in these cases means that they should constitute an "easy" test for realist theories of war outcomes. I test three measures of war-fighting capacity in this chapter: material strength, combat effectiveness, and assistance from allies.

Material Strength. I use the Correlates of War (COW) Project's composite index of national military-industrial capabilities, or CINC, score as a measure of the intervening state's latent destructive capacity.[1] When the intervention target is a state, I also measure target state destructive capacity using the CINC score. But this measure is not available for nonstate actors like insurgents and terrorist groups. Therefore, I set nonstate target capabilities equal to the weakest state in the international system. Although this measure of nonstate actor capabilities is far from ideal, it would be extremely difficult to construct a measure comparable to the COW capabilities index for all of the nonstate targets in the dataset. In fact, one important attribute of nonstate actors that I address later in this chapter is that there is tremendous uncertainty about their strength. Because they typically do not have the institutional structures, control over resources, heavy equipment, firepower, or military personnel of states, terrorist organizations and guerilla insurgents are technically weaker on the material and industrial dimensions measured by the CINC score. But their mobility, limited resource requirements, and ability to blend into the civilian population and physical terrain may give nonstate actors *non*material advantages that compensate for their lack of brute strength. I discuss these attributes in more detail later in this chapter. In the statistical models, the intervening state's military strength relative to that of the target is calculated as the ratio of the major power's military-industrial capabilities to the combined capabilities of the two sides. I also construct an alternative measure of intervention target destructive capacity that divides intervention targets into three categories: minor power states, weak states, and nonstate actors.

Combat Effectiveness. The loss-exchange ratio (LER)—a measure of battlefield combat effectiveness commonly used by defense analysts—is created by dividing the number of target state troops killed in action by intervening state fatalities. It is used here as another measure of intervening state destructive capacity and military effectiveness. The higher the LER, the more effective the intervening state military is relative to the target.

Assistance from Allies. Because either side's war-fighting capabilities can be augmented by allies, the realist school would also predict that military assistance provided to one side or the other could change the probability of intervention success. Moreover, a significant body of research provides evidence that, although initiators are more likely to win wars, their probability of winning declines precipitously if the target receives help from allies.[2] Because the intervening state is already significantly stronger than the target in the cases I am concerned with in this chapter, external intervention on behalf of the target is likely to be particularly important. Ideally, a measure of the contributions of allies would take into consideration the nature and magnitude of their role, as well as the timing of their intervention. Unfortunately, I was not able to find data at this level of detail for most cases. As a crude substitute, I create a series of dummy variables. One dichotomous variable indicates that the intervening state received assistance from one or more major power allies, whereas another indicates that the intervention target received direct military assistance from another state. A final variable indicates that the intervening state had a local government ally.

Resolve

A widely accepted alternative to the realist perspective contends that weak state and nonstate actors can prevail over strong states in war because they have much greater resolve, political will, or tolerance for costs than their powerful adversaries. In this chapter, I test the explanatory power of two measures of resolve. The first variable, issue salience, is based on the assumption that the human and material costs an actor is willing to bear in a war will vary with the importance of the interests at stake. This variable has the advantage of being observable to the belligerents either before a conflict has escalated to the use of force or shortly thereafter. The second variable, ground troop commitment, is an ex post measure of effort exerted by the intervening state. All else being equal, higher ground troop levels are expected to indicate a greater willingness on the part of the intervening state to incur costs in pursuit of its war aims.

Issue Salience. In chapter 4, I describe an ordinal variable that ranks how important the issues at stake are likely to be for each side. For the models in this chapter, I use the rank order to create dummy variables that indicate whether the issues at stake are of equal importance to each side (equal), the stakes are greater for the intervening state (higher), or the stakes are greater for the target (lower). The issues are of higher salience to the major power in only seven cases. The intervening state and target are coded as having equal stakes in twenty-eight cases. In ninety-five cases, the stakes are higher for the target.

Ground Troop Commitment. The number of troops deployed in post-WWII major power military interventions varies greatly. While 27 percent of the cases involve deployments of between 500 and 3,000 troops, in 33 percent of the cases, the intervening state committed more than 30,000 troops. The largest troop deployments, involving over 500,000 troops, occurred during the U.S. intervention in Vietnam and the Soviet intervention in Afghanistan. The ground troop commitment level variable captures the maximum number of major power ground combat troops deployed to the combat zone at any one time during the intervention. The assumption is that states that intervene with ground troops are signaling greater resolve than states that restrict their involvement to air strikes, naval bombardment, or small unit maneuvers. Evidence from recent history suggests that major powers sometimes choose air campaigns over ground combat in order to avoid the higher costs—and in particular the risk of casualties—inherent in the commitment of ground troops even when decision-makers acknowledge that air strikes are less likely to be successful than a ground campaign. In cases like the NATO intervention in Kosovo, the decision not to commit ground troops was one symptom of low tolerance for costs among NATO members. Because of the extreme right skew of the troop commitment variable and my expectation that additional troops have a greater effect when troop levels are low, I use the natural log of the number of troops committed when estimating the statistical models.

Strategic Approach

Although we can point to more and less effective military strategies and tactics throughout history, and military strategy is a major focus in the military history literature, it is often difficult to make the case that an actor that lost a war could have won by simply choosing a different military strategy. The military strategies adopted in a particular war may have little independent explanatory power, because military strategy choice is often severely constrained. In asymmetric wars, a weak target's military strategy is largely determined by the nature of the strong state's objectives and the target's own war-fighting capabilities. In the late stages of an insurgency, an armed independence or separatist movement may hold territory and begin direct military attacks on government and intervening armed forces with the intent of destroying their military capacity—but most insurgents must use primarily "punishment" strategies, because they do not have the capacity to defeat their adversaries on the battlefield. On the other hand, while the leadership of a state can employ an indirect strategy of raising costs when their adversary has a coercive war aim, they cannot physically defend their territorial integrity or defend the regime against an external invasion with anything but a denial strategy.

My aim in this analysis is to test three hypotheses. The first is drawn from arguments suggesting that punishment strategies are simply less effective than maneuver and attrition strategies. Intervening states that adopt punishment strategies will be less likely to achieve their objectives. The second, based on Arreguín-Toft's theory, predicts that a strong state will be more likely to prevail against a weak target if it uses the same strategic approach as the target. The final expectation is derived from the war aims model. I expect that the major powers will be less likely to attain brute-force objectives if they adopt a punishment strategy, but that employing a punishment strategy will have no effect on the probability of strategic success when the intervening state has a coercive political objective.

I use several variables as proxy measures of the military strategy employed by the intervening state and another variable to indicate the interaction between initiator and target strategies. My first measure attempts to replicate Allan Stam's maneuver-attrition-punishment typology.[3] The second measure collapses attrition and maneuver strategies into a denial strategy category and contrasts that category with punishment strategies. Following Biddle, the third measure employs country dummies in order to capture the possibility that the major powers have different force employment doctrines that would impact their military effectiveness.[4] A final strategy variable is created by interacting the dichotomous denial/punishment strategy indicator for intervening states with a dichotomous variable indicating whether the target adopted a primarily punishment or a primarily denial strategy. The result is a dummy variable that equals one when the major power and the target have the same strategic approach.

CONTROL VARIABLES

Target Type. Regardless of the primary political objective of an operation, a strong state's success is partially dependent upon the extent to which its target has assets that are (1) essential to its physical and/or political capacity to sustain the war effort, and (2) susceptible to the attacker's destructive capacity. A target's physical vulnerability is determined in large part by its level of political and economic development. As the organizational complexity of an actor increases, so does its susceptibility to attacks that can cripple the actor's capacity to maintain a campaign of organized violence. At the most basic level, states are expected to be more vulnerable to military force than nonstate actors. State targets have (1) a permanent population, (2) a defined territory, and (3) a government capable of maintaining effective control over its territory.[5] Terrorist organizations, civilian rioters, political opposition movements, and insurgents do not possess these attributes. Although state targets have strategic resources (defensible terrain, military installations, standing armies, equipment) and assets (cities, industrial and communications centers, transportation systems) that can be easily destroyed, degraded, or captured by the armed forces of strong states, terrorists and guerilla armies have small, mobile strategic assets, limited resource requirements, and unsophisticated leadership, supply, and communication infrastructure. Nonstate actors like insurgents can use the natural terrain and the civilian population as a means of concealment and avoid pitched battles with stronger foes. Since the termination of the United States' unsuccessful intervention in Vietnam, a substantial volume of case study literature has maintained that fighting nonstate actors like guerilla insurgencies is especially difficult for large, conventional armies.[6] More recent quantitative studies have provided additional evidence in support of this conjecture.[7] In the multivariate analyses below, a dummy variable indicates that the target was not a state. Forty-five percent of the targets in the major power military interventions since 1945 were nonstate actors.

Regime Type. A substantial body of recent research has advanced the argument that democratic states are more selective about the military contests they initiate because of the domestic political costs of failure.[8] There is evidence that democracies select wars that are shorter and less costly, and that they are more likely to win the wars they fight.[9] Some have even argued that democratic states are more militarily effective.[10] The theory of asymmetric war outcomes I am testing is agnostic about how regime type affects strong states' decisions to use military force against weak adversaries. I suspect that the uncertainty surrounding the cost of attaining coercive political objectives through the use of force puts both democracies and nondemocracies at risk for selecting into conflicts they cannot sustain to victory. But this first school of thought on the effects of democratic political institutions is consistent with my approach. If democratic governments are more cautious about the circumstances under which they will use military force, democratic major powers should be more likely than nondemocratic major powers to prevail when they initiate foreign military interventions.

On the other hand, several scholars have argued that democratic states are especially prone to *losing* "small wars," because weak adversaries can exploit the casualty sensitivity or humanitarian sensibilities of democratic publics.[11] I am more skeptical of this claim than I am of the possibility that democracies are more cautious when choosing to use military force. Citizens in democratic states are unlikely to be more sensitive to the loss of life than citizens in autocratic states, but democratic publics may be more aware of the human and material costs of a particular war than their counterparts in autocratic countries due to the transparency of their political institutions, freedom of the press, and opportunities for open political dissent. At the same time, the leaders of democratic states may be particularly vulnerable to losing office for fighting costly and/or losing wars, because the removal of political leaders is institutionalized and relatively easy in democracies, and democratic leaders must satisfy a larger proportion of the population in order to retain their positions.[12]

Nevertheless, as I have argued, strong states do not lose asymmetric wars simply because they have low tolerance for the costs of war. They fail to attain their war aims when they underestimate the cost of victory and select themselves into an armed conflict they cannot sustain to victory. If democracies are more "sensitive" to the costs of war, they should be more selective about the circumstances under which they use force. And there is no reason to believe that democratic governments are any worse (or better) than non-democratic governments in their ability to estimate the cost and likelihood of victory under uncertainty.

I use the Polity IV dataset to obtain a continuous measure of major power regime type by subtracting a regime's autocracy score from its democracy score to produce a twenty-one-point scale that ranges from negative ten to positive ten.[13] A state's Polity score can vary from year to year. For military interventions that last more than one year, I use the state's score on the day troops were deployed. There are too few democratic targets of post-WWII major power interventions to include target regime type as a control variable.

STATISTICAL TESTS

The results of the statistical analyses are discussed in three parts. First, I present the results of a bivariate test of the relationship between war aims and war outcomes. The second section presents the results from tests for the correct specification of a multivariate model predicting asymmetric war outcomes. Following this, I test hypotheses about the effects of relative military capacity, political will, and the nature of the intervening state's war aims. A second set of models tests for the effects of several different measures of military strategy. The final section discusses the substantive effect of each statistically significant variable on major power military intervention outcomes.

WAR AIMS AND WAR OUTCOMES

Table 6.1 presents the median intervention duration and proportion of successful interventions across major power political objective categories. Although the median duration of interventions does not vary significantly across political objective type ($p = 0.13$), the proportion of successful interventions does. A Pearson chi-square test indicates that the null hypothesis that

Table 6.1. RATE OF SUCCESS AND MEDIAN DURATION BY POLITICAL OBJECTIVE

	Primary Political Objective	N	% Successful	Median Duration
Brute Force	Remove Foreign Regime	14	86%	188 days
↓	Acquire or Defend Territory	35	71%	118 days
	Maintain Regime Authority	36	67%	309 days
	Maintain Empire	14	43%	1,056 days
	Social Order	11	44%	296 days
Coercive	Policy Change	16	25%	195 days
	Total	126	60%	211 days

Test: Intervention Outcomes are independent of Political Objective type.
Pearson chi2(6) = 18.1963 Pr = 0.006.

intervention outcome and intervening state war aim are independent can be rejected at the $p < 0.01$ level of significance. Major power states are *most* likely to attain their war aims when they use military force to remove a foreign regime or acquire or defend territory. Major power states are *least* likely to be successful when they attempt to coerce a foreign government into changing its foreign or domestic policy. Peacekeeping operations and wars to maintain empire are also significantly less likely to be successful than interventions to acquire territory or overthrow an incumbent regime.

MILITARY INTERVENTION OUTCOME MODELS

Table 6.2 presents the results of logit estimations of three equations predicting the outcomes of post-World War II major power military operations. Model 1 can be thought of as a classic realist model of war outcomes grounded in measures of war-fighting capacity. It predicts major power military intervention success and failure employing a measure of relative military capacity, the number of ground troops the intervening state committed, several variables indicating the military assistance provided to each side by allies, and a variable indicating whether the target is a state or nonstate actor. Two alternative models, one including the loss-exchange ratio (LER) as an additional measure of the intervening state's destructive-capacity advantage over the target and another replacing the relative military capabilities variable with the LER, are tested but not shown in the table. Due to missing data on target casualties, twenty cases must be dropped from the estimation when LER is included in the model. The LER is never a statistically significant predictor of major power intervention outcomes, and both Wald and Bayesian Information Criterion

(BIC) tests provide no evidence that including the LER improves the ability of the model to predict intervention outcomes.

In the second model, which attempts to factor in the effects of each side's political will, I incorporate variables indicating the relative salience of the issues at stake for each actor. Two dummy variables compare military conflicts in which the issues at stake have higher salience for the target or equal salience for both sides to conflicts in which the initiator has greater stakes in the conflict. This model also includes a measure of the intervening state's level of democracy. Neither dropping the major power's Polity score, nor changing which issue salience category is excluded has a significant effect on the results.

Table 6.2. LOGIT ANALYSIS OF MAJOR POWER MILITARY INTERVENTION SUCCESS, 1946–2003

	Model 1 Relative Power	Model 2 Political Will	Model 3 War Aims
Relative military capabilities	1.222	0.606	3.702
	(0.55)	(0.22)	(1.34)
Military assistance to target	-1.996***	-2.212***	-2.761***
	(2.79)	(2.98)	(3.32)
Major power coalition	-0.302	-0.174	-0.329
	(0.57)	(0.32)	(0.55)
Local government ally	2.604***	2.579***	2.753***
	(4.36)	(4.27)	(4.25)
Nonstate target	-0.728	-0.583	-0.518
	(1.52)	(1.14)	(0.94)
Ground troops committed	-0.023	-0.053	-0.092
	(0.71)	(1.05)	(1.60)
Major power Polity score		-0.028	-0.018
		(0.85)	(0.51)
Higher salience for target		-0.376	
		(0.38)	
Equal salience		0.672	
		(1.20)	
Coercive objective			-2.551***
			(3.49)
Moderately coercive objective			-1.413**
			(2.24)
Constant	-0.819	0.034	-1.437
	(0.39)	(0.01)	(0.57)
Observations	124	123	123
Adjusted count R^2	.32	.30	.43

Note: Absolute value of z statistics in parentheses.
* significant at $p < 0.1$ ** significant at $p < 0.05$ *** significant at $p < 0.01$

The final model in Table 6.2 tests for the impact of the nature of the intervening state's war aims on the probability of intervention success. I replace the two variables intended to measure the relative salience of the issues at stake with variables indicating the extent to which the intervening state's war aims are dependent on target compliance.

Neither relative military capabilities nor assistance provided to the intervening state by major power coalition partners approach statistical significance in any of the models. In fact, neither of these variables is statistically significant at even the 0.1 level of significance in bivariate models including only the dependent variable and the explanatory variable of interest. In contrast, all three models indicate that the intervening state is much more likely to succeed when it has a local government ally. At the same time, the coefficient on external assistance provided to the intervention target is negative and statistically significant at $p < 0.01$ in all three of the models.

Perhaps most surprisingly, whether the target is a state or a nonstate actor does not appear to be correlated with the probability that the intervening state will attain its objectives. The coefficient on the variable indicating that the target is not a state is negative, but it does not approach standard levels of statistical significance in any of the models in Table 6.2. There is also no support for arguments that attribute paradoxical war outcomes to a lack of effort or commitment on the part of powerful states. The coefficient on the ground troop commitment variable is also negative but statistically insignificant.

Based on my analysis of a number of goodness-of-fit statistics, model 2, which contains variables expected to be correlated with relative resolve and intervening state cost tolerance, is the weakest model of major power military intervention outcomes. None of the variables indicating the relative salience of the issues at stake for the actors is significant. Moreover, although some scholars have argued that democratic societies are less able to tolerate the human costs of war, and others have maintained that democratic leaders select more "winnable" wars, there is no evidence in Table 6.2 that the regime type of the major power has any effect on the probability it will attain its primary political objective. This is in contrast to the results from chapter 5 in which I found that democratic countries were significantly more likely than autocratic countries to attain their war aims in the broader population of all violent conflicts between states from 1919 to 2001.

Unlike model 2, the fit of model 3 is strong, correctly predicting 78 percent of intervention outcomes, an improvement in predictive accuracy of 43 percent over simply choosing the modal outcome category (success). Both variables indicating the extent to which the intervening state's war aims are dependent on target compliance are statistically significant, and the effects are in the predicted direction. Moreover, this model is 40 percent more accurate in predicting military intervention outcomes than the two models that do not include measures of the nature of the intervening state's war aims.

In Table 6.3, I compare four different models testing for the effects of major power military strategy, force employment doctrine, and strategic interaction. In model 4, the military strategy employed by the intervening state is indicated by two dummy variables and an excluded category (attrition). In model 5, I collapse the attrition and maneuver strategies into one excluded category to test whether major power states are particularly disadvantaged by employing a punishment strategy. In a bivariate model that does not control for the nature of the intervening state's war aims or military assistance provided to either side, the effect of employing a maneuver strategy is positive and marginally statistically significant ($p = 0.07$). However, in models 4 and 5, which do control for these factors, the probability of intervention success does not appear to be affected by whether the state employs a maneuver, punishment, or attrition strategy. Moreover, controlling for military strategy does not affect the magnitude, direction, or statistical significance of the coefficients on the variables indicating the nature of the state's war aims.

The estimation results from model 6 indicate that the probability of military intervention success also does not vary significantly from state to state. Including dummy variables for four of the five major powers—so that the coefficients measure the effects of each state's unique characteristics relative to the United States—slightly improves the fit of the model and the magnitude of the effect of war aims, but a Wald test confirms that we cannot reject the null hypothesis that the coefficients on all of the state dummy variables are equal to zero ($p = 0.36$). In model 7, we can see that whether the intervening state employs the same strategic approach as the target also has no effect on the likelihood that the major power will prevail.

To test for the possibility that the effect of military strategy varies with the nature of the intervening state's primary political objective—as anticipated by the war aims model—I construct an interaction term indicating that the state employed a punishment strategy to attain a brute-force political objective. I estimate a logit regression with a dichotomous measure of the nature of the intervening state's primary political objective (brute-force versus coercive/ moderately coercive), a dichotomous indicator of the state's strategic approach (punishment versus denial), the interaction term, and controls for military assistance provided to the target by an external actor and to the intervening state by a local government. I use this model to calculate the predicted probability of intervention success as both the intervening state war aim and military strategy vary. The results are displayed in Table 6.4.

Table 6.3. LOGIT ANALYSIS OF MAJOR POWER MILITARY INTERVENTION SUCCESS WITH MILITARY STRATEGY VARIABLES, 1946–2003

	Model 4	Model 5	Model 6	Model 7
Coercive objective	-2.361***	-2.296***	-2.380***	-2.449***
	(3.32)	(3.30)	(3.31)	(3.41)
Moderately coercive objective	-1.200*	-1.308**	-1.122*	-1.394**
	(1.96)	(2.16)	(1.89)	(2.31)
Relative military capabilities	3.476	3.259		5.160
	(1.37)	(1.30)		(1.36)
Military assistance to target	-2.260***	-2.221	-2.514***	-2.278***
	(3.01)	(3.00)	(3.16)	(3.14)
Local government ally	2.751***	2.623***	2.684***	2.622***
	(4.44)	(4.30)	(4.27)	(4.28)
Nonstate target	-0.333	-0.536	-0.230	-0.515
	(0.60)	(1.01)	(0.42)	(0.97)
Punishment strategy	0.020	-0.231		
	(0.04)	(0.47)		
Maneuver strategy	0.920			
	(1.28)			
United Kingdom			0.133	
			(0.18)	
France			-0.845	
			(1.12)	
China			0.217	
			(0.28)	
Russia			-0.257	
			(0.35)	
Same strategy				0.950
				(0.76)
Constant	-2.530	-1.889	1.222*	-3.818
	(1.08)	(0.83)	(1.89)	(1.06)
Observations	124	124	125	124
Adjusted count R^2	.45	.49	.49	.45

Note: Absolute value of z statistics in parentheses.
* significant at $p < 0.1$ ** significant at $p < 0.05$ *** significant at $p < 0.01$

Overall, the estimates from this model are in the expected direction—the coefficient on the variable indicating that the state has a brute-force objective is positive and the coefficients on the punishment variable and the interaction term are both negative—but the effect of strategy is not statistically significant. In Table 6.4, there is no difference between employing a punishment strategy and employing a denial strategy when the intervening state has a coercive or moderately coercive political objective. Major powers that employ punishment strategies when they have brute-force war aims appear to have a lower probability of success (68 percent vs.

Table 6.4. PREDICTED PROBABILITY OF INTERVENTION SUCCESS

	Punishment Strategy	Denial Strategy
Coercive objective	.35	.35
Brute-force objective	.68	.72

Note: The difference in the predicted probability of intervention success between coercive and brute-force objectives is statistically significant ($p < 0.1$) in both strategy categories. The difference in the predicted probability between strategy types is not significant for either type of objective.

72 percent). However, the 90 percent confidence intervals around the two predictions overlap. Pursuing a brute-force war aim, as opposed to a coercive or moderately coercive war aim, has a positive effect on the probability of intervention success across both military strategy categories. But the effect is only marginally statistically significant when the major power employs a punishment strategy. I discuss the significance of these results in the next section.

DISCUSSION OF RESULTS

The results of this analysis provide strong support for a model of asymmetric conflict outcomes that accounts for the degree of target compliance required to attain the strong state's primary political objective. Not only are the coefficients on the war aims variables significant and in the predicted direction, they are robust to a variety of changes in model specification and have large substantive effects on intervention outcomes. Coefficient estimates from all model specifications indicate that the major powers are significantly more likely to achieve brute-force war aims than more compliance-dependent objectives.

In contrast, many of the variables commonly employed to predict war outcomes are not correlated with major power military intervention outcomes. The major power states prevail more often than their weak targets, attaining their primary political objective in about 60 percent of their military interventions since 1946. But there is no relationship between intervention outcomes and the magnitude of the intervening state's destructive-capacity advantage over the target, and intervening states are no more likely to succeed when they have major power allies. The likelihood of success also does not improve with greater troop commitments. Moreover, democratic major powers do not appear to be any more or less likely to prevail in asymmetric wars than nondemocracies—although it is possible that democratic governments are both more sensitive to the costs of wars with weak adversaries and more selective about the use of military force against these adversaries so that the two attributes effectively cancel each other out. Contrary to expectations from the political will perspective, the relative salience of the issues at stake for each of the actors is not a significant predictor of military intervention outcomes. And militarily preponderant states do not appear to be significantly disadvantaged when they use military force against nonstate actors. Counterinsurgencies and wars of empire have a relatively low probability of success, not because they target nonstate actors, but because their objectives are dependent on target compliance.

Table 6.5 contains logit regression estimates for the final war aims model of major power military intervention outcomes. The far right column in the table displays the effect of each statistically significant variable on the probability that the intervening state will achieve its primary political objective.[14] I briefly describe the effect of each variable on intervention outcomes and then conclude with a broader discussion of the implications of these results for our understanding of asymmetric conflict and the utility and limitations of military force as an instrument of statecraft.

War Aims. The primary political objective sought by the major power state is at least moderately coercive in approximately half of post-WWII major power military interventions. Holding all other variables constant, a militarily strong intervening state is 37 percent less likely to achieve moderately coercive objectives, and 58 percent less likely to achieve the most coercive objectives, than it is to attain brute-force political objectives. When the intervening state has a brute-force war aim, the predicted probability of success is almost 79 percent. The probability that the intervening state will prevail declines to only 23 percent when the major power has an entirely compliance-dependent political objective.

Assistance from Allies. Not surprisingly, foreign military assistance provided to an intervention target significantly reduces the probability of success for

Table 6.5. LOGIT ANALYSIS RESULTS WITH CHANGE IN THE PREDICTED PROBABILITY OF INTERVENTION SUCCESS

Variable	Coef.	Std. Err.	p > |z|	Δ in variable	Δ in pr(success)
Moderately coercive	-1.623	.568	0.004	0 → 1	-.37
Coercive objective	-2.620	.738	0.000	0 → 1	-.58
Military assistance to target	-2.702	.788	0.001	0 → 1	-.59
Local government ally	2.737	.641	0.000	0 → 1	+.19
Ground troops	-0.094	.060	0.099	+/- sd/2	-.07
Relative destructive capacity	2.748	2.600	0.290	n.s.	
Constant	-.744	2.434	0.760		

Note: N = 123. Changes in predicted probabilities are calculated when each of the dichotomous variables is held constant at its median value and each of the continuous variables is held constant at its mean.

intervening states. When another state commits troops to assist the target of a major power military operation, the likelihood that the major power will achieve its objectives declines by 59 percent. Whereas the major power may have initially determined that the costs of pursuing its objectives vis-à-vis a weak foreign target would be low, when that target begins to receive help from another state, the major power's war costs are likely to increase significantly. This rise in the current or anticipated cost of attaining its war aims may push the intervening state beyond its cost-tolerance threshold and lead to withdrawal short of victory. It is rare, however, for another state to intervene on behalf of the target of a major power military intervention. Only twenty-one out of one hundred twenty-four of the targets received military assistance from an external ally.

Although intervening with major power allies does not significantly affect the probability of intervention success, intervening in support of a weak state has a positive effect on the probability of intervention success for major powers. All else being equal, major power military interventions in support of a local government ally are 19 percent more likely to achieve their objectives than military operations undertaken solely on the major power's own behalf.

Level of Troop Commitment. The coefficient on the log of the number of ground troops committed is negative and only marginally statistically significant in this final model. In previous models, this variable does not appear to have a statistically significant effect on intervention outcomes. Most importantly, there is no evidence that a failure to commit sufficient resources to the war effort can account for cases in which militarily preponderant states lose small wars. In fact, the probability of intervention success may slightly decline as troop levels increase. It is unlikely that increases in troop strength *cause* failure, because troop commitment levels are likely to be correlated with other, unobserved variables that are themselves correlated with an increase in failure rates. In other words, the intervening state's troop commitment is likely to be higher in the most "difficult" cases. We cannot conclude that strong states lose because they commit too many troops, or that committing more troops to a particular intervention would decrease the probability of success. But the pattern is clearly not consistent with standard arguments that explain paradoxical war outcomes by pointing to a lack of commitment or effort on the part of the militarily preponderant state.[15]

Military Strategy. Although employing a maneuver strategy appears to marginally improve the likelihood of intervention success in a model without controls for the nature of the intervening state's war aims, the punishment-attrition-maneuver distinction does not significantly improve our ability to predict major power military intervention outcomes in more fully specified models. In chapter 4, I predicted that strong states would be less likely to attain brute-force political objectives if they lacked the cost tolerance to employ a denial strategy. I suspected that a strong state that seeks to win cheaply by employing a punishment strategy would surrender its primary advantage—the ability to use battlefield results to convince its target that resistance is futile—and provide its target with an opportunity to employ its preferred strategy—imposing costs, avoiding pitched battles, and prolonging the fight until the strong state decides that the costs of continuing its military operations will exceed the value of attaining its objectives. However, a model estimating the effects of military strategy across war aim categories failed to reveal any statistically significant effects. As expected, major powers appear marginally more likely to attain brute-force war aims when they employ denial strategies, but the difference is statistically indistinguishable from zero.

CONCLUSION

In this chapter, I tested two hypotheses derived from my theory of war outcomes and six hypotheses from alternative explanations of war outcomes with an original dataset of all post-WWII major power military interventions. Consistent with my theoretical expectations, these models reveal that major power states are most likely to succeed in acquiring or defending territory and in removing foreign regimes, and least likely to convince an adversary to change a foreign or domestic policy. Territorial acquisition and regime change are historically difficult and costly to achieve through the use of military force. The overthrow of an incumbent regime in a foreign country is a particularly extreme war aim. But militarily strong states can seize territory or remove foreign regimes without changing a weak adversary's behavior.

Table 6.6 contains statistics on troop levels, intervening state and target casualties, and the percentage of interventions in which the major power committed ground troops to combat by primary political objective type. It is clear that interventions to attain brute-force war aims are not systematically "cheaper" or "easier" than interventions to attain coercive war aims. The most costly military interventions on all counts were the major powers' attempts to maintain their political authority in territories they claimed as colonies or protectorates. Military interventions to maintain empire involved the largest mean and median number of troops, extracted the highest toll in intervening state troops killed in action, and always entailed the commitment of ground combat troops. However, after operations to maintain empire, military interventions to seize or defend

Table 6.6. TROOP COMMITMENT LEVELS AND TYPE OF FORCE BY POLITICAL OBJECTIVE

	Primary Political Objective	Mean Number Troops	Median Number Troops	Median MP Casualties	Median Target Casualties	Ground Combat
Brute Force	Regime Change	50,125	27,500	26	382	69%
↓	Territory	63,360	12,000	50	998	63%
	Regime Maintenance	45,794	3,150	47	600	43%
	Maintain Empire	84,563	30,500	141	950	100%
	Social Order	9,902	5,750	29	356	50%
Coercive	Policy Change	55,017	18,000	2	235	44%
	Total	58,838	12,658	35	847	56%

territory or to remove a foreign regime were most likely to involve ground combat, and the major powers also tended to deploy relatively large numbers of troops and to suffer moderately high human losses in interventions to secure these objectives. When a state's objectives can be attained with brute force alone, the *cost* may be high, but *prewar uncertainty about the cost* of attaining these objectives is relatively low. Consequently, states are less likely to initiate the use of force to achieve these war aims with insufficient cost tolerance to sustain the war to victory. In contrast, policy change objectives are entirely dependent on target compliance, and uncertainty about what it will cost to convince a resolute adversary to change its behavior is likely to be high.

The results of this analysis suggest that the "best case" scenario for an intervening state is a military operation to obtain a brute-force political objective against a target that does not receive external assistance. Thirty-eight of the military interventions in the MIPS dataset (31 percent) fit this pattern. The major power attained its primary political objective in all but seven of these cases. Why would weak actors choose to fight major powers with brute-force objectives if their odds are so poor? When a strong adversary's war aims require target compliance, the weak can employ their preferred strategy of evading direct combat with superior forces while attempting to convince the challenger that the costs of attaining compliance will exceed the price the strong state is willing to pay. But this is not a strategy that can succeed against a strong state employing its military to forcibly seize territory or drive the ruling regime from power. In general, the weak should avoid threatening strong state interests that can be held with brute force alone.

Table A3 in the appendix to this chapter provides actual values for the key explanatory variables in the war aims model for all major power military interventions since 1979. The last two columns of the table list the intervention outcome predicted by the statistical model and the actual outcome of the conflict. It is relatively rare for weak states to try to seize territory from significantly stronger adversaries, and even less common for weak states to attempt to forcibly overthrow regimes in stronger states. Weak states are more likely than their strong enemies to make territorial concessions and even to surrender power when threatened with military action by a strong state. Nevertheless, weak actors do sometimes choose to fight much stronger opponents over brute-force objectives. How can we explain this?

In the cases in the MIPS dataset, it appears that weak actors tend to select themselves into armed contests over brute-force objectives because they doubt a more powerful rival has the cost tolerance to employ the full measure of its capabilities in a direct attempt to seize the objective. Sometimes, as in the case of Argentina's invasion of the Falkland Islands, the leaders of weak states believe that the powerful state's resolve is so low that it will fail to use force at all. On April 2, 1982, the military leaders that ruled Argentina decided to end a long-running dispute with Britain over the Falkland Islands (the Islas Malvinas to Argentineans) by seizing them in a surprise raid. The Argentine government knew that their armed forces were no match for the British military, but decision-makers believed that the British did not care enough about the largely uninhabited territory 8,000 miles away to bear the costs of retaking the land by force. According to Richard Thornton, the junta was "absolutely, viscerally, convinced that the British would not fight" once the Argentine military had occupied the islands.[16]

Initially, the invasion went well. The small British marine contingent on the islands quickly surrendered to the Argentine military, recognizing that—given their current strength—military defeat was inevitable. But the British government surprised the Argentineans by declaring war and dispatching a large military force to reclaim the islands. Argentina spent the two weeks it took for the British Navy to arrive reinforcing its positions in the hope of making it too difficult and costly for the United Kingdom to retake the territory. The first of the British forces arrived in the South Atlantic on April 25. The British ground invasion came on May 21. Although Argentina's Air Force conducted relentless attacks on the British Navy, the Argentine ground troops stationed on the islands were ill-prepared, and most quickly surrendered to much smaller British contingents. On June 12, the main British force captured the capital city on East Falklands. On June 14, the Argentine governor of the islands requested a ceasefire. The remaining Argentine troops surrendered the next day.

In sharp contrast to the remarkable success rate of major powers that use military force to seize territory or overthrow foreign regimes, in the MIPS dataset the intervening state *failed* to attain its primary political objective in all but seven of the twenty-two interventions with a coercive war aim. Sixty thousand ground troops failed to convince the Iranian government to make economic concessions to the Soviets in 1946; China could not coerce the Democratic Republic of Vietnam into withdrawing from Cambodia (1979–1984); and years of a significant U.S. troop presence and air campaigns against the Iraqi regime failed to produce consistent cooperation with UN weapons inspections. Although a major power's overwhelming destructive capacity can make resistance tremendously costly for a weak adversary, killing people and breaking things will not necessarily convince that adversary to change its behavior.

CHAPTER 7

Conclusion

I have with me two gods, Persuasion and Compulsion.
—Themistocles

In the weeks leading up to Operation Desert Storm, many Western military experts and scholars feared a difficult and costly campaign.[1] Military historians predicted the "most lethal war since 1945" and "a conflict as prolonged as that of Korea and possibly as unwinnable as Vietnam."[2] Retired General William Odom, head of the National Security Agency during the Reagan administration, warned of a "large, costly, and bloody campaign."[3] In a Senate Armed Services Committee hearing before the war, Admiral William Crowe, former chairman of the Joint Chiefs of Staff, maintained that "from the military standpoint, the least desirable U.S. action is to go in and dig the Iraqis out of Kuwait. I mean, they're well dug in, they've reinforced."[4] Senator Edward Kennedy noted: "Most military experts tell us that a war with Iraq will not be quick and decisive, as President Bush suggests; it'll be brutal and costly. . . . The Administration refuses to release casualty estimates, but the 45,000 body bags the Pentagon has sent to the region are all the evidence we need of the high price in lives and blood that we will have to spare."[5] In early January Gallup polls, less than a quarter of respondents believed that fewer than 10,000 American troops would be killed in a war between Iraq and the United States.

In reality, Operation Desert Storm was a quick and decisive victory for the United States, and the U.S.-led coalition suffered far fewer casualties than anyone had predicted. Instead of filling thousands of hospital beds in a protracted conflict, the United States liberated Kuwait after a six-week air campaign and a one-hundred-hour ground war, losing only 146 soldiers killed in action. After the war, political and military leaders in the United States hailed the conflict as a model for the future of warfare. Many analysts attributed the extraordinarily lopsided victory to a technological revolution in warfare. The U.S. Joint Chiefs of Staff began developing a vision of future war-fighting that would allow American forces to dominate any opponent across the full spectrum of military operations.[6] Perhaps not coincidentally, the United States engaged in unprecedented levels of military activism in the decade that followed the war.

More than twenty years and twelve U.S. military interventions later, what lessons should we draw from the first Gulf War? There is no question that technological advances in the stealth and precision of weaponry and command and control on the battlefield contributed to the low level of U.S. casualties and the speed with which U.S. objectives were attained. But it is less clear that the first Gulf War "vindicated air power" or put to rest post-Vietnam concerns about excessive reliance on technology in war.[7] Does the Revolution in Military Affairs (RMA) give the United States the ability to prevail quickly and cheaply in all forms of conflict? The historical record suggests that a state's ability to achieve its political objectives in war is dependent on more than superior war-fighting capabilities. Advances in military technology may make acquiring and defending territory or overthrowing foreign regimes less costly for militarily preponderant states, but such advantages in war-fighting capabilities are less applicable to conflicts in which one's primary war aims can be attained only with target compliance.

THEORETICAL IMPLICATIONS

My intent in this project was to explore the utility and limitations of military force as an instrument of statecraft. In particular, I sought to explain why militarily strong states frequently fail to achieve even limited objectives when they use military force against weaker adversaries. Research on how violent conflicts are terminated and what is gained or lost in the fighting are less prevalent within the field of political science than studies about the causes of war. Those studies of conflict outcomes that have been conducted have tended to focus on wars between states, ignoring more limited uses of force and wars involving nonstate actors. At the same time, conflict outcomes are usually conceived of in terms of combatants winning or losing relative to one another, rather than being successful or unsuccessful in relation to their war aims. Finally, there has been a divide between the quantitative and qualitative literature on the determinants of war outcomes. The large-*n* research has focused its attention on factors like material resources, war-fighting capabilities, strategic selection, and military strategy. In the case study literature, there is a greater emphasis on the impact of resolve and the importance of less tangible aspects of military effectiveness like unit cohesion and morale. In this study, I build on previous research in an attempt to develop a generalizable theory of armed conflict outcomes that can both explain past war outcomes and predict the likelihood of success and failure in future military operations.

The approach I adopt in this study employs deductive logic to predict the effects of strategic selection—in this case, decisions to use military force—on the outcomes of violent conflicts. I extend the implications of rationalist models of war initiation to explore how prewar uncertainty affects war outcomes.[8] In the model I present, actors select themselves into armed conflicts only when their prewar estimates of the cost of attaining their political objectives through the use of force fall below the threshold of their tolerance for costs. The more the actual costs of victory exceed a state's prewar expectations, the greater the risk that it will be pushed beyond its cost-tolerance threshold and forced to terminate its war effort before it attains its war aims.

My approach differs from existing theories of war outcomes in an important way. I argue that actors do not fail to attain their war aims simply because they have inferior war-fighting capacity or less tolerance for the costs of war than their adversary. Actors fail to achieve their objectives in war when they *underestimate* the cost or *overestimate* the likelihood of victory and select themselves into wars they cannot sustain to victory. The *extent* of prewar uncertainty therefore becomes an important predictor of war outcomes through its effect on decisions about the initiation of war.

The theory of armed conflict outcomes that I develop unifies previous theoretical work regarding the effects of military capability, resolve, and strategic selection on violent conflict outcomes. By acknowledging the impact of war aims on uncertainty about the cost of victory in war, this model is able to specify the conditions under which strong states are likely to achieve their political objectives when they use force against weak adversaries, and those under which militarily strong states are likely to select themselves into wars they cannot sustain to victory.

The Utility of Force

Common wisdom, particularly within professional military circles, holds that the ambiguity of civilian war aims is a common cause of defeat for otherwise capable states.[9] Policymakers and scholars have also argued that a state's war aims influence war outcomes through their effect on domestic support for the war effort or the strength of an opponent's motivation to resist.[10] Some scholars maintain that states are more likely to achieve their objectives in war if they limit the magnitude of their demands.[11]

I reject both the magnitude and ambiguity of objectives as causes of defeat for strong states. It is true that the magnitude of a challenger's demand is likely to affect the target's motivation to resist that demand. And it is reasonable to suggest that states should attempt to make their demands large enough to satisfy their own objectives but no larger than what could reasonably be accepted by an opponent given the distribution of capabilities and resolve between the two sides.[12] However, once a demand has been made and a conflict has escalated to war, we are unlikely to observe a positive correlation between smaller demands and the probability of victory because, although larger demands are more likely to be countered with stiff resistance, larger demands also imply greater motivation on the part of the challenger. It is therefore unclear in what direction increasingly bold war aims should tip the balance of resolve.

Moreover, although there are always innumerable personal, domestic political, and grand strategic *motivations* for using force, the desired political outcome of a military operation is rarely as vague as many arguments imply. What is more often ambiguous is the connection between the *military* objectives of an operation and attainment of the desired *political* outcome. During the U.S. intervention in Indochina, for example, the desired political outcome was unambiguous: The United States sought an independent, noncommunist South Vietnam. The relationship between achieving military objectives, such as the attrition of Viet Cong, and the attainment of that political outcome was much less clear. The U.S. intervention in Lebanon from 1982 to 1984 is another example. In a nationally televised speech on September 20, 1982, President Reagan announced that he was ordering the U.S. Marines back to Beirut to serve as part of a new multinational force "with the mission of enabling the Lebanese government to resume full sovereignty over its capital—the essential precondition for extending its control over the entire country."[13] The Reagan administration had a relatively unambiguous political objective, but it was never apparent how, in the context of a civil war between factions of Shiite, Druze, and Maronite militias, the Marines could use force to accomplish that objective. In a White House news conference the day before the Marines landed in Beirut, Reagan declared that "[t]he Lebanese government will be the ones that tell us when they feel that they're in charge and [the Marines] can go home."[14] Seventeen months later, as U.S. troops left Lebanon to be "redeployed" on ships offshore, Reagan maintained that the United States was "not bugging out" but simply "going to a more defensible position."[15] Nevertheless, although the United States launched naval and air attacks until withdrawing completely, the political objective was not obtained, and the Lebanese civil war continued until 1990.

Neither the magnitude nor the ambiguity of a strong state's war aims can explain why it fails to prevail over a much weaker target. Rather, the important distinction is the degree to which those *political* objectives are amenable to *military* solutions. The idea that some political objectives are more easily attained than others through the use of military force is not novel. Both war-fighters and scholars have recognized that military power is more useful for realizing some goals than others.[16] Millett, Murray, and Watman note that "an age-old problem is the employment of military forces to achieve objectives for which they are largely unsuited."[17] My contribution is an attempt to identify the precise quality of political objectives that makes them more or less amenable to military solutions. This study develops a broadly generalizable method of categorizing political objectives according to the degree to which attaining them requires target compliance. I then compare across a wide range of cases, including both interstate and civil wars, and operations against both state and non-state actors, to uncover systematic relationships between war aims and war outcomes. The results advance our understanding of the determinants of war outcomes, but they also speak more broadly to the utility and fungibility of military power. Much of the theory in international relations—about the formation of alliances, arms races, the success and failure of deterrence, and the causes of violent conflict—is based on an implicit assumption that power is largely a matter of military capabilities. I offer a theory about when military capabilities are likely to be the most important determinant of conflict outcomes and when an adversary's tolerance for costs can mitigate the effectiveness of force.

Resolve and Conflict Outcomes

The theoretical model and empirical results I present also introduce a significant new perspective on the relationship between "resolve" and conflict outcomes. The existing literature on the effect of resolve on conflict outcomes implies a straightforward, linear relationship between the extent of the asymmetry in "interests at stake," "motivation," or "tolerance for costs" between two belligerents and the probability that one side will prevail over the other. I argue that two factors complicate this relationship. First, as an actor's advantage in military capabilities grows, the human and material costs that actor can expect to bear in the fighting decline, so that stronger actors can afford to have lower tolerance for costs than their weaker adversaries. The key metric, therefore, is not the distance between an actor's cost-tolerance threshold and the cost-tolerance threshold of its adversary, but the distance between the *price an actor is willing to pay* and the *actual cost* of attaining that objective through the use of force. The gap between a strong state's tolerance for costs and that of its weak adversary does not influence war outcomes unless the strong state underestimates the cost of achieving its objectives and chooses to use military force without sufficient resolve to sustain military operations to victory.

Second, the relative magnitude of the effect of material capabilities versus resolve on victory and defeat in war varies with the nature of the object at stake. An actor's advantage in cost tolerance is unlikely to compensate for its material weakness when a much stronger adversary pursues an objective it can seize and hold with physical force alone. But the strength of a target's resolve can mitigate the effectiveness of military might if the materially stronger actor is dependent on target compliance. As a result, we see that strong states are most likely to succeed in forcibly removing an adversarial regime from power, where we can assume that the issues at stake for the target are extraordinarily salient, and least likely convince a weak adversary to change its domestic or foreign policy, even after controlling for variance in troop commitment levels and military strategy.

POLICY IMPLICATIONS

Every model of how the world works has policy implications. But not every policy is based on a clear view of how the world works.

—Robert Art

The implications of this research for policymaking are somewhat less straightforward than they may at first appear. The probability of success is much higher for militarily strong states that pursue objectives they can seize and hold with physical force alone (i.e., *brute-force* objectives) than for strong states that pursue objectives that can only be attained with target compliance. Powerful states are more likely to prevail when they seek to overthrow a foreign regime than when they use military force to convince a foreign government to change the way it treats a minority population within its borders, to stop sponsoring international terrorism, or to dismantle its nuclear weapons programs. But governments cannot simply switch from a coercive to a brute-force objective to increase the likelihood of victory in war. Theoretically, a strong state always has the option of choosing a brute-force political objective (e.g., annihilating its adversary) instead of a coercive objective (e.g., compelling the adversary to change its behavior). But pursuing a brute-force objective is frequently costly and inefficient, risks inciting other states to intervene on behalf of the target, and can be counterproductive to furthering the strong state's long-term security and prosperity interests. The reality is that, in most circumstances, a state's war aims are constrained by the underlying interests at stake in the conflict and domestic and international political concerns. Because the costs and risks of pursuing complete disarmament or destruction of an adversary are often prohibitive when strong states have conflicts with weak targets over less-than-vital interests, the state's ability to disarm, defeat, or even destroy an adversary is not always relevant, given the political objectives that are politically feasible to pursue.

The results presented here must be seen in their proper context—as the result of a selection process in which intervening states choose political objectives to pursue through the use of force based on an assessment of the importance of the issues at stake and the price they are willing to pay to secure those interests. Militarily strong states fail to attain their war aims vis-à-vis militarily weak actors when they select themselves into armed conflicts on the basis of prewar estimates of the cost of victory that are too low and subsequently find that they have initiated a war they do not have the cost tolerance to sustain to victory. Miscalculations of this sort are less likely to occur when states have brute-force objectives. As a result, strong states are more likely to attain brute-force objectives than coercive objectives in the asymmetric wars we observe. But this does not imply that states can or should always choose to pursue brute-force war aims. A state that has insufficient cost tolerance to sustain a coercive campaign until a coercive objective is attained is unlikely to have sufficient resolve to use the force that would be necessary to achieve a brute-force objective.

The results of this study do, however, caution leaders against underestimating the importance of a weak adversary's resolve when they choose to pursue war aims that are dependent on target compliance. Although the extent of a target's tolerance for costs is inherently unknowable, decision-makers should assume that a militarily weak actor that risks war to resist the demands of a much stronger opponent is prepared to bear extraordinarily high costs to defend its interests. The cost and difficulty of persuading a resolute enemy to change its behavior through the use of military force should not be taken lightly. By recognizing the fundamental difference between military operations in pursuit of brute-force and coercive political objectives, political leaders can gain an appreciation for the serious challenges posed by attempts to attain target compliance through the application of physical force.

When military operations go unexpectedly well, or unexpectedly poorly, military observers often begin to talk of a shift in the fundamental nature of war. A "Revolution in Military Affairs" is credited for the ease with which the United States evicted Iraq from Kuwait in 1991;[18] an innovative military strategy incorporating local forces and U.S. special operations troops is praised for a quick victory over the Taliban in 2002;[19] and poor military strategy and performance against guerilla insurgents is blamed for U.S. failure in Vietnam.[20] All of these factors likely contributed to the costliness, difficulty, and duration of these military operations, but neither the initial U.S. success in Afghanistan, nor its failure in Vietnam, mark a break from the past. The outcome of these operations is consistent with the historical record, which suggests that there is a fundamental difference in the nature of war across *purposes* for which force is employed.

APPENDIX TO CHAPTER 4

Table A1. POST-WWII MAJOR POWER MILITARY INTERVENTIONS

MP	Target	Location	Initiation	Termination
FRN	Syrian rioters	Syria	2 Apr 1945	15 Apr 1946
FRN	rioting nationalists/ villagers	Algeria	8 May 1945	31 May 1945
FRN	Viet Minh nationalists	Vietnam	1 Oct 1945	1 Apr 1946
UKG	Indonesian insurgents	Indonesia	1 Oct 1945	29 Nov 1946
RUS	Iranian government	Iran	12 Dec 1945	9 May 1946
RUS	Turkish government	Turkey	15 Mar 1946	5 Apr 1946
FRN	Lao Issara regime/rebels	Laos	17 Mar 1946	1 Oct 1946
FRN	Viet Minh nationalists	Vietnam	20 Nov 1946	7 May 1954
FRN	DMRM Rebels	Madagascar	29 Mar 1947	1 Dec 1948
UKG	Guatemalan army	BR Honduras	26 Feb 1948	5 Mar 1948
USA	Communist guerilla movement	Greece	28 Feb 1948	16 Oct 1949
UKG	MPLA (Communist insurgents)	Malaysia	16 Jun 1948	31 Jul 1960
RUS	West Berlin	E. Germany	22 Jun 1948	30 May 1949
UKG	Yemen	Aden	1 Mar 1949	31 Oct 1963
UKG	Shifta terrorists	Eritrea	3 Jan 1950	31 Aug 1951
CHN	Nationalist army	Hainan Island	18 Apr 1950	2 May 1950
CHN	Tibet	Tibet	1 May 1950	19 May 1951
USA	N. Korea (DPRK)	S. Korea	27 Jun 1950	1 Oct 1950
USA	N. Korea, China	N. Korea	1 Oct 1950	27 Jul 1953
CHN	United States/UN (15)	N. Korea	19 Oct 1950	24 Dec 1950
CHN	S. Korea/U.S./UN (15)	S. Korea	31 Dec 1950	27 Jul 1953
CHN	Chinese Nationalists	Burma	31 Jan 1951	31 Dec 1953
FRN	National Liberation Army	Tunisia	20 Jan 1952	19 Jun 1955
UKG	Mau Mau guerillas	Kenya	20 Oct 1952	19 Oct 1956
FRN	rioters	French Morocco	7 Dec 1952	31 Dec 1952
RUS	rioters	E. Germany	16 Jun 1953	17 Jun 1953
CHN	Nationalist army	Taiwan Strait	16 Jul 1953	17 Jul 1953

(*continued*)

Table A1. (*continued*)

MP	Target	Location	Initiation	Termination
FRN	Moroccan Lib Army, rioters	French Morocco	15 Aug 1953	2 Mar 1956
UKG	PPP regime, rioters	British Guiana	6 Oct 1953	26 May 1966
CHN	Khampa guerilla groups	Tibet	1 Apr 1954	31 Dec 1973
CHN	ROC (Nationalist forces)	Taiwan Strait	3 Sep 1954	1 May 1955
CHN	ROC (Nationalist forces)	Taiwan Strait	3 Sep 1954	1 May 1955
USA	China	Taiwan	4 Sep 1954	1 May 1955
FRN	nationalist movements (FLN)	Algeria	1 Nov 1954	3 Jul 1962
UKG	EOKA	Cyprus	26 Nov 1955	19 Feb 1959
UKG	rioters	Bahrain	11 Mar 1956	1 Jan 1957
FRN	Tunisia/Algerian rebels	Tunisia	19 May 1956	26 Oct 1960
RUS	Rioters/ protesters	Poland	28 Jun 1956	29 Jun 1956
FRN	national liberation movement	Morocco	3 Jul 1956	30 Sep 1961
RUS	Rioters/ protesters	Poland	20 Oct 1956	24 Oct 1956
RUS	Imre Nagy & mass protesters	Hungary	24 Oct 1956	31 Mar 1958
UKG	Egyptian government	Egypt	31 Oct 1956	6 Nov 1956
FRN	insurgents	Morocco	13 Dec 1956	1 Feb 1957
FRN	UPC independence movement	French Cameroun	15 Dec 1957	1 Jan 1960
FRN	Moroccan Liberation Army	Spanish Sahara	24 Feb 1958	30 May 1958
USA	UAR (Syria); leftist insurgents	Lebanon	15 Jul 1958	24 Oct 1958
UKG	UAR; communist insurgents	Jordan	17 Jul 1958	29 Oct 1958
CHN	ROC (Nationalist forces)	Taiwan Strait	23 Aug 1958	19 Dec 1958
USA	China	Taiwan	23 Aug 1958	31 Dec 1958
CHN	Nepal	Nepal	22 Apr 1959	31 Jul 1960
FRN	UPC guerillas & rioters	Cameroun	12 Jan 1960	31 Dec 1962
USA	new Trujillista regime	Dominican Rep	3 Jun 1961	16 Nov 1961
UKG	rioters	Zanzibar	3 Jun 1961	28 Feb 1963
UKG	Iraqi Army	Kuwait	1 Jul 1961	19 Oct 1961
FRN	Tunis govt, army, demonstrators	Tunisia	18 Jul 1961	22 Jul 1961
CHN	India	India	2 Nov 1961	21 Nov 1962
USA	new Trujillista regime	Dominican Rep	16 Nov 1961	30 Jan 1962
USA	NVA and VietCong	Vietnam	1 Feb 1962	27 Jan 1973
USA	Pathet Lao, N. Vietnamese, PRC	Thailand	16 May 1962	23 Jul 1962
USA	USSR and Cuba (Castro)	Cuba	24 Oct 1962	28 Oct 1962
UKG	TNKU rebels (w/Indonesia)	Brunei	10 Dec 1962	31 May 1963

Table A1. *(continued)*

MP	Target	Location	Initiation	Termination
UKG	Indonesian army/guerillas	Malaysia	19 Apr 1963	19 May 1965
UKG	rioters from labor movement	Swaziland	13 Jun 1963	30 Nov 1966
UKG	Tribes in the Radfan	Yemen AR	3 Aug 1963	18 Apr 1965
FRN	opposition rioters	Congo (FR)	13 Aug 1963	17 Aug 1963
UKG	Turkish and Greek communities	Cyprus	17 Dec 1963	27 Mar 1964
UKG	Mutinying military troops	E. African states	25 Jan 1964	31 Jul 1964
FRN	coup leaders /provisional govt	Gabon	19 Feb 1964	31 Dec 1965
USA	NVA, VC, and Pathet Lao	Laos	30 Apr 1964	14 Aug 1973
UKG	NLF, FLOSY	South Arabia	25 Nov 1964	30 Nov 1967
USA	leftist opposition	Dominican Rep	28 Apr 1965	20 Sep 1966
UKG	S. Rhodesia (Zimbabwe)	Zambia	3 Dec 1965	30 Apr 1966
RUS	Yemen Royalists	Yemen AR	30 Nov 1967	15 Mar 1968
RUS	Dubcek government	Czechoslovakia	20 Aug 1968	17 Apr 1969
FRN	FROLINAT insurgents	Chad	28 Aug 1968	30 Aug 1971
RUS	China	China	2 Mar 1969	11 Sep 1969
CHN	USSR	China	1 May 1969	11 Sep 1969
UKG	IRA, PIRA, rioters	N. Ireland	1 Sep 1969	22 May 1998
UKG	Guatemalan army	Br. Honduras	1 Jan 1970	31 Dec 1973
RUS	Israel	Egypt	31 Mar 1970	7 Aug 1970
USA	Khmer Rouge	Cambodia	30 Apr 1970	14 Aug 1973
USA	Palestinian fedayeen, Syria	Turkey	10 Sep 1970	25 Sep 1970
RUS	rioters	Poland	15 Dec 1970	20 Dec 1970
RUS	Anya-Nya guerillas	Sudan	1 Jan 1971	31 Aug 1971
RUS	Iraqi Kurds	Iraq	15 Mar 1973	30 Mar 1975
CHN	Republic of Vietnam	China	15 Jan 1974	20 Jan 1974
RUS	UNITA, FNLA opposition	Angola	14 Nov 1975	31 Dec 1988
UKG	Guatemalan army	Br. Honduras	7 Jul 1977	7 Aug 1977
FRN	POLISARIO/SPLA rebels	Mauritania	12 Dec 1977	30 May 1978
RUS	Somalian army and WSLF	Ethiopia	31 Dec 1977	9 Mar 1978
FRN	FROLINAT	Chad	28 Apr 1978	16 May 1980
FRN	Congolese rebels (FLNC)	Zaire	19 May 1978	22 Jun 1978
RUS	PRC	Vietnam	1 Jan 1979	1 Jun 1982
CHN	DRV	DRV	17 Feb 1979	17 Mar 1979
FRN	Bokassa regime	CAR/CAE	20 Sep 1979	21 Sep 1979
RUS	Mujahideen rebels	Afghanistan	25 Dec 1979	15 Feb 1989
UKG	Argentina	Argentina	25 Apr 1982	14 Jun 1982
USA	Shiite & Druze opposition, Syria	Lebanon	29 Sep 1982	26 Feb 1984
FRN	Libya & GUNT/FAP rebels	Chad	9 Aug 1983	9 Nov 1984

(continued)

Table A1. (*continued*)

MP	Target	Location	Initiation	Termination
USA	New Jewel/PRG regime	Grenada	25 Oct 1983	12 Dec 1983
CHN	DRV	DRV	2 Apr 1984	12 Jul 1984
FRN	Libya & GUNT/FAP rebels	Chad	16 Feb 1986	11 Sep 1987
USA	Libyan govt (Qaddafi)	Libya	23 Mar 1986	27 Mar 1986
USA	Nicaraguan govt (Sandinista)	Honduras	17 Mar 1988	31 Mar 1988
USA	Panamanian govt (Noriega)	Panama	11 May 1989	20 Dec 1989
USA	Panamanian govt (Noriega)	Panama	20 Dec 1989	31 Jan 1990
RUS	Azerbaijani Popular Front	Azerbaijan	20 Jan 1990	1 Feb 1990
USA	Iraqi government	Saudi Arabia	14 Aug 1990	28 Feb 1991
USA	Iraqi government	Kuwait	16 Jan 1991	28 Feb 1991
USA	Iraqi government	Iraq	6 Apr 1991	19 Mar 2003
FRN	Habre rebels	Chad	1 Dec 1991	7 Jan 1992
USA	Iraqi government	Iraq	27 Aug 1992	19 Mar 2003
USA	warring clans	Somalia	3 Dec 1992	4 May 1993
USA	Somali National Alliance	Somalia	4 May 1993	31 Dec 1993
RUS	rebels in breakaway republic	Russia/Chechnya	1 Jan 1994	30 Apr 1996
USA	Haitian military regime	Haiti	19 Sep 1994	31 Mar 1995
USA	Iraqi government	Kuwait	14 Oct 1994	21 Dec 1994
CHN	Taiwan	Taiwan Strait	21 Jul 1995	25 Mar 1996
USA	Bosnian Serbs	Bosnia	30 Aug 1995	21 Sep 1995
FRN	mercenaries/coup leaders	Comoros	15 Sep 1995	15 Oct 1995
USA	China	Taiwan	8 Mar 1996	25 Mar 1996
FRN	army mutineers/rioting soldiers	CAR	23 May 1996	2 Jun 1997
USA	Iraqi government	Kuwait	3 Sep 1996	19 Mar 2003
USA	Iraqi government	Iraq	1 Feb 1998	20 Dec 1998
USA	Federal Republic of Yugoslavia	Yugoslavia	24 Mar 1999	10 Jun 1999

Table A2. OPERATIONAL DEFINITIONS OF POLITICAL OBJECTIVES

Remove Foreign Regime	Military force is employed with the intention of removing a foreign regime from power. The intervening state may overthrow and replace a foreign government itself, fight alongside insurgent groups that seek to replace the regime in power, or support foreign invasions by other states attempting to seize power.
Maintain Foreign Regime Authority	Military force is employed in an attempt to preserve the governing authority of an incumbent regime or the existing political institutions in another state. This includes both operations to assist a foreign government with the elimination of a domestic insurgent threat and operations to defend a foreign government against an external threat. This category should also be chosen if the intervening state is attempting to establish and then maintain the political authority of a particular regime or create particular political institutions in a state (i.e., state-building). Military operations do not have to seek the preservation of any particular incumbent *leader* to be considered interventions for the maintenance of regime authority. Foreign regime building and maintenance may follow, but should be distinguished from the use of force to remove a foreign regime from power. Cases should be coded as defense of territory, rather than maintenance of political authority, if a piece of land, rather than political authority over an entire nation, is in dispute.
Maintain Empire	Military force is employed in an attempt to reassert or maintain the intervening state's own political authority over territory claimed as national homeland by another ethnic group.
Acquire or Defend Territory	Military force is employed to defend, acquire, or reclaim territory. The state may intervene to defend the territory of an ally from an external threat, help an ally acquire territory or reassert authority over previously held territory, or seize territory for itself.
Policy Change	Military force is employed in an attempt to coerce an incumbent regime, group, or leader into changing specific policies (foreign or domestic) or behaviors. Although many conflicts stem from policy disputes, the primary political objective of an intervention is only policy change when the intervening state wants the targeted adversary to change an objectionable policy of its own accord.
Social Protection and Order	Military force is used to protect civilians from violence and/or other human rights abuses; restore social order in a situation of unrest (e.g. violent protests, rioting, looting); or to suppress violence between armed groups within another state. "Peacekeeping" operations that are actually intended to prop up an incumbent regime or maintain empire should not be coded as social protection and order operations. Similarly, "humanitarian" operations in which military force is used in an attempt to coerce the incumbent government into changing the way it is treating a minority group within its borders should be coded as policy change operations.

APPENDIX TO CHAPTER 6

Table A3. PREDICTED PROBABILITY OF SUCCESS AND ACTUAL OUTCOME OF MILITARY INTERVENTION CASES, 1979–2002

MP	Location	Start Year	Objective	Target Assistance	Pr(Success)	Outcome
CHN	DRV	1979	policy change	no	0.10	failure
FRN	CAR/CAE	1979	regime change	no	0.94	success
RUS	Afghanistan	1979	maintain regime	no	0.27	failure
UKG	Argentina	1982	territory	no	0.82	success
USA	Lebanon	1982	maintain regime	yes	0.44	failure
FRN	Chad	1983	maintain regime	no	0.88	success
USA	Grenada	1983	regime change	no	0.93	success
CHN	DRV	1984	territory	no	0.16	failure
FRN	Chad	1986	maintain regime	no	0.88	success
USA	Libya	1986	policy change	no	0.37	failure
USA	Honduras	1988	territory	yes	0.94	success
USA	Panama	1989	policy change	no	0.14	failure
USA	Panama	1989	regime change	no	0.92	success
RUS	Azerbaijan	1990	order/protection	no	0.78	success
USA	Saudi Arabia	1990	territory	no	0.99	success
USA	Kuwait	1991	territory	no	0.94	success
USA	Iraq	1991	order/protection	no	0.78	failure
FRN	Chad	1991	maintain regime	no	0.92	success
USA	Iraq	1992	policy change	no	0.35	failure
USA	Somalia	1992	order/protection	no	0.17	failure
USA	Somalia	1993	order/protection	no	0.21	failure
RUS	Chechnya	1994	maintain empire	no	0.30	failure
USA	Haiti	1994	regime change	no	0.92	success
USA	Kuwait	1994	territory	no	0.95	success
CHN	Taiwan Strait	1995	policy change	yes	0.03	failure
USA	Bosnia	1995	policy change	no	0.37	success
FRN	Comoros	1995	regime change	no	0.97	success
USA	Taiwan	1996	maintain regime	no	0.92	success

(*continued*)

Table A3. *(continued)*

MP	Location	Start Year	Objective	Target Assistance	Pr(Success)	Outcome
FRN	CAR	1996	maintain regime	no	0.89	success
USA	Kuwait	1996	territory	no	0.98	success
USA	Iraq	1998	policy change	no	0.12	failure
USA	Yugoslavia	1999	policy change	no	0.37	success

ENDNOTES

CHAPTER 1

1. Michael Clodfelter, *Warfare and Armed Conflicts: A Statistical Reference to Casualty and Other Figures, 1500–2000*, 671–672.
2. Rick B. Andres, Craig Wills, and Thomas E. Griffith Jr., "Winning with Allies: The Strategic Value of the Afghan Model," 160.
3. "Secretary-General Report to the UN Security Council on the Situation in Afghanistan and its Implications for International Peace and Security," March 18, 2005.
4. Pew Research Center, "Record Number Favors Removing U.S. Troops from Afghanistan," June 23, 2011.
5. See, for example, U.S. House Armed Services Committee, "Statement of General David H. Petraeus, U.S. Army Commander, International Security Assistance Force and U.S. Forces Afghanistan before the House Armed Services Committee on Afghanistan," March 16, 2011.
6. For a recent debate about whether overly optimistic expectations about the likelihood of victory constitute a logically coherent rationalist explanation of war, see Mark Fey and Kristopher W. Ramsay, "Mutual Optimism and War," and Branislav L. Slantchev and Ahmer Tarar, "Mutual Optimism as a Rationalist Explanation of War."
7. Yuen Foong Khong, *Analogies at War: Korea, Munich, Dien Bien Phu, and the Vietnam Decisions of 1965*; Ernest R. May, *"Lessons" of the Past; the Use and Misuse of History in American Foreign Policy*; Dan Reiter and Curtis Meek, "Determinants of Military Strategy, 1903–1994: A Quantitative Empirical Test."
8. Ivan Arreguín-Toft, *How the Weak Win Wars: A Theory of Asymmetric Conflict*; D. S. Bennett and A. C. Stam, "The Declining Advantages of Democracy: A Combined Model of War Outcomes and Duration"; Stephen Biddle, *Military Power: Explaining Victory and Defeat in Modern Battle*; Risa Brooks and Elizabeth A. Stanley, *Creating Military Power: The Sources of Military Effectiveness*; Robert Anthony Pape, *Bombing to Win: Air Power and Coercion in War*; Dan Reiter and Allan C. Stam, *Democracies at War*; Allan C. Stam, *Win, Lose, or Draw: Domestic Politics and the Crucible of War*.
9. Andrew Mack, "Why Big Nations Lose Small Wars: The Politics of Asymmetric Conflict," 177.
10. See James Lee Ray, *Global Politics*, for an excellent discussion of the promise and perils of "resolve" as an explanation for paradoxical war outcomes.
11. See, for example, Ivan Arreguín-Toft, "How the Weak Win Wars: A Theory of Asymmetric Conflict"; Andrew F. Krepinevich, *The Army and Vietnam*; Pape, *Bombing to Win: Air Power and Coercion in War*; Stam, *Win, Lose, or Draw: Domestic Politics and the Crucible of War*; Harry G. Summers, *On Strategy: A Critical Analysis of the Vietnam War*.
12. Geoffrey Blainey, *The Causes of War*; Kelly M. Kadera, *The Power-Conflict Story: A Dynamic Model of Interstate Rivalry*; Douglas Lemke and Jacek Kugler, "The Evolution of

the Power Transition Perspective," in *Parity and War: Evaluations and Extensions of the War Ledger*, eds. Jacek Kugler and Douglas Lemke; Jack S. Levy, "The Causes of War and the Conditions of Peace"; A.F.K. Organski and Jacek Kugler, *The War Ledger*; Kenneth Neal Waltz, *Theory of International Politics*.

13. Robert Art, "To What Ends Military Power"; Vesna Danilovic, "Conceptual and Selection Bias Issues in Deterrence"; Alexander L. George and Richard Smoke, *Deterrence in American Foreign Policy: Theory and Practice*; Robert Jervis, *Perception and Misperception in International Politics*; Robert Jervis, "Cooperation under the Security Dilemma"; Thomas C. Schelling, *Arms and Influence*.
14. Bruce Bueno de Mesquita, *Principles of International Politics*.
15. Zeev Maoz, "Resolve, Capabilities, and the Outcomes of Interstate Disputes, 1816–1976."
16. Zeev Maoz, "Power, Capabilities, and Paradoxical Conflict Outcomes," 247.
17. Bruce Bueno de Mesquita, *The War Trap*.
18. Cynthia A. Cannizzo, "The Costs of Combat: Death, Duration, and Defeat," in *The Correlates of War II: Testing Some Realpolitik Models*, ed. J. David Singer.
19. Stam, *Win, Lose, or Draw: Domestic Politics and the Crucible of War*.
20. Bennett and Stam, "The Declining Advantages of Democracy: A Combined Model of War Outcomes and Duration"; Ken Boulding, *Conflict and Defense: A General Theory*; Bueno de Mesquita, *The War Trap*; Michael C. Desch, "Democracy and Victory: Why Regime Type Hardly Matters"; David A. Lake, "Powerful Pacifists: Democratic States and War"; Organski and Kugler, *The War Ledger*; Dan Reiter and Allan C. Stam III, "Democracy and Battlefield Military Effectiveness"; Reiter and Stam, *Democracies at War*; Frank W. Wayman, J. David Singer, and Gary Goertz, "Capabilities, Allocations, and Success in Militarized Interstate Disputes and Wars, 1816–1976."
21. Alastair Smith, "Fighting Battles, Winning Wars."
22. Reiter and Stam, *Democracies at War*.
23. Steven Rosen, "War Power and the Willingness to Suffer," in *Peace, War, and Numbers*, ed. Bruce M. Russett.
24. Rosen, "War Power and the Willingness to Suffer."
25. Biddle, *Military Power: Explaining Victory and Defeat in Modern Battle*.
26. Jason Lyall and Isaiah Wilson III, "Rage against the Machines: Explaining Outcomes in Counterinsurgency Wars."
27. Colin S. Gray, *Irregular Enemies and the Essence of Strategy: Can the American Way of War Adapt*; Richard Lock-Pullan, *U.S. Intervention Policy and Army Innovation: From Vietnam to Iraq*; Jeffrey Record, "Collapsed Countries, Casualty Dread, and the New American Way of War"; Jeffrey Record, "*The American Way of War: Cultural Barriers to Successful Counterinsurgency*"; Russell F. Weigley, *The American Way of War: A History of United States Strategy and Policy*.
28. John J. Mearsheimer, *Conventional Deterrence*.
29. Stam, *Win, Lose, or Draw: Domestic Politics and the Crucible of War*.
30. Pape, *Bombing to Win: Air Power and Coercion in War*.
31. Pape, *Bombing to Win: Air Power and Coercion in War*, 10.
32. Michael Horowitz and Dan Reiter, "When Does Aerial Bombing Work?: Quantitative Empirical Tests, 1917–1999."
33. Arreguín-Toft, *How the Weak Win Wars: A Theory of Asymmetric Conflict*.
34. Krepinevich, *The Army and Vietnam*.
35. Summers, *On Strategy: A Critical Analysis of the Vietnam War*.
36. Scott S. Gartner, *Strategic Assessment in War*.
37. Rupert Smith, *The Utility of Force: The Art of War in the Modern World*.
38. Michael I. Handel, *Clausewitz and Modern Strategy*.
39. Rosen, "War Power and the Willingness to Suffer."

40. Rosen, "War Power and the Willingness to Suffer," 169.
41. John E. Mueller, "The Search for the 'Breaking Point' in Vietnam: The Statistics of a Deadly Quarrel."
42. Mueller, "The Search for the 'Breaking Point' in Vietnam: The Statistics of a Deadly Quarrel," 517.
43. Mack, "Why Big Nations Lose Small Wars: The Politics of Asymmetric Conflict."
44. Mack, "Why Big Nations Lose Small Wars: The Politics of Asymmetric Conflict," 177.
45. Alexander L. George and William E. Simons, eds., *The Limits of Coercive Diplomacy.*
46. Maoz, "Resolve, Capabilities, and the Outcomes of Interstate Disputes, 1816–1976"; Rosen, "War Power and the Willingness to Suffer."
47. Mack, "Why Big Nations Lose Small Wars: The Politics of Asymmetric Conflict"; Maoz, "Resolve, Capabilities, and the Outcomes of Interstate Disputes, 1816–1976"; Rosen, "War Power and the Willingness to Suffer."
48. Erik Gartzke, "War Is in the Error Term."

CHAPTER 2

1. Gartzke, "War Is in the Error Term."
2. Militarized Interstate Disputes (MID) dataset (v 3.02). This data collection compiled by the Correlates of War Project provides information about conflicts in which one or more states threaten, display, or use force against one or more other states between 1816 and 2001. See Faten Ghosn and Scott Bennett, "Codebook for the Dyadic Militarized Interstate Incident Data, Version 3.10"; Faten Ghosn, Glenn Palmer, and Stuart Bremer, "The MID3 Data Set, 1993–2001: Procedures, Coding Rules, and Description"; Daniel M. Jones, Stuart A. Bremer, and J. David Singer, "Militarized Interstate Disputes, 1816–1992: Rationale, Coding Rules, and Empirical Patterns."
3. Dominic P. Johnson, *Overconfidence and War: The Havoc and Glory of Positive Illusions.*
4. Blainey, *The Causes of War*, 114.
5. Robert Jervis, "War and Misperception," 676; Stephen Van Evera, *Causes of War: Power and the Roots of Conflict*, 16.
6. Hedley Bull, *The Anarchical Society: A Study of Order in World Politics*, 178. See also John A. Vasquez, *The War Puzzle.*
7. James D. Fearon, "Rationalist Explanations for War"; Darren Filson and Suzanne Werner, "A Bargaining Model of War and Peace: Anticipating the Onset, Duration, and Outcome of War"; Robert Powell, "Bargaining Theory and International Conflict"; Dan Reiter, "Exploring the Bargaining Model of War"; Alastair Smith and Allan C. Stam, "Bargaining and the Nature of War."
8. Carl von Clausewitz, *On War*, 605.
9. Smith, "Fighting Battles, Winning Wars"; Harrison Wagner, "Bargaining and War."
10. Fearon, "Rationalist Explanations for War"; Filson and Werner, "A Bargaining Model of War and Peace: Anticipating the Onset, Duration, and Outcome of War"; Darren Filson and Suzanne Werner, "Sensitivity to Costs of Fighting Versus Sensitivity to Losing the Conflict: Implications for War Onset, Duration, and Outcomes."
11. Schelling, *Arms and Influence*, 34.
12. Data come from the Militarized Interstate Disputes (MID) dataset (v 3.02) and the Military Interventions by Powerful States (MIPS) dataset. Violent interstate disputes are MIDs that have escalated to mutual hostilities. For documentation on the datasets, see Ghosn and Bennett, "Codebook for the Dyadic Militarized Interstate Incident Data, Version 3.10"; Ghosn, Palmer, and Bremer, "The MID3 Data Set, 1993–2001: Procedures, Coding Rules, and Description"; Jones, Bremer, and Singer, "Militarized Interstate Disputes, 1816–1992: Rationale, Coding Rules, and Empirical Patterns"; Patricia L. Sullivan and Michael T. Koch, "Military Intervention by Powerful States, 1945–2003."

13. See, for example, Paul F. Diehl, *A Road Map to War: Territorial Dimensions of International Conflict*; Paul R. Hensel, "Territory: Theory and Evidence on Geography and Conflict," in *What Do We Know About War?*, ed. John A. Vasquez; Paul K. Huth, *Standing Your Ground: Territorial Disputes in International Conflict.*
14. Isaiah Wilson, *Thinking Beyond War: Civil-Military Relations and Why America Fails to Win the Peace.*
15. Clausewitz, *On War*, 97.
16. Tanisha Fazal counts fifty violent "state deaths" from conquest or occupation by another state since 1816. However, even "formal loss of control over foreign policy making to another state," as Fazal defines state death, does not necessarily indicate that the state was militarily defeated. Even though states tend to value their sovereignty highly, it is not uncommon for leaders to surrender the state before (sometimes well before) their armed forces are rendered incapable of fighting (e.g., Poland in 1939 and Kuwait in 1990). Tanisha M. Fazal, *State Death: The Politics and Geography of Conquest, Occupation, and Annexation*. See also, Fred Charles Iklé, *Every War Must End*; Dan Reiter, *How Wars End*; Wagner, "Bargaining and War."
17. This is not to imply that leaders always make concessions as soon as they realize that victory is either unlikely or too costly. For a number of reasons—including concerns about their own political fortunes or the state's international reputation—leaders may choose to prolong an ill-fated war. However, although such delays increase the cost and duration of wars, they rarely change the ultimate outcome. Most states still concede far short of complete military defeat. See George W. Downs and David M. Rocke, "Conflict, Agency, and Gambling for Resurrection: The Principal-Agent Problem Goes to War"; H. E. Goemans, *War and Punishment: The Causes of War Termination and the First World War*; Michael Koch and Patricia Sullivan, "Should I Stay or Should I Go Now? Partisanship, Approval, and the Duration of Major Power Democratic Military Interventions"; Reiter, *How Wars End.*
18. Biddle, *Military Power: Explaining Victory and Defeat in Modern Battle*; Brooks and Stanley, *Creating Military Power: The Sources of Military Effectiveness*; Allan R. Millett, Williamson Murray, and Kenneth H. Watman, "The Effectiveness of Military Organizations," in *Military Effectiveness; Volume I: The First World War*, eds. Allan R. Millett and Williamson Murray.
19. Greg Jaffe, "War of Persuasion: The Modern U.S. Officer Emerges in Afghanistan."
20. For a similar definition, see Rosen, "War Power and the Willingness to Suffer."
21. Bruce Russett, "Why Democratic Peace?," in *Debating the Democratic Peace*, eds. Michael E. Brown, Sean M. Lynn-Jones, and Steven E. Miller; Kenneth A. Schultz, "Do Democratic Institutions Constrain or Inform? Contrasting Two Institutional Perspectives on Democracy and War"; Randolph M. Siverson, "Democracies and War Participation: In Defense of the Institutional Constraints Argument."
22. Adam Jones, "Kosovo: Orders of Magnitude"; Meredith Reid Sarkees and Frank Whelon Wayman, *Resort to War: 1816–2007.*
23. Horowitz and Reiter, "When Does Aerial Bombing Work?: Quantitative Empirical Tests, 1917–1999," 156. For analyses of the U.S. intervention in Panama, see Conrad C. Crane, *Landpower and Crises: Army Roles and Missions in Smaller-Scale Contingencies During the 1990s*; Thomas Donnelly, Margaret Roth, and Caleb Baker, *Operation Just Cause: The Storming of Panama*; Seth G. Jones et al., *Establishing Law and Order after Conflict*; and Roy Licklider, "The American Way of State Building: Germany, Japan, Somalia and Panama."
24. Alastair Smith and Allan Stam make a similar argument when they maintain that weak actors can achieve better settlements by fighting if they can impose *unexpected* costs on their adversary. Smith and Stam, "When Likely Losers Go to War," in *New Direction for International Relations*, eds. Alex Mintz and Bruce Russett.

25. Peter D. Feaver and Christopher Gelpi, *Choosing Your Battles: American Civil-Military Relations and the Use of Force*; Christopher Gelpi and Peter D. Feaver, "Speak Softly and Carry a Big Stick? Veterans in the Political Elite and the American Use of Force."
26. Clodfelter, *Warfare and Armed Conflicts: A Statistical Reference to Casualty and Other Figures, 1500–2000*; Richard P. Hallion, *Storm over Iraq: Air Power and the Gulf War*; U.S. Dept. of Defense, *Conduct of the Persian Gulf War*.
27. Alexander L. George, *Forceful Persuasion: Coercive Diplomacy as an Alternative to War*.
28. Charles A. Duelfer and Stephen Benedict Dyson, "Chronic Misperception and International Conflict: The U.S.-Iraq Experience"; Richard Herrmann, "Coercive Diplomacy and the Crisis over Kuwait, 1990–1991," in *The Limits of Coercive Diplomacy*, eds. Alexander L. George and William E. Simons; Jerrold M. Post and Amatzia Baram, "Saddam Is Iraq: Iraq Is Saddam"; Kevin M. Woods, David D. Palkki, and Mark E. Stout. *The Saddam Tapes: The Inner Workings of a Tyrant's Regime, 1978–2001*.
29. Janice Gross Stein, "Deterrence and Compellence in the Gulf, 1990–1991," 173.
30. A number of government reports and scholarly accounts provide evidence that the Iraqi leader underestimated U.S. military capabilities. See, for example, U.S. Dept. of Defense, *Conduct of the Persian Gulf War*, "Interview with Yevgenni Primakov"; Lawrence Freedman and Efrain Karsh, "How Kuwait Was Won: Strategy in the Gulf War"; and Michael R. Gordon and Bernard E. Trainor, *The Generals' War: The Inside Story of the Conflict in the Gulf*. Woods et al., *The Saddam Tapes: The Inner Workings of a Tyrant's Regime, 1978–2001* and Kevin M. Woods and Mark E. Stout, "Saddam's Perceptions and Misperceptions: The Case of 'Desert Storm'" provide evidence from primary source material that Saddam also grossly overestimated the capabilities of his own armed forces. As these authors note, the Iraqi leader was able to remain deluded about Iraq's capabilities in large part because he would not tolerate receiving bad news from his advisors. With good reason, both military leaders and political officials within the regime feared for their lives if they made reports questioning Iraq's military capabilities or Saddam's judgment.
31. "Excerpts from Iraqi Document on Meeting with U.S. Envoy," *The New York Times International* (September 23, 1990).
32. "Audio tape of Lt. Gen. Husayn Rashid Muhammad discussing 1991 Gulf War, dated 11 May 1995," cited in Woods and Stout, "Saddam's Perceptions and Misperceptions: The Case of 'Desert Storm,'" 21.
33. Freedman and Karsh, "How Kuwait Was Won: Strategy in the Gulf War"; Kenneth M. Pollack, *Arabs at War: Military Effectiveness, 1948–1991*; Stein, "Deterrence and Compellence in the Gulf, 1990–1991."
34. Post and Baram, "Saddam Is Iraq: Iraq Is Saddam," 21.
35. On page 180 of *The General's War*, Gordon and Trainor maintain that "Iraq did not have to defeat the allies or even come out ahead in the body count. There was no hope of that. But if Iraq could not scare the American-dominated coalition out of attacking in the first place, it had to cause the coalition enough pain so that the popularly elected Western governments would seek a compromise." Also see page 269: "Convinced that the Americans would not tolerate heavy casualties, the Iraqis' hope had been to force a stalemate on the battlefield in which the Americans took steady losses, which would stir up political opposition to the war at home."
36. Freedman and Karsh, "How Kuwait Was Won: Strategy in the Gulf War," 15.
37. "Saddam and His Advisers Discussing the Soviet Union and the State of the Iraqi Military," quoted in Woods et al., *The Saddam Tapes*, 195–196. See also "Saddam and Iraqi Officials Discussing a U.S.-Led Attack on Faylakah Island and the Condition of the Iraqi Army," and "Saddam and His Advisers Discussing the U.S. Ground Attack during the 1991 Gulf War, Garnering Arab and Iraqi Support, and a Letter to Gorbachev," in Woods et al., *The Saddam Tapes*, 191–194.

38. Freedman and Karsh, "How Kuwait Was Won: Strategy in the Gulf War," 19–20.
39. Gordon and Trainor, *The General's War*, 80. In U.S. House of Representatives, *Interim Report of the Committee on Armed Services Dated March 30, 1992 by Mr. Les Aspin (Chairman) and Mr. Dickinson*, Les Aspin notes that "[d]uring the planning stage of Operation Desert Storm, air power advocates hoped that a concentrated strategic air campaign against Saddam's political, economic and military centers would force Iraq to withdraw from Kuwait and eliminate the threat to the region posed by the Baath regime without resorting to ground warfare. These were hoped-for results, never official objectives, and they were not achieved." See also Williamson Murray and Robert H. Scales, *The Iraq War: A Military History*, 11.
40. U.S. General Accounting Office, "Operation Desert Storm: Evaluation of the Air Campaign, Gao/Nsiad-97-134," 197.
41. Gordon and Trainor, 139–140; *New York Times*, February 5, 1991.
42. Andrew J. Bacevich, "'Splendid Little War': America's Persian Gulf Adventure Ten Years On," in *The Gulf War of 1991 Reconsidered*, eds. Andrew J. Bacevich and Efraim Inbar; Department of Defense, *Conduct of the Persian Gulf War: Final Report to Congress*; Thomas A. Keaney and Eliot A. Cohen, *Gulf War Air Power Survey Summary Report.*
43. U.S. Dept. of Defense, *Conduct of the Persian Gulf War.*
44. There is some debate about whether Saddam Hussein's offer to withdraw from Kuwait in February 1991 was sincere. See, for example, Herrmann, "Coercive Diplomacy and the Crisis over Kuwait, 1990–1991"and Stephen T. Ganyard, "Strategic Air Power Didn't Work." Transcripts from audio recordings of meetings between Saddam and his advisors, captured after the fall of the regime, suggest that Saddam agreed to the Soviet proposal in good faith and that he was genuinely surprised that the United States initiated its ground campaign even after Iraq indicated it would accept the proposal. See Woods et al., *The Saddam Tapes*, 191–195. Three of the translated transcripts, records SH-SHTP-A-000-630, SH-SHTP-A-000-931, and SH-SHTP-A-000-666, are available at the Institute for National Strategic Studies (INSS) Conflict Records Research Center (CRRC) website: http://www.ndu.edu/inss/index.cfm?secID=172&pageID=4&type=section.
45. "RCC Statement of Bush's 'Disgraceful' Ultimatum, February 22, 1991," *FBIS-NESA*, February 25, 1991, 33–34; Pape, *Bombing to Win: Air Power and Coercion in War*, 218.
46. Although the conventional wisdom is that air power was decisive in the Gulf War, a number of scholars and military experts have questioned the effectiveness and/or centrality of the strategic air campaign. See, for example, Stephen Biddle, "Victory Misunderstood: What the Gulf War Tells Us About the Future of Conflict"; Ganyard, "Strategic Air Power Didn't Work"; Thomas G. Mahnken and Barry D. Watts, "What the Gulf War Can (and Cannot) Tell Us About the Future of Warfare"; Pape, *Bombing to Win: Air Power and Coercion in War*; Jeffrey Record, *Hollow Victory: A Contrary View of the Gulf War*; U.S. House of Representatives, *Interim Report of the Committee on Armed Services Dated March 30, 1992 by Mr. Les Aspin (Chairman) and Mr. Dickinson.*
47. Keaney and Cohen, *Gulf War Air Power Survey Summary Report.*
48. Pape, *Bombing to Win: Air Power and Coercion in War*, 213.
49. Freeman and Karsh, "How Kuwait Was Won," 35.
50. Biddle, *Military Power: Explaining Victory and Defeat in Modern Battle*; Murray and Scales, *The Iraq War: A Military History*; Record, *Hollow Victory: A Contrary View of the Gulf War.*
51. Murray and Scales maintain that the air campaign phase of Operation Desert Storm "was an exercise in overkill and lasted far too long" because most U.S. military leaders seriously overrated Iraqi strength and some "believed that an air campaign by itself could dispense with the need for a costly ground campaign." *The Iraq War: A Military History*, 8–11.
52. Dilip Hiro, *Secrets and Lies: Operation Iraqi Freedom and After.*
53. Johnson, *Overconfidence and War: The Havoc and Glory of Positive Illusions*, 191–192.

54. Quoted in Kevin Woods, James Lacey, and Murray Williamson, "Saddam's Delusions: The View from the Inside," 3. The authors also note that "the evidence now clearly shows that Saddam and those around him believed virtually every word issued by their own propaganda machine," 4.
55. See, for example, Ali A. Allawi, *The Occupation of Iraq: Winning the War, Losing the Peace*; Ivo H. Daalder and James M. Lindsay, *America Unbound: The Bush Revolution in Foreign Policy*; Michael R. Gordon and Bernard E. Trainor, *Cobra II: The Inside Story of the Invasion and Occupation of Iraq*; Jeffrey Record and W. Andrew Terrill, *Iraq and Vietnam: Differences, Similarities, and Insights*; Bob Woodward, *Plan of Attack*.
56. William D. Nordhaus, "The Economic Consequences of a War in Iraq."
57. *WSJ*, September 15, 2002.
58. U.S. House Budget Committee, Democratic Caucus, "Assessing the Cost of Military Action against Iraq: Using Desert Shield/Desert Storm as a Basis for Estimates."
59. Johnson, *Overconfidence and War*, 200.
60. Allawi, *The Occupation of Iraq*, 185–187.
61. Allawi, *The Occupation of Iraq*, 240.
62. U.S. Senate Armed Services Committee, "Hearing to Consider the Nomination of Hon. Leon E. Panetta to Be Secretary of Defense; Statement of Hon. Leon E. Panetta, Director, U.S. Central Intelligence Agency."
63. Jim Michaels, "19,000 Insurgents Killed in Iraq since '03."
64. Iraq Body Count documents over 100,000 violent civilian deaths in Iraq since the U.S. invasion in 2003, http://www.iraqbodycount.org/about/. A 2006 study in *The Lancet* estimated that 650,000 more Iraqis died in the period between the invasion in March 2003 and June 2006 than would be expected based on the pre-invasion mortality rate in Iraq. Gilbert Burnham et al., "Mortality after the 2003 Invasion of Iraq: A Cross-Sectional Cluster Sample Survey."

CHAPTER 3

1. Barry M. Blechman and Stephen S. Kaplan, *Force without War: U.S. Armed Forces as a Political Instrument*. See chapter 4 for a more extensive discussion of how I determine states' war aims in particular conflicts.
2. A similar distinction is made in Bruce Bueno de Mesquita et al., *The Logic of Political Survival*, 409–418. The authors posit two types of war aims: those requiring active compliance and those that require only the passive compliance of the defeated state. The defeated state can most easily revise the outcome of a war when the victor's terms necessitate active compliance. A territorial gain, for example, requires only passive compliance, because the loser would have to challenge the postwar status quo openly through either diplomatic or military means in order to revise the new borders.
3. Schelling, *Arms and Influence*, 1.
4. Schelling, *Arms and Influence*.
5. Our current perspective on the frequency with which foreign-imposed regime change leads to military commitments to secure the replacement regime is unduly influenced by the current conflicts in Iraq and Afghanistan—in which regime removal was accomplished rapidly but the United States became bogged down in costly occupations. Although foreign governments sometimes engage in long military occupations and nation-building after removing a regime, many times the foreign intervener simply leaves the target state to its own devices after toppling the leadership. In fact, an empirical analysis by Nigel Lo, Barry Hashimoto, and Dan Reiter finds that interstate wars that end in foreign-imposed regime change are *less* likely to restart than armed conflicts that terminate with the governments of both sides still in power. See N. Lo, B. Hashimoto, and D. Reiter, "Ensuring Peace: Foreign-Imposed Regime Change and Postwar Peace Duration, 1914–2001."

6. Mack, "Why Big Nations Lose Small Wars: The Politics of Asymmetric Conflict," 178.
7. Stephen J. Cimbala, *Military Persuasion: Deterrence and Provocation in Crisis and War*, 178.
8. Robert C. Art and Robert Jervis, *International Politics: Enduring Concepts and Contemporary Issues*, 150.
9. Mueller, "The Search for the 'Breaking Point' in Vietnam: The Statistics of a Deadly Quarrel."
10. The literature on the role of overly optimistic prewar beliefs in preventing states from reaching a negotiated settlement that would prevent escalation to war is well developed. See Fearon, "Rationalist Explanations for War"; Gartzke, "War Is in the Error Term"; Slantchev and Tarar, "Mutual Optimism as a Rationalist Explanation of War."
11. Susan Hannah Allen and Tiffiny Vincent, "Bombing to Bargain? The Air War for Kosovo"; Bruce R. Nardulli, *Disjointed War: Military Operations in Kosovo, 1999*.
12. Allen and Vincent, "Bombing to Bargain? The Air War for Kosovo," 5. Other scholars maintain that Milošević only backed down because of the increasing threat of a ground invasion. See, for example, Daniel Byman and Matthew Waxman, *The Dynamics of Coercion: American Foreign Policy and the Limits of Military Might*.
13. See, for example, Mark Clodfelter, *The Limits of Air Power: The American Bombing of North Vietnam*; Horowitz and Reiter, "When Does Aerial Bombing Work?: Quantitative Empirical Tests, 1917–1999"; Iklé, *Every War Must End*; Pape, *Bombing to Win: Air Power and Coercion in War*; Summers, *On Strategy: A Critical Analysis of the Vietnam War*.
14. Christopher M. Gacek, *The Logic of Force: The Dilemma of Limited War in America*; Jason Lyall and Isaiah Wilson, "The American Way of War and Peace in Comparative Perspective." The most recent Army Field Manual, FM 3-24/Marine Corps War-fighting Publication 3–33.5, *Counterinsurgency*, is an important exception (Washington DC: HQ, Dept. of the Army; HQ, Marine Corps Combat Development Command, Dept. of the Navy, December 2006).
15. Biddle, *Military Power: Explaining Victory and Defeat in Modern Battle*, 28.
16. Pape, *Bombing to Win: Air Power and Coercion in War*, 10. Numerous scholars distinguish between military strategies that are intended to render an opponent physically incapable of maintaining an organized offense or defense—which are often called *direct, denial*, or *counterforce* strategies—and military strategies that are principally concerned with convincing an adversary that the costs of prosecuting the armed conflict to victory will be too high—which are labeled *punishment* or *countervalue* strategies. Maneuver (e.g., blitzkrieg) strategies are the most obvious example of the former, but attrition strategies that have as their goal the piecemeal destruction of the enemy's war-making capacity also fall into this category. Guerilla hit-and-run tactics, terrorist attacks, and the carpet-bombing of enemy population centers are examples of the latter.
17. Martin Kitchen, *A World in Flames: A Short History of the Second World War in Europe and Asia, 1939–1945*; George Sanford, *Katyn and the Soviet Massacre of 1940: Truth, Justice and Memory*.
18. Richard Shultz, "Breaking the Will of the Enemy during the Vietnam War: The Operationalization of the Cost-Benefit Model of Counterinsurgency Warfare," 109.
19. Robert Jackman, *Power without Force: The Political Capacity of Nation-States*, 111.
20. Mack, "Why Big Nations Lose Small Wars: The Politics of Asymmetric Conflict," 180–181.
21. Bacevich, "'Splendid Little War': America's Persian Gulf Adventure Ten Years On."
22. U.S. Joint Chiefs of Staff, *Joint Vision 2020: America's Military: Preparing for Tomorrow*, 6.
23. Gray, *Irregular Enemies and the Essence of Strategy: Can the American Way of War Adapt?*
24. U.S. Senate Armed Services Committee, "Crisis in the Persian Gulf Region. Testimony of Admiral William Crowe."
25. Steven J. Davis, Kevin M. Murphy, and Robert H. Topel, "War in Iraq Versus Containment."

26. Duelfer and Dyson, "Chronic Misperception and International Conflict: The U.S.-Iraq Experience"; Federal News Service. Section: Special Conference or Speech about the Middle-East, "United States Senate Debate on the Persian Gulf Crisis and the Use of Force. Opening Remarks of Senate Majority Leader Senator Mitchell."
27. Global Security, "Operation Southern Watch."
28. Brogan, *World Conflicts*, 301–303; Woods, Palkki, and Stout, *The Saddam Tapes: The Inner Workings of a Tyrant's Regime, 1978–2001*, 265–268.
29. Sarah Graham-Brown, *Sanctioning Saddam: The Politics of Intervention in Iraq*.
30. George A. Lopez and David Cortright, "Containing Iraq: Sanctions Worked," 91.
31. Charles Duelfer, "Comprehensive Report of the Special Advisor to the DCI on Iraq's WMD."
32. Duelfer, "Comprehensive Report of the Special Advisor to the DCI on Iraq's WMD," Volume 1, 44. See also Duelfer and Dyson, "Chronic Misperception and International Conflict: The U.S.-Iraq Experience."
33. Duelfer, "Comprehensive Report of the Special Advisor to the DCI on Iraq's WMD," Key Findings, Regime Strategic Intent, 2.
34. Duelfer, "Comprehensive Report of the Special Advisor to the DCI on Iraq's WMD," Volume 1, 51.
35. Department of the Army, "Field Manual 3–24: Counterinsurgency," 1–25.

CHAPTER 4

1. S. A. Bremer, "Dangerous Dyads: Conditions Affecting the Likelihood of Interstate War, 1816–1965."
2. Michael C. Desch, *Power and Military Effectiveness: The Fallacy of Democratic Triumphalism*, 174.
3. See, for example, Brooks and Stanley, *Creating Military Power: The Sources of Military Effectiveness*; Pollack, *Arabs at War: Military Effectiveness, 1948–1991*; Reiter and Stam, *Democracies at War*; Wilson, *Thinking Beyond War: Civil-Military Relations and Why America Fails to Win the Peace*.
4. See, for example, George and Simons, eds., *The Limits of Coercive Diplomacy*; James D. Morrow, "Capabilities, Uncertainty, and Resolve: A Limited Information Model of Crisis Bargaining"; Rosen, "War Power and the Willingness to Suffer."
5. George and Simons, eds., *The Limits of Coercive Diplomacy*; Rosen, "War Power and the Willingness to Suffer."
6. Mack, "Why Big Nations Lose Small Wars: The Politics of Asymmetric Conflict"; J Record, *Beating Goliath: Why Insurgencies Win*.
7. Rosen, "War Power and the Willingness to Suffer."
8. Arreguín-Toft, "How the Weak Win Wars: A Theory of Asymmetric Conflict"; Arreguín-Toft, *How the Weak Win Wars: A Theory of Asymmetric Conflict*; Biddle, *Military Power: Explaining Victory and Defeat in Modern Battle*; Krepinevich, *The Army and Vietnam*; Reiter and Meek, "Determinants of Military Strategy, 1903–1994: A Quantitative Empirical Test"; Stam, *Win, Lose, or Draw: Domestic Politics and the Crucible of War*; Summers, *On Strategy: A Critical Analysis of the Vietnam War*.
9. Clodfelter, *The Limits of Air Power: The American Bombing of North Vietnam*; Pape, *Bombing to Win: Air Power and Coercion in War*.
10. Byman and Waxman, *The Dynamics of Coercion: American Foreign Policy and the Limits of Military Might*; Pape, *Bombing to Win: Air Power and Coercion in War*.
11. Arreguín-Toft, *How the Weak Win Wars: A Theory of Asymmetric Conflict*, 34.
12. Fearon, "Rationalist Explanations for War."
13. I use the Expected Utility Generation and Data Management Program (*EUGene*) with Zeev Maoz's version of the Militarized Interstate Dispute data to generate a dataset consisting of one case per dyadic dispute initiation. Maoz examined the multiparty disputes in the MID

dataset to eliminate dyads in which the states did not actually threaten or use force against each other and to correct dates, hostility levels, and dispute outcomes for each dyad in a multiparty dispute. D. S. Bennett and A. C. Stam, "EUGene: A Conceptual Manual"; Ghosn, Palmer, and Bremer, "The MID3 Data Set, 1993–2001: Procedures, Coding Rules, and Description"; Zeev Maoz, "Dyadic Militarized Interstate Disputes (Dymid1.1) Dataset—Version 1.1."

14. Sarkees and Wayman, *Resort to War: 1816–2007*, 40. For the original definition, see J. David Singer and Melvin Small, *The Wages of War, 1816–1965*.
15. Peter Wallensteen and Margareta Sollenberg, "Armed Conflict 1989–2000," 649.
16. Robert Powell, *In the Shadow of Power: States and Strategy in International Politics*; Donald Wittman, "How a War Ends: A Rational Model Approach."
17. I initiated the data project with support from the Institute on Global Conflict and Cooperation (IGCC) at the University of California and a Doctoral Dissertation Research Improvement Grant from the National Science Foundation (SES 0242022). In 2008, my colleague Michael Koch at Texas A&M University joined the project, allowing for additional data collection, refinement of several measures, and reliability testing on key variables. Patricia Sullivan and Michael Koch, "Military Intervention by Powerful States: 1945–2003."
18. Melvin Small and J. David Singer, *Resort to Arms: International and Civil Wars, 1816–1980*.
19. Patrick M. Regan, *Civil Wars and Foreign Powers: Outside Intervention in Intrastate Conflict*.
20. Blechman and Kaplan, *Force without War: U.S. Armed Forces as a Political Instrument*.
21. Military operations that target a state's own citizens and are conducted within a state's internationally recognized borders (e.g., China's use of force against Tiananmen Square protesters in 1989) are excluded unless both citizenship and borders are in dispute by an armed independence movement in territory claimed as national homeland by a distinct ethnic group (e.g., Tibet).
22. For a similar definition of "combat readiness," see Herbert Tilemma, "Overt Military Intervention and International Conflict."
23. International Military Intervention, 1946–1988 Ver. ICPSR Study No. 6035, Inter-University Consortium for Political and Social Research.
24. See Alexander L. George and Andrew Bennett, eds., *Case Studies and Theory Development in the Social Sciences* for a discussion of the value of selecting "most-likely" and "least-likely" cases. Asymmetric wars are most-likely cases for realist explanations of war outcomes because the "independent variables are at values that strongly posit an outcome," 121.
25. Clausewitz, *On War*, 193.
26. Biddle, *Military Power: Explaining Victory and Defeat in Modern Battle*, 28.
27. Patrick M. Regan, "Conditions of Successful Third-Party Intervention in Intrastate Conflicts."
28. For example, Arreguín-Toft, *How the Weak Win Wars: A Theory of Asymmetric Conflict*; Small and Singer, *Resort to Arms: International and Civil Wars, 1816–1980*; Stam, *Win, Lose, or Draw: Domestic Politics and the Crucible of War*; Kevin Wang and James Lee Ray, "Beginners and Winners: The Fate of Initiators of Interstate Wars Involving Great Powers since 1495." An exception is Maoz, "Resolve, Capabilities, and the Outcomes of Interstate Disputes, 1816–1976."
29. This coding scheme was first adopted in Patricia Sullivan and Scott Gartner, "Disaggregating Peace: Domestic Politics and Dispute Outcomes," 12.
30. David Baldwin, "Success and Failure in Foreign Policy," 178.
31. The date of intervention termination is the date that (1) a peace treaty or other agreement between the parties ends the intervening state's combat role, or (2) the intervening state has reduced its combat troop levels to no more than 30 percent of their level at the height of the conflict.
32. Blechman and Kaplan, *Force without War: U.S. Armed Forces as a Political Instrument*.

33. Blechman and Kaplan, *Force without War: U.S. Armed Forces as a Political Instrument*, 59.
34. Blechman and Kaplan, *Force without War: U.S. Armed Forces as a Political Instrument*, 65.
35. Clodfelter, *Warfare and Armed Conflicts: A Statistical Reference to Casualty and Other Figures, 1500–2000*; Gordon and Trainor, *The Generals' War: The Inside Story of the Conflict in the Gulf*; U.S. Senate Armed Services Committee, "Statement of William E. Odom."
36. Gary R. Hess, "The Military Perspective on Strategy in Vietnam."
37. A more detailed discussion of the case selection criteria and a complete bibliography of sources used to identify and code the data are available in the codebook provided on the author's website. For a description of coding procedures and inter-coder reliability, see Sullivan and Koch, "Military Intervention by Powerful States: 1945–2003." The codebook contains the decision algorithm, and the dataset (also available on the author's website) identifies the sources used to code each individual case.
38. Jones, Bremer, and Singer, "Militarized Interstate Disputes, 1816–1992: Rationale, Coding Rules, and Empirical Patterns," 179.
39. Maoz, "Resolve, Capabilities, and the Outcomes of Interstate Disputes, 1816–1976."
40. Rosen, "War Power and the Willingness to Suffer."
41. Rosen does recognize that cost tolerance is only partially observable and that battle deaths are not a direct measure of willingness to absorb costs. He acknowledges two problems with battle deaths as a measure of cost tolerance in particular: (1) Wars may end because the loser anticipates great losses but has not yet suffered great losses, and (2) battle deaths are not the only costs in war.
42. The Militarized Interstate Dispute Location (MIDLOC) dataset records the precise geographic onset location of Militarized Interstate Disputes (MIDs). I thank Alex Braithwaite for sharing his original data on distances from MID participant capital cities to MID onset locations with me.
43. Carter Malkasian, *A History of Modern Wars of Attrition*, 213.
44. In *Military Power*, Biddle argues that "in practice, attrition is difficult to separate from a tautological characterization of failure or unimaginative conduct," 19. Biddle, *Military Power: Explaining Victory and Defeat in Modern Battle.*
45. Stam, *Win, Lose, or Draw: Domestic Politics and the Crucible of War*, 53.
46. Biddle, *Military Power: Explaining Victory and Defeat in Modern Battle.*
47. Smith, *The Utility of Force: The Art of War in the Modern World.*
48. James D. Campbell, "French Algeria and British Northern Ireland: Legitimacy and the Rule of Law in Low-Intensity Conflict"; Robert M Cassidy, "The British Army and Counterinsurgency: The Salience of Military Culture"; John A. Nagl, *Counterinsurgency Lessons from Malaya and Vietnam: Learning to Eat Soup with a Knife*; U.S. Dept. of Defense, *Conduct of the Persian Gulf War.*
49. The primary sources used to code the ground combat variable were "Facts on File"; "Keesing's Contemporary Archives"; "Keesing's Record of World Events"; Clodfelter, *Warfare and Armed Conflicts: A Statistical Reference to Casualty and Other Figures, 1500–2000*; Sarkees and Wayman, *Resort to War: 1816–2007.*
50. Byman and Waxman, *The Dynamics of Coercion: American Foreign Policy and the Limits of Military Might*; Pape, *Bombing to Win: Air Power and Coercion in War.*

CHAPTER 5

1. Militarized Interstate Disputes are defined as conflicts in which at least one state threatens, displays, or uses force against one or more other states. States that become part of a MID after the first day ("joiners") are captured in the analyses by variables that count the number of allies on each side of the dispute, but only dispute originators are used to create dispute dyads. Jones, Bremer, and Singer, "Militarized Interstate Disputes, 1816–1992: Rationale, Coding Rules, and Empirical Patterns."

2. The MID dataset's hostility level variables are used to determine whether the target used military force. The MID "revisionist state" and "outcome" variables are used to code whether the dispute initiator attained its primary objective using the procedure described in chapter 4.
3. The logit model uses maximum likelihood estimation to calculate the probability of intervention success using the following functional form: $\Pr(y_i = 1 | x_i) = 1/(1 + \exp(-x_i \beta))$, where x_i is a vector of independent variable values for the *i*th observation and β is a vector of parameters. See J. Scott Long, *Regression Models for Categorical and Limited Dependent Variables.*
4. A variable indicating the extent of power parity/disparity between the two states is created by taking the absolute value of the distance between the states' relative military capabilities and 0.5 (a value 0.5 on relative military capabilities indicates perfect parity in military capabilities between the two states).
5. Unless otherwise stated, I evaluate the statistical significance of all variables at the 0.05 level of significance using Wald tests. Because the effects of independent variables on the outcome variable are dependent on the values of other variables in logit models, I test for the statistical significance of effects across the range of a variable.
6. The issue salience measure for each state is the five category ordinal variable described in chapter 4. I obtain democracy scores for the states in each dispute dyad from the Polity IVe dataset (Monty G. Marshall and Keith Jaggers, "Polity IV Dataset [Computer File; Version P4v2002]"). I also create dummy variables that code a state as a democracy if its democracy score minus its autocracy score is seven or above. The interaction of the two dummy variables creates a variable that equals one if both states are democracies. Only 4 percent of the militarized disputes since 1918 have been between two democracies.
7. The highest number of target fatalities recorded in a militarized interstate dispute between two democracies is 500, far below the threshold at which a violent conflict qualifies as a war in the Correlates of War interstate war dataset.
8. I calculate relative distance by dividing initiator distance by target distance, adding one kilometer to each distance to avoid dividing by zero when the dispute begins in the target state's capital.
9. I calculate the conditional probability of success (i.e., the probability the initiator achieves its primary political objective given that the dispute has escalated to violence). Neither alternative measure of relative destructive capacity—the ratio of initiator to target military personnel or the ratio of target to initiator battle deaths—is significant as a control variable in any specification of the model. Because including these variables does not significantly change the effects of other variables in the models, and many cases are missing values for casualties, I do not show results with these variables in the table.
10. The effect of relative capabilities is significant at $p < 0.05$ for both coercive and brute-force objectives.
11. Because a statistically significant product term does not necessarily indicate a substantively meaningful interaction among independent variables, and the marginal effects of independent variables on the outcome variable are dependent on the values of other variables in logit models, I test for statistical significance across the range of capability distributions using nonlinear Wald tests (William D. Berry, Jacqueline H. R. DeMeritt, and Justin Esarey, "Testing for Interaction in Binary Logit and Probit Models: Is a Product Term Essential?"). The null hypothesis is that, at a given value of relative military capabilities, the probability of success is equal for initiators pursuing policy (coercive) and land or governance (brute-force) objectives. The difference between the probability of success when the dispute initiator has coercive objectives and the probability of success when the

initiator has brute-force objectives is significant at $p < 0.05$ when the initiator's proportion of dyad capabilities is below 0.36 and above 0.92. When the dispute initiator possesses between 36 and 92 percent of dyad capacity, its probability of attaining the two types of objectives is approximately the same.

CHAPTER 6

1. Correlates of War (COW) Project, "National Material Capabilities Dataset" (version 3.02), http://correlatesofwar.org; J. David Singer, Stuart Bremer, and John Stuckey, "Capability Distribution, Uncertainty, and Major Power War, 1820–1965," in *Peace, War, and Numbers*, ed. Bruce Russett; J. David Singer, "Reconstructing the Correlates of War Dataset on Material Capabilities of States, 1816–1985."
2. Bueno de Mesquita, *The War Trap*; Scott Sigmund Gartner and Randolph M. Siverson, "War Expansion and War Outcome"; Wang and Ray, "Beginners and Winners: The Fate of Initiators of Interstate Wars Involving Great Powers since 1495."
3. Stam, *Win, Lose, or Draw: Domestic Politics and the Crucible of War.*
4. Biddle, *Military Power: Explaining Victory and Defeat in Modern Battle.*
5. Campbell, "French Algeria and British Northern Ireland: Legitimacy and the Rule of Law in Low-Intensity Conflict."
6. Richard Duncan Downie, *Learning from Conflict: The U.S. Military in Vietnam, El Salvador, and the Drug War*; John M. Gates, "The Limits of Power: The U.S. Conquest of the Philippines," in *Great Powers and Little Wars: The Limits of Power*, eds. A. Hamish Ion and E. J. Errington; Krepinevich, *The Army and Vietnam*; Ariel Levite, Bruce W. Jentleson, and Larry Berman, eds., *Foreign Military Intervention: The Dynamics of Protracted Conflict*; Record and Terrill, *Iraq and Vietnam: Differences, Similarities, and Insights*; Sam C. Sarkesian, "U.S. Strategy and Unconventional Conflicts: The Elusive Goal," in *The U.S. Army in a New Security Era*, eds. Sam C. Sarkesian and John Allen Williams.
7. Lyall and Wilson, "Rage against the Machines: Explaining Outcomes in Counterinsurgency Wars."
8. Bruce Bueno de Mesquita and David Lalman, *War and Reason: Domestic and International Imperatives*; David Lektzian and Mark Souva, "A Comparative Theory Test of Democratic Peace Arguments, 1946—2000"; Reiter and Stam, *Democracies at War*; David L. Rousseau et al., "Assessing the Dyadic Nature of the Democratic Peace, 1918–88."
9. Bennett and Stam, "The Declining Advantages of Democracy: A Combined Model of War Outcomes and Duration"; Lake, "Powerful Pacifists: Democratic States and War"; Reiter and Stam, "Democracy and Battlefield Military Effectiveness"; Reiter and Stam, *Democracies at War*; Siverson, "Democracies and War Participation: In Defense of the Institutional Constraints Argument."
10. Reiter and Stam, "Democracy and Battlefield Military Effectiveness"; Reiter and Stam, *Democracies at War.*
11. Daniel Byman and Matthew Waxman, "Defeating U.S. Coercion"; Gil Merom, *How Democracies Lose Small Wars.*
12. Bueno de Mesquita et al., *The Logic of Political Survival.*
13. Marshall and Jaggers, "Polity IV Dataset [Computer File; Version P4v2002]."
14. I calculate changes in the predicted probability of intervention success as each dichotomous variable varies from zero to one and the log of troop commitment changes one standard deviation, centered on the mean. All other variables are held constant at either their mean (continuous variables) or median (dichotomous variables) values in the dataset.
15. Hess, "The Military Perspective on Strategy in Vietnam"; Summers, *On Strategy: A Critical Analysis of the Vietnam War.*
16. Richard C. Thornton, *The Falklands Sting: Reagan, Thatcher, and Argentina's Bomb*, 147.

CHAPTER 7

1. Stephen Biddle observes that "All published results radically overestimated casualties: the best got no closer than a factor of three; the next best missed by a factor of six." Biddle, "Victory Misunderstood: What the Gulf War Tells Us about the Future of Conflict", 142. See also Murray and Scales, *The Iraq War: A Military History*; Record, *Hollow Victory: A Contrary View of the Gulf War*.
2. Michael Howard, "Why UN Sanctions Are Better Than a Prolonged War"; Philip Towle, *Pundits and Patriots: Lessons from the Gulf War*.
3. U.S. Senate Armed Services Committee, "Statement of William E. Odom."
4. Jeffrey McCausland, "The Gulf Conflict: A Military Analysis."
5. "Confrontation in the Gulf; War and Peace: A Sampling from the Debate on Capitol Hill," *The New York Times* (January 11, 1991).
6. U.S. Joint Chiefs of Staff, *Joint Vision 2020: America's Military: Preparing for Tomorrow*.
7. Keaney and Cohen, *Gulf War Air Power Survey Summary Report*.
8. Fearon, "Rationalist Explanations for War"; Robert Powell, "Bargaining and Learning While Fighting"; Branislav Slantchev, "How Initiators End Their Wars: The Duration of Warfare and the Terms of Peace."
9. Hess, "The Military Perspective on Strategy in Vietnam"; Gary R. Hess, "The Unending Debate: Historians and the Vietnam War."
10. George and Simons, eds., *The Limits of Coercive Diplomacy*; Iklé, *Every War Must End*; B. W. Jentleson, "The Pretty Prudent Public: Post Post-Vietnam American Opinion on the Use of Military Force"; Stam, *Win, Lose, or Draw: Domestic Politics and the Crucible of War*.
11. Cimbala, *Military Persuasion: Deterrence and Provocation in Crisis and War*; Iklé, *Every War Must End*; Suzanne Werner, "Negotiating the Terms of Settlement: War Aims and the Bargaining Leverage."
12. Powell, "Bargaining and Learning While Fighting."
13. National Security Decision Directive 103.
14. *The New York Times*, September 28, 1982
15. Congressional Quarterly Weekly, February 25, 1985.
16. See, for example, Art, "To What Ends Military Power"; Blechman and Kaplan, *Force without War: U.S. Armed Forces as a Political Instrument*; Richard Hobbs, *The Myth of Victory: What Is Victory in War*; Schelling, *Arms and Influence*; Smith, *The Utility of Force: The Art of War in the Modern World*; Wilson, *Thinking Beyond War: Civil-Military Relations and Why America Fails to Win the Peace*.
17. Millett, Murray, and Watman, "The Effectiveness of Military Organizations," 18.
18. Bacevich, "'Splendid Little War': America's Persian Gulf Adventure Ten Years On"; Thomas A. Keaney and Eliot A. Cohen, *Revolution in Warfare? Air Power in the Persian Gulf*; Colin Powell, *My American Journey*; Record and Terrill, *Iraq and Vietnam: Differences, Similarities, and Insights*.
19. "The Invasion of Iraq. Interview with Thomas E. Ricks." See Stephen Biddle, "Afghanistan and the Future of Warfare" for a contrary argument; O'Hanlon, "A Flawed Masterpiece"; Gen. David H. Petraeus, "Transcript: General Petraeus on the Way Ahead in Iraq."
20. Clodfelter, *The Limits of Air Power: The American Bombing of North Vietnam*; Downie, *Learning from Conflict: The U.S. Military in Vietnam, El Salvador, and the Drug War*; Hess, "The Military Perspective on Strategy in Vietnam"; Hess, "The Unending Debate: Historians and the Vietnam War"; Krepinevich, *The Army and Vietnam*; Sarkesian, "U.S. Strategy and Unconventional Conflicts: The Elusive Goal"; Summers, *On Strategy: A Critical Analysis of the Vietnam War*.

BIBLIOGRAPHY

Allawi, Ali A. *The Occupation of Iraq: Winning the War, Losing the Peace*. New Haven, CT: Yale University Press, 2007.

Allen, Susan Hannah, and Tiffiny Vincent. "Bombing to Bargain? The Air War for Kosovo," *Foreign Policy Analysis* 7, No. 1 (2011): 1–26.

Andres, Rick B., Craig Wills, and Thomas E. Griffith Jr. "Winning with Allies: The Strategic Value of the Afghan Model," *International Security* 30, No. 3 (2006): 124–160.

Army, Department of the. "Field Manual 3–24, Counterinsurgency." Washington, DC: U.S. Government Printing Office, 2006.

Arreguín-Toft, Ivan. *How the Weak Win Wars: A Theory of Asymmetric Conflict*. New York: Cambridge University Press, 2005.

Arreguín-Toft, Ivan. "How the Weak Win Wars: A Theory of Asymmetric Conflict," *International Security* 26, No. 1 (2001): 93–128.

Art, Robert. "To What Ends Military Power," *International Security* 4 (1980): 4–35.

Art, Robert C., and Robert Jervis. *International Politics: Enduring Concepts and Contemporary Issues*, 4th ed. New York: HarperCollins College Publishers, 1996.

Bacevich, Andrew J. "'Splendid Little War': America's Persian Gulf Adventure Ten Years On," in *The Gulf War of 1991 Reconsidered*, eds. Andrew J. Bacevich and Efraim Inbar, 149–164. London: Frank Cass, 2003.

Baldwin, David. "Success and Failure in Foreign Policy," *Annual Review of Political Science* 3 (2000): 167–182.

Bennett, D. Scott, and Allan C. Stam. "The Declining Advantages of Democracy: A Combined Model of War Outcomes and Duration," *Journal of Conflict Resolution* 42, No. 3 (1998): 344–366.

Bennett, D. Scott, and Allan C. Stam. "EUGene: A Conceptual Manual," *International Interactions* 26, No. 2 (2000): 179–204.

Berry, William D., Jacqueline H.R. DeMeritt, and Justin Esarey. "Testing for Interaction in Binary Logit and Probit Models: Is a Product Term Essential?" *American Journal of Political Science* 54, No. 1 (2010): 248–266.

Biddle, Stephen. "Afghanistan and the Future of Warfare," *Foreign Affairs* 82, March/April (2003): 31–46.

Biddle, Stephen. *Military Power: Explaining Victory and Defeat in Modern Battle*. Princeton, NJ: Princeton University Press, 2004.

Biddle, Stephen. "Victory Misunderstood: What the Gulf War Tells Us about the Future of Conflict," *International Security* 21, No. 2 (1996): 139–180.

Blainey, Geoffrey. *The Causes of War*. New York: Free Press, 1973.

Blechman, Barry M., and Stephen S. Kaplan. *Force without War: U.S. Armed Forces as a Political Instrument*. Washington, DC: Brookings Institution, 1978.

Boulding, Ken. *Conflict and Defense: A General Theory*. New York: Harper and Row, 1963.

Bremer, S. A. "Dangerous Dyads—Conditions Affecting the Likelihood of Interstate War, 1816–1965," *Journal of Conflict Resolution* 36, No. 2 (1992): 309–341.

Brooks, Risa, and Elizabeth A. Stanley. *Creating Military Power: The Sources of Military Effectiveness*. Stanford, CA: Stanford University Press, 2007.

Bueno de Mesquita, Bruce. *Principles of International Politics*. Washington, DC: CQ Press, 2000.

Bueno de Mesquita, Bruce. *The War Trap*. New Haven, CT: Yale University Press, 1981.

Bueno de Mesquita, Bruce, and David Lalman. *War and Reason: Domestic and International Imperatives*. New Haven, CT: Yale University Press, 1992.

Bueno de Mesquita, Bruce, Alastair Smith, Randolph M. Siverson, and James D. Morrow. *The Logic of Political Survival*. Cambridge, MA: MIT Press, 2003.

Bull, Hedley. *The Anarchical Society: A Study of Order in World Politics*. New York: Columbia University Press, 1977.

Burnham, Gilbert, Riyadh Lafta, Shannon Doocy, and Les Roberts. "Mortality after the 2003 Invasion of Iraq: A Cross Sectional Cluster Sample Survey," *The Lancet* 368, No. 9545 (2006): 1421–1428.

Byman, Daniel, and Matthew Waxman. "Defeating U.S. Coercion," *Survival* 41, No. 2 (1999): 107.

Byman, Daniel, and Matthew Waxman. *The Dynamics of Coercion: American Foreign Policy and the Limits of Military Might*. Cambridge, UK: Cambridge University Press, 2002.

Campbell, James D. "French Algeria and British Northern Ireland: Legitimacy and the Rule of Law in Low-Intensity Conflict," *Military Review* 85, No. 2 (2005): 2–5.

Cannizzo, Cynthia A. "The Costs of Combat: Death, Duration, and Defeat," in *The Correlates of War II: Testing Some Realpolitik Models*, ed. J. David Singer, 233–57. New York: Free Press, 1980.

Cassidy, Robert M. "The British Army and Counterinsurgency: The Salience of Military Culture," *Military Review* 85, No. 3 (2005): 53–59.

Cimbala, Stephen J. *Military Persuasion: Deterrence and Provocation in Crisis and War*. University Park, PA: Pennsylvania State University Press, 1994.

Clausewitz, Carl von. *On War*, eds. Michael Eliot Howard and Peter Paret. Princeton, NJ: Princeton University Press, 1976 [1832].

Clodfelter, Mark. *The Limits of Air Power: The American Bombing of North Vietnam*. New York: Free Press, 1989.

Clodfelter, Michael. *Warfare and Armed Conflicts: A Statistical Reference to Casualty and Other Figures, 1500–2000*. 2nd ed. Jefferson, NC: McFarland & Company, 2002.

Correlates of War (COW) Project. "National Material Capabilities Dataset" (version 3.02), http://correlatesofwar.org.

Crane, Conrad C. *Landpower and Crises: Army Roles and Missions in Smaller-Scale Contingencies during the 1990s*. Carlisle, PA: Strategic Studies Institute, U.S. Army War College, 2001.

Daalder, Ivo H., and James M. Lindsay. *America Unbound: The Bush Revolution in Foreign Policy*. Washington, DC: Brookings Institution Press, 2003.

Danilovic, Vesna. "Conceptual and Selection Bias Issues in Deterrence," *Journal of Conflict Resolution* 45, No. 1 (2001): 97–125.

Davis, Steven J., Kevin M. Murphy, and Robert H. Topel. "War in Iraq Versus Containment," *NBER Working Paper Series* No. W12092 (2006): Available at SSRN http://ssrn.com/abstract=889882.

Defense, Department of. *Conduct of the Persian Gulf War: Final Report to Congress*. Washington, DC: U.S. Government Printing Office, 1992.

Desch, Michael C. "Democracy and Victory: Why Regime Type Hardly Matters," *International Security* 27, No. 2 (2002): 5–47.

Desch, Michael C. *Power and Military Effectiveness: The Fallacy of Democratic Triumphalism*. Baltimore, MD: Johns Hopkins University Press, 2008.

Diehl, Paul F. *A Road Map to War: Territorial Dimensions of International Conflict.* 1st ed. Nashville, TN: Vanderbilt University Press, 1999.

Donnelly, Thomas, Margaret Roth, and Caleb Baker. *Operation Just Cause: The Storming of Panama.* New York: Lexington Books, 1991.

Downie, Richard Duncan. *Learning from Conflict: The U.S. Military in Vietnam, El Salvador, and the Drug War.* Westport, CT: Praeger, 1998.

Downs, George W., and David M. Rocke. "Conflict, Agency, and Gambling for Resurrection: The Principal-Agent Problem Goes to War," *American Journal of Political Science* 38, No. 2 (1994): 362–380.

Duelfer, Charles. "Comprehensive Report of the Special Advisor to the DCI on Iraq's WMD." Washington, DC: U.S. Government Printing Office, 2004.

Duelfer, Charles A., and Stephen Benedict Dyson. "Chronic Misperception and International Conflict: The U.S.-Iraq Experience," *International Security* 36, No. 1 (2011): 73–100.

"Excerpts from Iraqi Document on Meeting with U.S. Envoy," *The New York Times International,* September 23, 1990.

Facts on File World News Digest. New York: Facts on File News Service, 1940–2005.

Fazal, Tanisha M. *State Death: The Politics and Geography of Conquest, Occupation, and Annexation.* Princeton, NJ: Princeton University Press, 2007.

Fearon, James D. "Rationalist Explanations for War." *International Organization* 49, No. 3 (1995): 379–414.

Feaver, Peter D., and Christopher Gelpi. *Choosing Your Battles: American Civil-Military Relations and the Use of Force.* Princeton, NJ: Princeton University Press, 2004.

Federal News Service. "United States Senate Debate on the Persian Gulf Crisis and the Use of Force. Opening Remarks of Senate Majority Leader Senator Mitchell." Special Conference or Speech about the Middle-East. January 10, 1991.

Fey, Mark, and Kristopher W. Ramsay. "Mutual Optimism and War," *American Journal of Political Science* 51, No. 4 (2007): 738–754.

Filson, Darren, and Suzanne Werner. "A Bargaining Model of War and Peace: Anticipating the Onset, Duration, and Outcome of War," *American Journal of Political Science* 46, No. 4 (2002): 819–837.

Filson, Darren, and Suzanne Werner. "Sensitivity to Costs of Fighting Versus Sensitivity to Losing the Conflict: Implications for War Onset, Duration, and Outcomes," *Journal of Conflict Resolution* 51, No. 5 (2007): 691–714.

Freedman, Lawrence, and Efrain Karsh. "How Kuwait Was Won: Strategy in the Gulf War," *International Security* 16, No. 2 (1991): 5–41.

Gacek, Christopher M. *The Logic of Force: The Dilemma of Limited War in America.* New York: Columbia University Press, 1994.

Ganyard, Stephen T. "Strategic Air Power Didn't Work," *U.S. Naval Institute Proceedings* 121, No. 8 (1995): 31–35.

Gartner, Scott S. *Strategic Assessment in War.* New Haven, CT: Yale University Press, 1997.

Gartner, Scott Sigmund, and Randolph M. Siverson. "War Expansion and War Outcome," *Journal of Conflict Resolution* 40, No. 1 (1996): 4–15.

Gartzke, Erik. "War Is in the Error Term," *International Organization* 53, No. 03 (1999): 567–587.

Gates, John M. "The Limits of Power: The U.S. Conquest of the Philippines," in *Great Powers and Little Wars: The Limits of Power,* eds. A. Hamish Ion and E. J. Errington, 124–143. Westport, CT: Praeger Publishers, 1993.

Gelpi, Christopher, and Peter D. Feaver. "Speak Softly and Carry a Big Stick? Veterans in the Political Elite and the American Use of Force," *American Political Science Review* 96, No. 4 (2002): 779–793.

George, Alexander L. *Forceful Persuasion: Coercive Diplomacy as an Alternative to War.* Washington, DC: United States Institute of Peace Press, 1992.

George, Alexander L., and Andrew Bennett, eds. *Case Studies and Theory Development in the Social Sciences*, 2nd ed. Cambridge, MA: MIT Press, 2004.

George, Alexander L., and William E. Simons, eds. *The Limits of Coercive Diplomacy*, 2nd ed. Boulder, CO: Westview Press, 1994.

George, Alexander L., and Richard Smoke. *Deterrence in American Foreign Policy: Theory and Practice*. New York: Columbia University Press, 1974.

Ghosn, Faten, and Scott Bennett. "Codebook for the Dyadic Militarized Interstate Incident Data, Version 3.10," http://cow2.la.psu.edu.

Ghosn, Faten, Glenn Palmer, and Stuart Bremer. "The MID3 Data Set, 1993–2001: Procedures, Coding Rules, and Description," *Conflict Management and Peace Science* 21, (2004): 133–154.

Global Security. "Operation Southern Watch," http://www.globalsecurity.org.

Goemans, H. E. *War and Punishment: The Causes of War Termination and the First World War*. Princeton, NJ: Princeton University Press, 2000.

Gordon, Michael R., and Bernard E. Trainor. *Cobra II: The Inside Story of the Invasion and Occupation of Iraq*. New York: Pantheon Books, 2006.

Gordon, Michael R., and Bernard E. Trainor. *The Generals' War: The Inside Story of the Conflict in the Gulf*, 1st ed. Boston: Little Brown, 1995.

Graham-Brown, Sarah. *Sanctioning Saddam: The Politics of Intervention in Iraq*. London: I. B. Tauris & Co., 1999.

Gray, Colin S. *Irregular Enemies and the Essence of Strategy: Can the American Way of War Adapt?* Carlisle, PA: Strategic Studies Institute, 2006.

Hallion, Richard P. *Storm over Iraq: Air Power and the Gulf War*. Washington, DC: Smithsonian Institution Press, 1992.

Handel, Michael I. *Clausewitz and Modern Strategy*. London; Totowa, NJ: F. Cass, 1986.

Hensel, Paul R. "Territory: Theory and Evidence on Geography and Conflict," in *What Do We Know About War?*, ed. John A. Vasquez, 57–84. Lanham, MD: Rowman & Littlefield, 2000.

Herrmann, Richard. "Coercive Diplomacy and the Crisis over Kuwait, 1990–1991," in *The Limits of Coercive Diplomacy*, eds. Alexander L. George and William E. Simons, 229–264. Boulder, CO: Westview Press, 1994.

Hess, Gary R. "The Military Perspective on Strategy in Vietnam," *Diplomatic History* 10, Winter (1986): 91–106.

Hess, Gary R. "The Unending Debate: Historians and the Vietnam War," *Diplomatic History* 18, No. 2 (1994): 239.

Hiro, Dilip. *Secrets and Lies: Operation Iraqi Freedom and After*. New York: Thunder's Mouth Press/Nation Books, 2004.

Hobbs, Richard. *The Myth of Victory: What Is Victory in War? (Westview Special Studies in Peace, Conflict, and Conflict Resolution)*. Boulder, CO: Westview Press, 1979.

Horowitz, Michael, and Dan Reiter. "When Does Aerial Bombing Work?: Quantitative Empirical Tests, 1917–1999," *Journal of Conflict Resolution* 45, No. 2 (2001): 147–173.

Howard, Michael. "Why UN Sanctions Are Better Than a Prolonged War." *The London Times*, August 17, 1990.

Huth, Paul K. *Standing Your Ground: Territorial Disputes in International Conflict*. Ann Arbor, MI: University of Michigan Press, 1996.

Iklé, Fred Charles. *Every War Must End*, rev. ed. New York: Columbia University Press, 1991.

"Interview with Yevgenni Primakov," *Paris Europe Number One*, April 28, 1991.

"The Invasion of Iraq. Interview with Thomas E. Ricks," on *PBS Frontline*, 2004.

Jackman, Robert. *Power without Force: The Political Capacity of Nation-States, Analytical Perspectives on Politics*. Ann Arbor, MI: University of Michigan Press, 1993.

Jaffe, Greg. "War of Persuasion: The Modern U.S. Officer Emerges in Afghanistan," *The Washington Post*, May 16, 2010.

Jentleson, B. W. "The Pretty Prudent Public: Post Post-Vietnam American Opinion on the Use of Military Force," *International Studies Quarterly* 36, No. 1 (1992): 49–74.

Jervis, Robert. "Cooperation under the Security Dilemma," *World Politics* 30, January (1978): 167–214.

Jervis, Robert. *Perception and Misperception in International Politics*. Princeton, NJ: Princeton University Press, 1976.

Jervis, Robert. "War and Misperception," *Journal of Interdisciplinary History* 18, No. 4 (1988): 675–700.

Johnson, Dominic P. *Overconfidence and War: The Havoc and Glory of Positive Illusions*. Cambridge, MA: Harvard University Press, 2004.

Jones, Adam. "Kosovo: Orders of Magnitude," *IDEA-A Journal of Social Issues* 5, No. 1 (2000).

Jones, Daniel M., Stuart A. Bremer, and J. David Singer. "Militarized Interstate Disputes, 1816–1992: Rationale, Coding Rules, and Empirical Patterns," *Conflict Management and Peace Science* 15, No. 2 (1996): 163–213.

Jones, Seth G., Jeremy M. Wilson, Andrew Rathmell, and K. Jack Riley. *Establishing Law and Order after Conflict*. Santa Monica, CA: RAND Corporation, 2005.

Kadera, Kelly M. *The Power-Conflict Story: A Dynamic Model of Interstate Rivalry*. Ann Arbor, MI: University of Michigan Press, 2001.

Keaney, Thomas A., and Eliot A. Cohen. *Gulf War Air Power Survey Summary Report*. Washington, DC: U.S. Government Printing Office, 1993.

Keaney, Thomas A., and Eliot A. Cohen. *Revolution in Warfare? Air Power in the Persian Gulf*. Annapolis, MD: Naval Institute Press, 1995.

"Keesing's Contemporary Archives [serial]." London: Keesing's Limited [c1945–1986].

"Keesing's Record of World Events [serial]." London: Longman [c1987–2005].

Khong, Yuen Foong. *Analogies at War: Korea, Munich, Dien Bien Phu, and the Vietnam Decisions of 1965*. Princeton, NJ: Princeton University Press, 1992.

Kitchen, Martin. *A World in Flames: A Short History of the Second World War in Europe and Asia, 1939–1945*. London: Longman Publishing Group, 1990.

Koch, Michael, and Patricia Sullivan. "Should I Stay or Should I Go Now? Partisanship, Approval, and the Duration of Major Power Democratic Military Interventions," *Journal of Politics* 72, No. 3 (2010): 1–14.

Krepinevich, Andrew F. *The Army and Vietnam*. Baltimore, MD: Johns Hopkins University Press, 1986.

Lake, David A. "Powerful Pacifists: Democratic States and War." *American Political Science Review* 86, No. 1 (1992): 24.

Lektzian, David, and Mark Souva. "A Comparative Theory Test of Democratic Peace Arguments, 1946–2000," *Journal of Peace Research* 46, No. 1 (2009): 17–37.

Lemke, Douglas, and Jacek Kugler. "The Evolution of the Power Transition Perspective," in *Parity and War: Evaluations and Extensions of the War Ledger*, eds. Jacek Kugler and Douglas Lemke, 3–34. Ann Arbor, MI: University of Michigan Press, 1996.

Levite, Ariel, Bruce W. Jentleson, and Larry Berman, eds. *Foreign Military Intervention: The Dynamics of Protracted Conflict*. New York: Columbia University Press, 1992.

Levy, Jack S. "The Causes of War and the Conditions of Peace," *Annual Review of Political Science* 1, No. 1 (1998): 139–165.

Licklider, Roy. "The American Way of State Building: Germany, Japan, Somalia and Panama," *Small Wars & Insurgencies* 10, No. 3 (1999): 82–115.

Lo, N., B. Hashimoto, and D. Reiter. "Ensuring Peace: Foreign-Imposed Regime Change and Postwar Peace Duration, 1914–2001," *International Organization* 62, No. 4 (2008): 717–736.

Lock-Pullan, Richard. *U.S. Intervention Policy and Army Innovation: From Vietnam to Iraq*. New York: Routledge, 2006.

Long, J. Scott. *Regression Models for Categorical and Limited Dependent Variables*. Thousand Oaks, CA: Sage, 1997.

Lopez, George A., and David Cortright. "Containing Iraq: Sanctions Worked," *Foreign Affairs* 83, No. 4 (2004): 90–103.

Lyall, Jason, and Isaiah Wilson III. "Rage against the Machines: Explaining Outcomes in Counterinsurgency Wars," *International Organization* 63, No. 01 (2009): 67–106.

Lyall, Jason, and Isaiah Wilson. "The American Way of War and Peace in Comparative Perspective," paper presented at the American Political Science Association annual meeting, Philadelphia, 2006.

Mack, Andrew. "Why Big Nations Lose Small Wars: The Politics of Asymmetric Conflict," *World Politics* 27, No. 2 (1975): 175–200.

Mahnken, Thomas G., and Barry D. Watts. "What the Gulf War Can (and Cannot) Tell Us About the Future of Warfare," *International Security* 22, No. 2 (1997): 151–162.

Malkasian, Carter. *A History of Modern Wars of Attrition, Studies in Military History and International Affairs*. Westport, CT: Praeger, 2002.

Maoz, Zeev. "Dyadic Militarized Interstate Disputes (DYMID 1.1) Dataset—Version 1.1 [Computer File]," 1999. Available at http://psfaculty.ucdavis.edu/zmaoz/.

Maoz, Zeev. "Power, Capabilities, and Paradoxical Conflict Outcomes," *World Politics* 41, No. 2 (1989): 239–266.

Maoz, Zeev. "Resolve, Capabilities, and the Outcomes of Interstate Disputes, 1816–1976," *Journal of Conflict Resolution* 27, No. 2 (1983): 195–229.

Marshall, Monty G., and Keith Jaggers. "Polity IV Dataset [Computer File; Version P4v2002]." College Park, MD: Center for International Development and Conflict Management, University of Maryland, 2002.

May, Ernest R. *"Lessons" of the Past: The Use and Misuse of History in American Foreign Policy*. New York: Oxford University Press, 1973.

McCausland, Jeffrey. "The Gulf Conflict: A Military Analysis," *Adelphi Papers*, No. 282 (1993).

Mearsheimer, John J. *Conventional Deterrence*: London: Cornell University Press, 1983.

Merom, Gil. *How Democracies Lose Small Wars*. Cambridge, UK: Cambridge University Press, 2003.

Michaels, Jim. "19,000 Insurgents Killed in Iraq since '03," *USA TODAY*, September 27, 2007.

Millett, Allan R., Williamson Murray, and Kenneth H. Watman. "The Effectiveness of Military Organizations," in *Military Effectiveness; Volume I: The First World War*, eds. Allan R. Millett and Williamson Murray. Boston: Allen & Unwin, 1988.

Morrow, James D. "Capabilities, Uncertainty, and Resolve: A Limited Information Model of Crisis Bargaining," *American Journal of Political Science* 33, No. 4 (1989): 941–972.

Mueller, John E. "The Search for the 'Breaking Point' in Vietnam: The Statistics of a Deadly Quarrel," *International Studies Quarterly* 24, No. 4 (1980): 497–519.

Murray, Williamson, and Robert H. Scales. *The Iraq War: A Military History*. Cambridge, MA: Harvard University Press, 2005.

Nagl, John A. *Counterinsurgency Lessons from Malaya and Vietnam: Learning to Eat Soup with a Knife*. Westport, CT: Praeger, 2002.

Nardulli, Bruce R. *Disjointed War: Military Operations in Kosovo, 1999*. Santa Monica, CA: Rand, 2002.

Nordhaus, William D. "The Economic Consequences of a War in Iraq," *NBER Working Paper Series*, No. W9361 (2002): Available at SSRN http://ssrn.com/abstract=359302.

O'Hanlon, Michael. "A Flawed Masterpiece," *Foreign Affairs* 81, No. 3 (2002): 47–63.

"Operation Desert Storm: Evaluation of the Air Campaign, GAO/NSIAD-97-134," Washington, DC: U.S. General Accounting Office, June 1997.

Organski, A. F. K., and Jacek Kugler. *The War Ledger*. Chicago: University of Chicago Press, 1980.

Pape, Robert Anthony. *Bombing to Win: Air Power and Coercion in War*. Ithaca, NY: Cornell University Press, 1996.

Pearson, Frederick S., and Robert A. Baumann. "International Military Intervention, 1946–1988 [Computer File] ICPSR Study No. 6035." Ann Arbor, MI: Inter-University Consortium for Political and Social Research, 1993.

Petraeus, Gen. David H. "Transcript: General Petraeus on the Way Ahead in Iraq," *Military Review* 87, No. 2 (2007).

Pew Research Center. "Record Number Favors Removing U.S. Troops from Afghanistan," Washington, DC: Pew Research Center for the People & the Press, June 21, 2011.

Pollack, Kenneth M. *Arabs at War: Military Effectiveness, 1948–1991*. Lincoln, NE: University of Nebraska Press, 2002.

Post, Jerrold M., and Amatiza Baram. "Saddam Is Iraq: Iraq Is Saddam," in *The Counterproliferation Papers, Future Warfare Series*. Montgomery, AL: USAF Counterproliferation Center, Air University, 2002.

Powell, Colin. *My American Journey*. New York: Random House, 1995.

Powell, Robert. "Bargaining and Learning While Fighting," *American Journal of Political Science* 48, No. 2 (2004): 344–361.

Powell, Robert. "Bargaining Theory and International Conflict," *Annual Review of Political Science* 5 (2002): 1–30.

Powell, Robert. *In the Shadow of Power: States and Strategy in International Politics*. Princeton, NJ: Princeton University Press, 1999.

Press, Daryl G. "The Myth of Air Power in the Persian Gulf War and the Future of Warfare," *International Security* 26, No. 2 (2001): 5–44.

Ray, James Lee. *Global Politics*, 7th ed. Boston: Houghton Mifflin, 1998.

Record, Jeffrey. *Beating Goliath: Why Insurgencies Win*. Dulles, VA: Potomac Books, 2007.

Record, Jeffrey. *The American Way of War: Cultural Barriers to Successful Counterinsurgency*. Washington, DC: Cato Institute, 2006.

Record, Jeffrey. "Collapsed Countries, Casualty Dread, and the New American Way of War," *Parameters: U.S. Army War College* 32, No. 2 (2002): 4–23.

Record, Jeffrey. *Hollow Victory: A Contrary View of the Gulf War*. Washington, DC: Brassey's (U.S.), 1993.

Record, Jeffrey, and W. Andrew Terrill. *Iraq and Vietnam: Differences, Similarities, and Insights*. Carlisle, PA: Strategic Studies Institute, 2004.

Regan, Patrick M. *Civil Wars and Foreign Powers: Outside Intervention in Intrastate Conflict*. Ann Arbor, MI: University of Michigan Press, 2000.

Regan, Patrick M. "Conditions of Successful Third-Party Intervention in Intrastate Conflicts," *Journal of Conflict Resolution* 40, No. 2 (1996): 336–359.

Reiter, Dan. "Exploring the Bargaining Model of War," *Perspectives on Politics* 1, No. 01 (2003): 27–43.

Reiter, Dan. *How Wars End*. Princeton, NJ: Princeton University Press, 2009.

Reiter, Dan, and Allan C. Stam. *Democracies at War*. Princeton, NJ: Princeton University Press, 2002.

Reiter, Dan, and Curtis Meek. "Determinants of Military Strategy, 1903–1994: A Quantitative Empirical Test," *International Studies Quarterly* 43, No. 2 (1999): 363–387.

Reiter, Dan, and Allan C. Stam III. "Democracy and Battlefield Military Effectiveness," *Journal of Conflict Resolution* 42, No. 3 (1998): 259–277.

Rosen, Steven. "War Power and the Willingness to Suffer," in *Peace, War, and Numbers*, ed. Bruce M. Russett, 352. Beverly Hills, CA: Sage, 1972.

Rousseau, David L., Christopher Gelpi, Dan Reiter, and Paul K. Huth. "Assessing the Dyadic Nature of the Democratic Peace, 1918–88," *American Political Science Review* 90, No. 3 (1996): 512–534.

Russett, Bruce. "Why Democratic Peace?" in *Debating the Democratic Peace*, eds. Michael E. Brown, Sean M. Lynn-Jones, and Steven E. Miller, 82–115. Cambridge, MA: MIT Press, 1996.

Sanford, George. *Katyn and the Soviet Massacre of 1940: Truth, Justice and Memory*. London: Routledge, 2005.

Sarkees, Meredith Reid, and Frank Whelon Wayman. *Resort to War: 1816–2007, Correlates of War Series*. Washington, DC: CQ Press, 2010.

Sarkesian, Sam C. "U.S. Strategy and Unconventional Conflicts: The Elusive Goal," in *The U.S. Army in a New Security Era*, eds. Sam C. Sarkesian and John Allen Williams. Boulder, CO: Lynne Rienner, 1990.

Schelling, Thomas C. *Arms and Influence*. New Haven, CT: Yale University Press, 1966.

Schultz, Kenneth A. "Do Democratic Institutions Constrain or Inform? Contrasting Two Institutional Perspectives on Democracy and War," *International Organization* 53, No. 2 (1999): 233–266.

Shultz, Richard. "Breaking the Will of the Enemy during the Vietnam War: The Operationalization of the Cost-Benefit Model of Counterinsurgency Warfare," *Journal of Peace Research* 15, No. 2 (1978): 109–129.

Singer, J. David. "Reconstructing the Correlates of War Dataset on Material Capabilities of States, 1816–1985," *International Interactions* 14, No. 2 (1987): 115–132.

Singer, J. David, and Melvin Small. *The Wages of War, 1816–1965*. Ann Arbor, MI: Inter-University Consortium for Political Research, 1974.

Singer, J. David, Stuart Bremer, and John Stuckey. "Capability Distribution, Uncertainty, and Major Power War, 1820–1965," in *Peace, War, and Numbers*, ed. Bruce Russett, 159–88. Beverly Hills, CA: Sage, 1972.

Siverson, Randolph M. "Democracies and War Participation: In Defense of the Institutional Constraints Argument," *European Journal of International Relations* 1, No. 4 (1995): 481–489.

Slantchev, Branislav. "How Initiators End Their Wars: The Duration of Warfare and the Terms of Peace," *American Journal of Political Science* 48, No. 4 (2004): 813–829.

Slantchev, Branislav L., and Ahmer Tarar. "Mutual Optimism as a Rationalist Explanation of War," *American Journal of Political Science* 55, No. 1 (2011): 135–148.

Small, Melvin, and J. David Singer. *Resort to Arms: International and Civil Wars, 1816–1980*, 2nd ed. Beverly Hills, CA: Sage, 1982.

Smith, Alastair. "Fighting Battles, Winning Wars," *Journal of Conflict Resolution* 42, No. 3 (1998): 301–320.

Smith, Alastair, and Allan C. Stam. "Bargaining and the Nature of War." *Journal of Conflict Resolution* 48, No. 6 (2004): 783–813.

Smith, Alastair, and Allan C. Stam. "When Likely Losers Go to War," in *New Direction for International Relations*, eds. Alex Mintz and Bruce Russett, 179–198. New York: Lexington Books, 2005.

Smith, Rupert. *The Utility of Force: The Art of War in the Modern World*. New York: Knopf, 2007.

Stam, Allan C. *Win, Lose, or Draw: Domestic Politics and the Crucible of War*. Ann Arbor, MI: University of Michigan Press, 1996.

Stein, Janice Gross. "Deterrence and Compellence in the Gulf, 1990–1991," *International Security* 17, No. 2 (1992): 147–179.

Sullivan, Patricia. "War Aims and War Outcomes: Why Powerful States Lose Limited Wars," *Journal of Conflict Resolution* 51, No. 3 (2007): 496–524.

Sullivan, Patricia, and Scott Gartner. "Disaggregating Peace: Domestic Politics and Dispute Outcomes," *International Interactions* 32, No. 2 (2006): 1–25.

Sullivan, Patricia L., and Michael T. Koch. "Military Intervention by Powerful States, 1945–2003," *Journal of Peace Research* 46, No. 5 (2009): 707–718.

Summers, Harry G. *On Strategy: A Critical Analysis of the Vietnam War*. Novato, CA: Presidio Press, 1982.

Thornton, Richard C. *The Falklands Sting: Reagan, Thatcher, and Argentina's Bomb*, 1st ed. Washington, DC; London: Brassey's, 1998.

Tilemma, Herbert. "Overt Military Intervention and International Conflict," paper presented at the Uppsala Conference on Conflict Data, Sweden, June 8–9, 2001.

Towle, Philip. *Pundits and Patriots: Lessons from the Gulf War*. London: The Institute for European Defence and Strategic Studies, 1991.

U.S. Dept. of Defense. *Conduct of the Persian Gulf War*. Washington, DC: U.S. Government Printing Office, 1992.

U.S. House Armed Services Committee. "Statement of General David H. Petraeus, U.S. Army Commander, International Security Assistance Force and U.S. Forces Afghanistan Before the House Armed Services Committee on Afghanistan," March 16, 2011.

U.S. House Budget Committee, Democratic Staff. *Assessing the Cost of Military Action against Iraq: Using Desert Shield/Desert Storm as Basis for Estimates*. Washington, DC: Democratic Caucus, 2002.

U.S. House of Representatives. "Interim Report of the Committee on Armed Services by Mr. Les Aspin (Chairman) and Mr. Dickinson," March 30, 1992.

U.S. Joint Chiefs of Staff. *Joint Vision 2020: America's Military: Preparing for Tomorrow*. Washington, DC: U.S. Government Printing Office, 2000.

U.S. Senate Armed Services Committee. "Hearing to Consider the Nomination of Hon. Leon E. Panetta to Be Secretary of Defense; Statement of Hon. Leon E. Panetta, Director, U.S. Central Intelligence Agency," 2011.

U.S. Senate Armed Services Committee. "Crisis in the Persian Gulf Region. Testimony of Admiral William Crowe," November 28, 1990.

U.S. Senate Armed Services Committee. "Statement of William E. Odom," 1990.

Van Evera, Stephen. *Causes of War: Power and the Roots of Conflict, Cornell Studies in Security Affairs*. Ithaca, NY: Cornell University Press, 1999.

Vasquez, John A. *The War Puzzle*. Cambridge, UK: Cambridge University Press, 1993.

Wagner, Harrison. "Bargaining and War," *American Journal of Political Science* 44, No. 3 (2000): 469–484.

Wallensteen, Peter, and Margareta Sollenberg. "Armed Conflict 1989–2000," *Journal of Peace Research* 38, No. 5 (2001): 629–644.

Waltz, Kenneth Neal. *Theory of International Politics*. Reading, MA: Addison-Wesley, 1979.

Wang, Kevin, and James Lee Ray. "Beginners and Winners: The Fate of Initiators of Interstate Wars Involving Great Powers since 1495," *International Studies Quarterly* 38, No. 1 (1994): 139–154.

Wayman, Frank W., J. David Singer, and Gary Goertz. "Capabilities, Allocations, and Success in Militarized Interstate Disputes and Wars, 1816–1976," *International Studies Quarterly* 27, No. 4 (1983): 497–515.

Weigley, Russell F. *The American Way of War: A History of United States Strategy and Policy*. New York: Macmillan, 1973.

Werner, Suzanne. "Negotiating the Terms of Settlement: War Aims and the Bargaining Leverage," *Journal of Conflict Resolution* 42, No. 3 (1998): 321–343.

Wilson, Isaiah. *Thinking beyond War: Civil-Military Relations and Why America Fails to Win the Peace*. New York: Palgrave Macmillan, 2007.

Wittman, Donald. “How a War Ends: A Rational Model Approach,” *Journal of Conflict Resolution* 23, No. 4 (1979): 743–763.

Woods, Kevin, James Lacey, and Williamson Murray. “Saddam’s Delusions: The View from the Inside,” *Foreign Affairs* 85, No. 3 (2006): 2–26.

Woods, Kevin M., David D. Palkki, and Mark E. Stout. *The Saddam Tapes: The Inner Workings of a Tyrant’s Regime, 1978–2001*. New York: Cambridge University Press, 2011.

Woods, Kevin M., and Mark E. Stout. “Saddam’s Perceptions and Misperceptions: The Case of ‘Desert Storm,’” *Journal of Strategic Studies* 33, No. 1 (2010): 5–41.

Woodward, Bob. *Plan of Attack*. London: Simon & Schuster, 2008.

INDEX